T0330233

# TRADE, MARKETS AND WELFARE

# Trade, Markets and Welfare

Kelvin Lancaster

*John Bates Clark Professor of Economics, Columbia University, US*

**Edward Elgar**

Cheltenham, UK • Brookfield, US

Published by
Edward Elgar Publishing Limited
8 Lansdown Place
Cheltenham
Glos GL50 2HU
UK

Edward Elgar Publishing Company
Old Post Road
Brookfield
Vermont 05036
US

**British Library Cataloguing in Publication Data**
Lancaster, Kelvin
    Trade, markets and welfare
    1. International trade 2. Monopolies 3. Competition, Imperfect
    4. Competition
    I. Title
    338.8'2

**Library of Congress Cataloguing in Publication Data**
Lancaster, Kelvin,
        Trade, markets, and welfare / Kelvin J. Lancaster.
            p.   cm.
        Includes bibliographical references and index.
        1. Industries. 2. Industrial organization. 3. Commerce.
    4. Monopolies. 5. Competition. 6. Diversification in industry.
    7. Markets. 8. Welfare economics. I. Title.
    HB241.L355 1996
    338.6'048—dc20                                      95–38731
                                                         CIP

ISBN  1 85278 975 1

Printed and bound in Great Britain by Hartnolls Limited, Bodmin, Cornwall

# Contents

# Figures

# Tables

# Acknowledgements

The author wishes to thank the following who have kindly given permission for the use of copyright material.

Basil Blackwell Ltd for articles: 'The Heckscher–Ohlin Trade Model, *Economica*, **24** (1957), 19–39; 'Protection and Real Wages', *The Economic Journal*, **67** (1957), 199–210; 'Innovative Entry: Profit Hidden beneath the Zero', *Journal of Industrial Economics*, **31** (1982), 41–56; 'Productivity-Geared Wage Policies', *Economica*, **25** (1958), 199–212.

Elsevier Science Publishers for articles: 'Intra-Industry Trade under Perfect Monopolistic Competition', *Journal of International Economics*, **10** (1980), 151–75; 'The 'Product Variety' Case for Protection', *Journal of International Economics*, **31** (1991), 1–26.

Harvester Wheatsheaf for article 'Two-Tiered Industries: Large and Small Firms in Simultaneous Competition' in *Market Structure and Strategy* (eds Alec J. Gee and George Norman), 1992.

Institute of Marketing Science for article: 'The Economics of Product Variety', *Marketing Science*, **9** (1990), 41–56.

Kluwer Academic Publishers for article: 'Information and Product Differentiation' in *Economics of Information* (eds M. Galatin and R.D. Leiter), Martinus Nijhoff, 1991.

Review of Economic Studies Ltd for article: 'The General Theory of Second Best', *Review of Economic Studies*, **24** (1956), 11–32.

University of Chicago Press for article: 'The Dynamic Inefficiency of Capitalism', *Journal of Political Economy*, **81** (1973), 1092–1109.

Every effort has been made to trace all the copyright holders but if any have been inadvertently overlooked the publishers will be pleased to make the necessary arrangements at the first opportunity.

# 1 Introduction

This is a second volume of selected papers by the author. The first selection, published as *Modern Consumer Theory*,[1] consisted of eleven papers which traced the development of the author's work on consumer theory and product characteristics, with its application to various aspects of the economy including quality measurement and the optimal degree of product variety in both private and public sectors. Partly for lack of space and partly because they lay outside the main time frame for selection (1966–80), some important applications (especially to international trade) were omitted from the first volume in anticipation of this second selection. The papers so omitted make up some of the fourteen papers in the current volume, along with related papers written after the first volume went to press.

In addition to papers related in theme or in descent from those in *Modern Consumer Theory*, the opportunity was taken to include in this volume some papers on other themes or written earlier than 1966. In selecting what to reprint out of a body of publications going back as far as 1953, it was decided to apply the 'market test' to papers published before 1980. A necessary (although not sufficient) condition for inclusion was that a paper should have been referenced non-trivially[2] since 1980. The four pre-1980 papers included here have passed this test.

**Trade**
The first four chapters in this part are from the period 1980–91, and are developments of the author's work on product differentiation[3] into international trade theory. Chapter 2, 'Intra-industry trade under perfect monopolistic competition', shows how intra-industry trade will develop even between *identical* economies, provided there are some economies of scale (they need only be minimal), products can be freely differentiated, and there is diversity of preferences within each country even though the distribution of preferences is identical between the two countries. The intra-industry trade may vanish, however, if the countries are sufficiently different to give rise to clear comparative advantage. Chapter 3, 'Protection and product differentiation', shows that the degree of product variety can be increased by protection, at least for the model simulated in the paper, and this may result in a welfare gain even for a country which is too small to exert an influence on the terms of trade. Chapter 4, 'Multi-product defensive monopoly in an open economy', is a short paper making the point that, under conditions of variable product specifications and diverse preferences, a firm which

is able to preserve a multi-product monopoly in a closed economy will generally be able to sustain it against lower-cost foreign competition, at least up to some limit of cost difference. Chapter 5, 'The "product variety" case for protection', shows that protection can sometimes increase both single-country and world welfare when consumers in a small open economy place more weight on the differences between product varieties than do consumers elsewhere. The interesting features of this case are that the welfare gain persists only so long as the tariff is in place (it is not an infant-industry case), and the protection must be partial only, and not prohibitive for any product.

The two remaining papers in the section are among the author's earliest publications and date from 1957. Both Chapter 6, 'The Heckscher–Ohlin trade model', and Chapter 7, 'Protection and real wages', are based on geometric analysis of the Heckscher–Ohlin trade model. The first developed the complete geometrical analysis of the two-good, two-factor world, while the second showed that the effect of protection on the real wage cannot be determined solely from the relative scarcity of the factors in the home economy.

**Markets**

The four papers in this part are all later than 1980, and are all concerned with imperfectly competitive markets under conditions of product differentiation. In Chapter 8, 'Innovative entry: profit hidden beneath the zero', it is shown that an industry may be at a local zero-profit equilibrium, yet a new firm may enter with an appropriately differentiated product and cause a restructuring in which it (and even existing firms) can make a positive profit. The theme of Chapter 9, 'Product differentiation in two-tiered industries', is that appropriate product differentiation permits very small and very large firms to coexist and compete without implicit collusion or price leadership, even though the small firms' prices are higher than those of the large firms. Chapter 10, 'Information and product differentiation', discusses product differentiation under conditions of imperfect information, while Chapter 11, 'The economics of product variety', surveys the development of the theory of product variety in economics from Chamberlin and Hotelling to 1990.

**Welfare**

The common thread through the otherwise diverse papers in this part is the existence of important welfare and policy implications in each case. Except for Chapter 13, which is a follow-up of a much older paper, all the papers date from before 1980.

Chapter 12, 'The general theory of second best' presents a corrected version[4] of the Lipsey and Lancaster 1956 paper on the theory of second-best optima. The basic thrust of the paper is that policies that would be optimal if they could be applied everywhere in the economy will not generally be so if they *cannot* be applied in some sectors, and the appropriate second-best policies may then diverge from standard policy rules like marginal cost pricing. The possibility of strategic behavior by large firms was not taken into account in that early paper, and Chapter 13, 'Strategic considerations in second best', is a recent paper in which such effects are explored for an important case.

Chapter 14, 'Productivity-geared wage policies', is an early paper showing that increasing each sector's wages in proportion to its increase in productivity will generally be suboptimal. Chapter 15 is published under its original title, 'The dynamic inefficiency of capitalism', although the author has long been unhappy with that title. This paper is really a differential game model[5] applied to a very simple economic example with two decision makers having different objectives and controlling different variables, but acting on a common economic model. The central theme is lack of credible commitment in a dynamic game. The context of both chapters 14 and 15 is that of an economy with a centralized wage policy or centralized wage bargaining.

**General**
The main texts of all the papers are presented here in their original form, with minor exceptions, except for the revision of a small part of Chapter 12 which has already been mentioned. Footnotes have been edited, however. All have been changed to endnotes, some have been omitted as no longer relevant, and some others have been changed in various ways. References have been changed to a common style and consolidated at the end of the book. The aim has been to bring all the papers, which vary considerably because of the 40-year time span and the variety of journals for which they were written, into a consistent style for publication in this book. The titles of Chapters 6, 7, 9 and 11 have been varied or shortened, but not changed in substance. The original title of Chapter 15 has been retained, in spite of the comment above.

**Notes**
1. Lancaster 1966.
2. Lancaster 1991.
3. That is, the paper was used directly or was cited as important in the historical development of the topic.
4. See Lancaster 1979, or Lancaster 1991, Chapter 11.
5. The modifications correct an algebraic error in the original, which did not affect the results in any important way. See the Chapter 12 endnotes for details.
6. This seems to be the earliest use of a differential game in a true economic model. It is certainly one of the very first, and perhaps the only one for which an explicit solution can be given.

# PART I

# TRADE

# 2 Intra-industry trade under perfect monopolistic competition[1]

## Introduction

Intra-industry trade on a large scale, an undeniable fact of trade between modern industrial economies,[2] is simply not a prediction of traditional trade theory. Nor is large-scale trade between economies with similar factor endowments, technologies, and (probably) underlying tastes, which is another fact of modern trade. In this paper it is shown that the kind of market structure generated within a high-technology industrialized economy will result in a great amount of intra-industry trade and, furthermore, such trade will take place even between economies which are absolutely identical in all respects. Indeed, more trade may take place if the economies are identical or similar than if they are significantly different.

The problem of intra-industry trade has received its share of attention in the literature,[3] a good overall survey of the possible solutions to the apparent conundrum which it poses being given by Grubel.[4] These include entrepôt trade and locational effects between large adjacent countries, the only cases in which exports and imports can consist of *absolutely* identical commodities, and a variety of models which involve some kind of increasing returns to scale. The best known of these is probably that of Linder,[5] in which economies with different income distributions produce goods of different qualities for their home markets and then have a competitive edge for these same products in sales to other countries. Grubel develops another version of this generic class of models. Throughout the literature are hints, explicit and implicit, that the intra-industry trade problem should be solvable in terms of monopolistic competition and product differentiation theory.[6]

Monopolistic competition theory, in its original Chamberlin form, unfortunately lacked the firm general equilibrium foundation without which it could not be incorporated into the theory of trade. In particular, the Chamberlin demand curves are not derivable from underlying preferences and budget constraints and thus float dangerously free from any analytical underpinning. The problems inherent in these curves are illustrated in the attempt by Gray,[7] shown to be incorrect by Davies,[8] to produce a monopolistic competition theory of intra-industry trade while assuming constant returns to scale.

Another problem in integrating monopolistic competition and product differentiation into pure trade theory has been the incorrect belief that these were associated essentially with 'imperfect' markets and that there was some perfect competition solution available under the same production and consumption technologies. Since basic trade theory is the theory of perfect competition in an international setting, anything involving imperfect competition was regarded as an aberrant, even pathological, case. The author's work[9] has shown that a market structure broadly similar to that of traditional monopolistic competition is, in fact, the *most competitive* structure possible when the number and design of goods are themselves equilibrium variables and not specified as initial data. Thus, perfect monopolistic competition is the most relevant form of competition in the analysis of modern high-technology economies. Traditional trade theory is irrelevant to such economies since perfect competition throughout the economy is an impossible market structure under conditions of diverse preferences and infinitely variable product specifications.

**The underlying economic structure**
Economies in which the number and design of the goods to be produced are part of the solution rather than part of the initial specification have been the subject of detailed study by the author in the work already cited. Since it is such economies with which this paper is concerned, it is necessary to summarize both the assumptions made in modeling these economies and those conclusions as to the operation of the economies which are relevant to the purpose of this paper. Only those aspects of the more general study which are concerned with operation of the economy under a competitive market system without 'imperfections' in information or flexibility are touched upon,[10] and no welfare or optimality aspects are considered.

No attempt is made to prove any propositions in this section. For the justification of any conclusions that do not seem intuitively plausible, the reader is referred to the cited study.

The economies with which this paper is concerned are those possessing a manufacturing sector which is characterized by product-differentiated groups. A 'group' in this sense is a product class in which all products, actual and potential, possess the same characteristics, different products within the group being defined as products having these characteristics in different proportions. All are considered to be either divisible or, if indivisible, to be of the same 'quality' so that no product dominates any other with respect to its content of the relevant characteristics. The proportions in which the characteristics are possessed by any product within the group define its *specification*, and specifications are assumed to be potentially variable in a continuous manner over some convex set which will be referred to as the product *spectrum* for that group, so that the group has an infinite number of potential products.

Individuals are assumed to have preferences over characteristics of goods rather than over collections of goods themselves[11] and the consumption technology over the groups being considered is taken to be *non-combinable*.[12] That is to say, the individual can choose any available good within the group and obtain characteristics in proportions represented by that good's specification, but cannot obtain characteristics in proportions not represented among available goods by buying two or more such goods and consuming them in combination. Thus, the context is that of groups in which the individual chooses one good out of the group, as in the case of most consumer durables. The analysis is not changed fundamentally if the goods are combinable, but the scope for differentiated products is lessened.

If all goods in the group, actual or potential, were available at their unit resource cost, each individual would find some good which he preferred under those circumstances, which is his *most preferred good*[13] or 'ideal product'. It is of the essence of the analysis that follows that there is *diversity* in consumer preferences so that the most preferred goods vary over consumers and, in particular, the set of all most preferred goods is taken to be a convex subset of the product spectrum. In any market situation a particular consumer will choose among these goods which are actually available on the basis of their relative prices and on the relationship of their specifications to that of his most preferred good. There is assumed to be some appropriate measure of spectral distance such that the price the consumer is willing to pay for a particular good, given income and other prices, is inversely proportional to a convex function of the spectral distance between the good in question and the consumer's most preferred good. To simplify the analysis it is assumed that the function referred to is the same for all consumers so that two consumers with quite different most preferred goods will have identical views with respect to two available goods which are at the same spectral distances from their respective most preferred goods. This key assumption is referred to as the *uniformity assumption*, and can be considered as comparable to the featureless plain assumption in location theory.[14]

The uniformity assumption is an assumption about a certain type of similarity between the preferences of different consumers and is roughly equivalent to assuming consumers have indifference surfaces over group characteristics which are of the same general shape but vary in their position over the spectrum so as to give different most preferred goods. This assumption must not be confused with the assumption of *uniform density* of consumers over the spectrum, which refers to the relative number of consumers having most preferred goods at each point in the spectrum. Although uniform density will also be assumed here, this is a property that can be relaxed without major difficulty, unlike that of uniformity of preferences.[15]

In a market situation with a finite number of goods actually available at given prices there will be boundary consumers between each pair of goods which are adjacent on the spectrum, i.e. consumers whose most preferred good is so located on the spectrum that, at the prices and specifications of the goods as given, these consumers are indifferent between buying one good or the other.

Owing to the assumed uniformity of preferences, all consumers having most preferred goods with specifications closer to an available good than those of the boundary consumers will buy that good. Thus, the market areas for goods will be convex subsets of the spectrum and it will be assumed that there are enough goods available for the market areas to form a partition of the spectrum.

Although the market area for a good, which depends on its price and specification relative to those of adjacent goods, shows which consumers will buy that good as compared with other goods in the group, it does not determine what quantity of the good each consumer will buy. This will depend on the consumer's income, obviously, and on the prices of goods outside the group which will be referred to collectively as *outside goods*. It is assumed that relative prices within the set of outside goods remain constant, so that they can be treated as a single aggregate good, that outside goods have no influence on the choice between group goods but only on how much of the group good is consumed relative to the outside good, and that all consumers have the same view of the relationship between their most preferred group good and outside goods, a view which is summarized in terms of two parameters, the elasticity of substitution between group and outside goods and the proportion of total expenditure devoted to group goods.

The quantity of the group good that will be purchased by a consumer within the market area will depend on how different is the specification of the available good from that of his most preferred good. For a consumer towards the boundary of the market area, the available good is some distance from his ideal product and so, for the same price, he will buy less of it and more of the outside good than will a consumer near the market center, provided the elasticity of substitution with respect to outside goods is greater than unity, as assumed throughout the analysis. Under the uniformity assumption, the quantity of any good purchased by any individual will be a function only of the market variables and the distance between the specifications of the available good and his ideal good. Since there is a single quantity function for all consumers, the demand properties for a specific good can be found by integrating the product of the quantity function and the density function (generally assumed to be a constant) over the market area. Some market variables, such as the price of the good, affect both the market area and the quantity function; some, such as the price of the outside good, affect only the market area.

The demand functions so calculated give the quantity of each group good as a function of its price and specification, the prices and specifications of adjacent goods and the price of the outside good, income and its distribution being assumed constant. The key properties are that

1. demand is a function of specifications as well as prices;

2. the own-price elasticity of demand is greater than unity if the elasticity of substitution with respect to outside goods is greater than unity; and
3. the price elasticity is a continuous decreasing function of the distance between adjacent goods and approaches infinity as the goods move towards identical specifications.

On the production side, it is assumed that there are *initial* economies of scale at the product level, defined as falling average cost of production of a good of constant specification for some range of output commencing at the origin. It is convenient to talk of the *degree of economies of scale* at a given output level, defined by the ratio of average to marginal cost. Obviously average cost is falling if the degree of economies of scale at the output is greater than unity. For a homogeneous production function of constant degree $k$, the degree of economies to scale is constant and equal to $k$, while for a cost curve of the conventional U-shape, the degree of economies of scale commences at some level above unity and declines to unity at the minimum average cost output. Any form for the cost function, including the homogeneous and U-shaped versions, is permissible provided the degree of economies of scale is greater than unity at zero output and does not increase with output. The U-shaped curve will, however, be regarded as the usual case, since this requires only the weakest assumption of economies of scale – the existence of such economies for very small outputs.

It is assumed that the economies of scale are lost completely if the good is changed in specification, the change resulting in a new good for which the scale must be measured again from zero. Subject to the loss of economies of scale, firms are free to choose to produce any good within the product spectrum.

All goods in the product spectrum are measured in units so chosen that the total cost of producing the first $Q_0$ units is the same for all goods, actual or potential.[16] It is further assumed that the cost functions for all goods within the group are identical when the goods are measured in this way, so that the total cost of producing $Q$ units of any good is independent of its specification.

In the context of the model set out above, the individual firm selling a product within the group has two decision variables, price and specification, instead of the single variable price as in the traditional analysis. The interrelation between the decisions with respect to the two variables is easily seen in the case of two characteristics, where the spectrum can be represented along a line and specification by a point on the line. Then each firm has two other firms adjacent to it, one in each direction along the line. The firm's market area consists of two independent half-markets, one to the left of its position on the spectrum in which the competition within the group comes primarily from the good adjacent on the left, the other to the right in competition with its right-hand neighbor. The profit-maximizing solution for the firm will be a joint price-specification pair such that

(a)    marginal revenue is equalized between the two half-markets, and
(b)    marginal revenue is equal to marginal cost.

The analogous result holds for more than two characteristics and a multidimensional spectrum.

With uniform preferences, identical cost functions, and, in addition, a uniform density of consumers over the spectrum, the market situations of firms will be identical if they have neighbors at the same distances selling at the same prices. The *Nash equilibrium* for a group containing $N$ firms can be shown to have the following properties:

1.  No two firms will produce to the same specification.[17]
2.  The specifications of the goods produced will be at equal distances from each other over the spectrum.
3.  The market areas of all goods will be the same.
4.  All goods will be sold at the same price and produced in the same quantity when units have been chosen in accordance with the rules given above.

All firms will equate marginal cost and marginal revenue (which will be the same over all firms) while the relationship between price and average cost, and thus the level of profit, will depend on $N$, the number of firms. It can easily be shown that the profit level is a decreasing function of $N$ so that free entry will result in an equilibrium number $N^*$ such that price equals average cost for all firms, as in the Chamberlin version of monopolistic competition.

The market structure derived here can be called *perfect monopolistic competition* since it represents the Nash equilibrium of perfectly informed firms facing perfectly informed consumers under conditions of perfect flexibility in choice of specification, absence of collusion, and free and willing entry. Since it can be shown that no two firms will ever produce identical goods if there is diversity of consumer preferences of a continuous kind, perfect competition is not a possible market structure and perfect monopolistic competition is the 'most perfect' market structure which can exist under the conditions of the model. It might be noted that market behavior resembling that of traditional perfect competition could be induced by *restricting* freedom of action, in particular by making it illegal to produce a good to any specification other than some government standard so that all firms were forced to produce the same product, but the result would be suboptimal in a welfare sense and would not result from the operation of a free market.

Some of the properties of the perfect monopolistic competition equilibrium which are relevant to the succeeding analysis are as follows:

1.  There is a viable and stable equilibrium only if the elasticity of substitution between group goods and outside goods is greater than unity and less than some maximum value which depends on the economies of scale properties. If cost curves are U-shaped with a minimum at a relatively low output level, however, there is no upper limit.
2.  The equilibrium number of goods, $n^*$, which is always finite, depends on the preference properties over the group characteristics, the elasticity of substitution with respect to outside goods, the economies of scale properties, the importance of the group in total expenditure, and the 'size of the market' in the sense of total consumer purchasing power. In particular, the number will be larger

    (i)     the more sensitive are consumers to differences in specification;
    (ii)    the lower the elasticity of substitution with respect to outside goods;
    (iii)   the lower the economies of scale at each output; and
    (iv)    the larger the market, unless the economies of scale are derived from a homogeneous production function of constant degree.

Some feeling for the underlying analysis of the model may be obtained by considering the last property given above. Suppose there is an initial equilibrium, with marginal revenue equal to marginal cost and price equal to average cost, so that the ratio of price to marginal revenue (a function of the elasticity of demand only) must equal the ratio of average to marginal cost. Now suppose the population increases by the addition of more consumers with preferences identical to those of the original population with no change in their distribution over the spectrum. The elasticity of demand will be unchanged, so the ratio of price to marginal revenue will be unchanged when quantity increases in proportion to the population. But the larger quantities for all goods will lower average costs relative to marginal costs unless the production function is homogeneous, so that firms will make profits if marginal revenue equals marginal cost. This will attract new entrants so that goods will be closer in specification and each will be produced in smaller quantity. When the goods are closer together the demand elasticities rise and thus the ratio of price to marginal cost falls, while the lower outputs increase the ratio of average to marginal cost. Thus, new entries move the group closer to a new equilibrium which will be reached at a higher value of $N^*$. In the homogeneous production function case the ratio of average to marginal cost is the same for all output levels, so that a population increase results in lower prices for group goods (since average cost falls) but no change in the equilibrium number.

Note that, although the analysis is given initially for an economy consisting of a single product-differentiated group and an amorphous 'outside good', the latter can itself contain additional product-differentiated groups provided these

are fully separable from the group being investigated (i.e. share no characteristics with it) and there is zero correlation between the positions of individuals'
most preferred goods in the various spectra. Thus, the analysis can be examined
to cover an economy consisting of many groups.

The economies whose trading patterns form the subject matter of the analysis
which follows will be considered to consist of a sector made up of product-differentiated groups ('manufacturing') and another sector in which there are no
economies of scale and no product differentiation ('agriculture'), the aggregate
good formed by the output of the latter playing the role of the outside good.
Within the product-differentiated manufacturing sector, firms are assumed to
behave non-collusively and to have no power to either prevent entry of new
firms or prevent other firms (new or existing) from varying their specifications
in any way, so that the long-run equilibrium market configuration is that of perfect
monopolistic competition in the sense discussed above.

### Trade between identical economies

By identical economies is meant economies which are truly identical in every
respect, possessing identical production technologies and identical resources
in kind and quantity, and having identical populations with identical distributions of consumers having the same preferences – that is, so that every individual
in one economy can be paired off with an individual having the same preferences and same income in the other. Each economy has the general structure
described in the previous section, with a product-differentiated manufacturing
sector (assumed initially to consist of a single group) subject to economies of
scale, at least up to some small output, and an outside goods sector (agriculture) without economies of scale or product differentiation. Preferences are diverse
within each economy, but uniform in the sense previously described.

In isolation, the equilibrium configurations of the two economies will be
identical. Uniform density will be assumed so that the equilibrium configuration of a perfect monopolistic competition structure in manufacturing and a perfect
competition structure in agriculture will give, for each country, some number
$n^0$ of products in the manufacturing group, each produced in the same quantity
$Q^0$ and sold at the same price $p^0 = C(Q^0)/Q^0$, where $C(Q)$ is the cost function,
and some output $X^0$ of agriculture.

If the countries trade freely without barriers or transport costs, they constitute
a single market having the same uniformity properties as each country in
autarky, but with double the population. The structure of the world market for
manufactures under conditions of free entry and perfect information will be that
of perfect monopolistic competition, in which no two firms will choose to
produce the same product. Thus, each manufactured good will be produced in
only one of the countries, but consumed in both. Since the quantity of each good
is given by world demand (the quantities of all manufactured goods being the

same due to uniformity), the relative sizes of the manufacturing sectors in the two countries are determined by, and proportional to, the respective numbers of products produced in each. Denote the number of manufactured products produced in country 1 by $n_1$ and the number in country 2 by $n_2$. Note that $n_1 + n_2$ is not necessarily equal to $n^0$, the number produced by each country in isolation, since the large market will lower average costs and give (generally) a larger number of products at equilibrium than for the smaller individual markets.

It is easy to see that a configuration in which $n_1 = n_2$ is *always* an equilibrium configuration because (1) both countries then have manufacturing sectors of equal size and, having identical resources, will have equal agricultural outputs and equal real incomes, (2) having identical preference structures will then consume the same quantities of each good in both countries, and (3) will therefore both have zero trade balances.

The equilibrium pattern with $n_1 = n_2$ will be one in which there is intra-industry trade *only*, each country exporting half the output of each of its manufactured products in exchange for half the output of the manufactured products produced in the other country, while each country covers its own agricultural needs. Note that the equilibrium solution predicts the *general pattern* of trade and the *level* of trade (determined by the importance of manufactures in total consumption), but not which *specific* good will be produced in each country. The predictions hold, however, only if it can be shown that the solution with $n_1 = n_2$ is a unique solution.

This solution is certainly unique if agriculture exhibits decreasing returns to scale at the economy-wide level or if it uses some specific factor ('land') in addition to the mobile factor ('labor plus capital') used by both agriculture and manufacturing, either of which is an eminently reasonable assumption to make in a simple model of this kind. The reason for uniqueness under such conditions is that adjustment of the identical economies to the world price ratio of manufactures to agriculture implies that the manufacturing sectors must be of the same size in both countries, which can only be achieved if $n_1 = n_2$.

For some purposes it would be sufficient to stop at this point, relying on the reasonableness of the above conditions on agriculture to guarantee uniqueness of the equilibrium with $n_1 = n_2$. However, in order to be able to generalize the 'outside good' so that it is not necessarily confined to agriculture, it is necessary to deal with the case in which 'agriculture' has constant returns to scale properties – and here some problems arise.

If there are constant returns to scale in agriculture, the competitive price of the agricultural good in terms of resources is constant (and will be taken to be unity), so that the resource price of manufactures, $p$, is also the price in terms of agriculture. Instead of two independent prices, there is now but one, and multiple equilibria become possible.

Consider the solutions possible in which both countries have the same incomes and thus the same consumption patterns, each consuming an amount $X$ of the agricultural product and an amount $Q$ of each manufactured good. If $X_i$ is the agricultural output of the $i$th country, and $n_i$ the number of manufactured goods it produces, its income is given by

$$Y_i = X_i + 2n_i pQ \tag{1}$$

and its resource use must satisfy the constraint[18]

$$V = X_i + n_i C(2Q) \tag{2}$$

where $V$ is the resource endowment and $C$ the cost function in manufacturing, each the same for both countries. If price equals average cost, which is the full equilibrium relationship for perfect monopolistic competition, then $Y_i = V$ for all $n_i$. That is, the level of income is independent of the division of the economy between agriculture and manufacturing – the source of the problems which arise when there are constant returns to scale in agriculture.

The trade balances for the two countries are given by the equations

$$T_1 = X_1 - X + 2pn_1 Q - p(n_1 + n_2)Q \tag{3a}$$

and

$$T_2 = X_2 - X + 2pn_2 Q - p(n_1 + n_2)Q \tag{3b}$$

Using the resource constraints, these can be written

$$T_1 = (V - X) - (n_1 C(2Q) - p(n_1 - n_2)Q) \tag{4a}$$

and

$$T_2 = (V - X) - (n_2 C(2Q) + p(n_1 - n_2)Q) \tag{4b}$$

Equilibrium trade, with $T_1 = T_2 = 0$, then implies the *balance condition*

$$(n_1 - n_2)(2pQ - C(2Q)) = 0 \tag{5}$$

In the constant returns case, therefore, an equilibrium is possible for any relationship between $n_1$ and $n_2$ if the monopolistic competition equilibrium $p = C(2Q)/2Q$ is satisfied.

The question now arises as to whether all the potential equilibrium configurations under constant returns are stable. Consider an initial situation in which $p = C(2Q)/2Q$ but $n_1 \neq n_2$, and suppose this to be disturbed by some shock that moves the price to $p' > p$. Assume that $n_1 > n_2$, so that the income in country 1 rises relative to the income in country 2 by an amount equal to $(n_1 - n_2)(2p'Q - C(2Q))$. If income determines expenditure in the next period (an appropriate dynamic for adjustment), then the balance condition cannot be satisfied in the initial period. But in the second period, country 1's expenditures will rise relative to those of country 2 by an amount equal to the income difference. Suppose that agricultural consumption becomes $X^1$, $X^2$ and the consumption of each manufactured good $Q^1$, $Q^2$ in the two countries (instead of $X$, $Q$ in each as in the equal income situation). Working through (3a), (3b) and (4a), (4b) in this case, it can be shown that

$$T_1 - T_2 = (n_1 - n_2)(p'(Q^1 + Q^2) - C(Q^1 + Q^2))$$
$$-[(X^1 - X^2) + p'(Q^1 - Q^2)] \qquad (6)$$

The last term is the difference in expenditure between the two countries and is equal to the difference in income $(n_1 - n_2)(2p'Q - C(2Q))$. Thus (6) becomes

$$T_1 - T_2 = (n_1 - n_2)[(p'(Q^1 + Q^2) - C(Q^1 + Q^2)) - (p'2Q - C(2Q))] \qquad (7)$$

Since average cost is a declining function of output in manufacturing, $T_1 - T_2 = 0$ if and only if $Q^1 + Q^2 = 2Q$. Since the changes in quantities purchased are due to income changes only, the relationship depends on the income elasticity of demand for manufactures. It is easy to show that

$$Q^1 + Q^2 \gtreqless 2Q, \text{ according as } e \gtreqless 1$$

where $e$ is the relevant elasticity. Thus, trade remains balanced if and only if the income elasticity of demand for manufactures is unity.

If the income elasticity is greater than unity (which would be a usual assumption), $Q^1 + Q^2 > 2Q$. Since average cost is falling at every monopolistic competition equilibrium, the right-hand side of (7) is positive in this case and thus $T_1 > 0$ (since $T_1 + T_2 = 0$). Thus, country 1 will move into a surplus position if $n_1 > n_2$, and the income elasticity is greater than unity. Any adjustment mechanism with non-perverse exchange markets and such that the more profitable industries expand before the less profitable will then move the countries towards an equilibrium in which $n_1 = n_2$. With flexible exchange rates, country 1's currency will appreciate. Manufacturing and agriculture in country 2 will both become more competitive, but the greater profit will be in manufacturing (since price exceeds average cost). Thus, manufacturing will expand in country 2, underselling country 1 in which manufacturing will contract, so that $n_1$ will move towards $n_2$. When $n_1 = n_2$, all unbalancing forces vanish. If the initial shock causes price to fall below average cost in manufacturing, country 1 will move into deficit, its currency will depreciate, its agriculture will become a profitable export, and its manufacturing will shrink relative to country 2, again moving $n_1$ and $n_2$ closer together.

If the income elasticity of demand for manufactures is *less* than unity, the initial increase in the price of manufactures will lead to a trade deficit for the country with the larger manufacturing sector and the consequent adjustments will increase the size of that sector relative to country 2, giving the unstable case in which all manufacturing will be concentrated in one of the countries and trade will be of the traditionally predicted kind, with exchange of manufactures for agriculture. If the income elasticity is unity, no unbalancing effects or adjustment processes will appear and the system is in neutral equilibrium at any relationship between $n_1$ and $n_2$.

For the case of identical economies in which manufacturing consists of a single group, the equilibrium pattern of trade will be as follows:

1.  If there are diseconomies of scale in agriculture or if there are constant returns to scale but the income elasticity of manufactures is greater than unity, the only long-run stable equilibrium will be such that: (i) there will be directional trade in manufacturing, each good being produced entirely within one country and sold equally in both; (ii) each country will produce half the total number of products within the group; (iii) there will be no trade in agriculture (if it is strictly an undifferentiated product), each country supplying its own domestic market; and (iv) the volume of trade will be equal to half the volume of manufactured output, and can therefore be expected to rise more rapidly than income, assuming an income elasticity greater than unity to be the regular case. The composition of an individual country's exports cannot be predicted, however, the specific products produced in each country being determined by historical or random factors.

    Since the conditions which give this case are those considered to be satisfied in general, this can be regarded as the 'normal' case.

2.  If there are constant returns to scale in agriculture *and* manufactures are an inferior good, the equilibrium with $n_1 = n_2$ will be unstable and the long-run trade pattern will correspond to a corner solution, with all manufactures produced in one country, no intra-industry trade (unless the demand for manufactures requires more resources than those of a single country), and exchange of manufactures for agricultural products.[19]

3.  If there are constant returns to scale in agriculture *and* the income elasticity of demand for manufactures is unity, manufacturing may be divided in any

way between the two countries and the trade may consist of anything from pure intra-industry trade to exchange of manufactures for agriculture.[20]

In the latter sections it will be assumed that either of the conditions for the 'normal' case is satisfied, and no further discussion will be given of the perverse case (2) or the neutral equilibrium (3).

In the 'normal' case the gains from trade are entirely due to the ability of the two countries to take advantage of economies of scale in manufacturing. Since real incomes are the same in both countries before trade and the same in both after trade, the gains from trade are equal in both countries – if price equals average cost in manufacturing, the equality of gains holds whatever the division of manufacturing and agriculture between the two countries. There is, in general, also a special kind of equity gain because, with the greater degree of product differentiation (except in the homogeneous production function case), the average difference in specification between available goods and consumers' most preferred ('ideal') goods will be lower as a result of trade.

## Multi-group manufacturing sectors

The preceding analysis was carried out for the case of a manufacturing sector consisting of a single group, such as automobiles. If there are a number of different groups (automobiles, refrigerators and shoes, for example), it is obvious that the general relationships between manufacturing as a whole and agriculture will be similar to those of the single-group case, with manufacturing split evenly between the two countries to give bidirectional trade in manufactures and no trade in agriculture, at least for a long-run stable equilibrium. It is not possible to deduce how the production and trade will be divided among the various groups in the manufacturing sector from the single-group model, however.

Both before and after trade, identical economies will have identical incomes and thus consumption levels for all goods in all groups. Denote the consumption levels of all goods in the $i$th group by $Q^i$, their prices by $p^i$, the cost functions for the group by $C^i(Q^i)$, where $Q^i$ is the production of the good, and the number of goods in the $i$th group produced in countries 1 and 2 by $n_1^i$ and $n_2^i$, respectively. Note that the uniformity and uniform density properties imply an equilibrium in which the quantities and prices are the same for all goods *within* each group when units are chosen in the appropriate way. The different groups are quite independent, however, with different cost functions and different preference relationships, and there is no necessary relationship between prices, quantities, units of measurement, or number of goods across different groups.

The balance condition for the multi-group case is derived in the same manner as for the single group, and is easily found to have the form:

$$\sum_i \left( n_1^i - n_2^i \right)\!\left( C^i\!\left( 2Q^i \right) - 2p^i Q^i \right) \tag{8}$$

where the summation is over all the groups in the manufacturing sector. In this case the balance condition can be satisfied in three different ways. The first and second correspond to those for the single-group case, that is either $n_1^i = n_2^i$ or $p^i = C^i(Q^i)/2Q^i$ for all $i$, so that all terms in the balance equation vanish simultaneously. As between these two possibilities, only $n_1^i = n_2^i$ gives a stable equilibrium. But there is a third possibility here, namely that the balance condition is satisfied by positive and negative terms to zero. This can occur with price greater than average cost in all groups if country 1 produces more of the goods in some groups than country 2 and less in others, so that there is balanced trade in manufacturing as a whole but not necessarily balance in intra-group trade. It is the stability of this solution that needs investigation.

It is sufficient to consider the case of two groups, and suppose that country 1 produces the majority of the goods in group 1 and country 2 the majority in group 2. Since the two groups represent quite different classes of goods with different demand and production conditions, the ratio of price to average cost (and thus the profitability) of the groups will, in general, differ. Suppose that the ratio of price to average cost is higher than in group 1, so that new entrants enter this group rather than group 2. If the group expands more rapidly in country 1 than in country 2, so that the absolute difference $n_1^1 - n_2^1$ increases, country 1's trade balance will be potentially in surplus and its currency will appreciate. The profitability of manufacturing in country 1 will diminish and expansion of the group will slow down or stop, but the profitability of manufacturing will increase in country 2. Although both groups in country 2 will become increasingly profitable, group 1 will remain the relatively more so and will expand. Thus, the difference $n_1^1 - n_2^1$ will diminish and the currencies move back towards par. When sufficient new entries have occurred in group 1, its profitability will have fallen below that of group 2 and new entrants will switch their attention to the latter. A similar process to that just described, with the relative roles of the two countries reversed, will take place and the difference $n_1^2 - n_2^2$ (negative) will move closer to zero. Thus, there will be an alternating series of entries (possibly combined with exits) until both countries are producing the same number of goods *in every group*, which is the only stable equilibrium.

The long-run stable equilibrium pattern of trade between identical economies having multi-group manufacturing sectors will thus be generally similar to that for the single-group case with the additional and very significant property that there will not only be bidirectional trade in manufacturing generally, but there will be bidirectional intra-industry trade in every group, with each country producing half the goods in each group.

## The crucial role of preference diversity

Before proceeding to discuss trade patterns between economies which are not identical, but possess the basic properties of the economies already investigated, we shall pause to consider the way in which the results already given (and those that are to follow) depend on the existence of populations within each country which are composed of individuals with diverse preferences.

Suppose that all individuals in each country had the same preferences, which would imply that all individuals in both countries had the same preferences if the economies were identical. Then there would be no product differentiation within the groups since there would be a single specification that was the most preferred specification for everybody, and the output of the group would consist of a homogeneous product made to this specification. Provided the economies of scale vanished at a relatively small output (as we have generally assumed), the market structure would be that of perfect competition, not of perfect monopolistic competition. The alternative market structure, if economies of scale persisted for large outputs, would be monopoly or possibly an oligopoly.

In the perfect competition case, no gains from trade at either the level of the firm or of the economy exist between identical economies, and thus there will be no trade. This can be compared with the relatively extensive intra-industry trade that would occur with diverse preferences.

In the monopoly case, there exist potential gains from trade if the economies of scale persist for outputs beyond those required to supply the market for a single country. Trade would take one of the following forms, or some mixture of the two.

1.  With a single group in manufacturing, an exchange of manufactures (all produced in one country) for agriculture but no bidirectional trade in manufacturing. Since the country producing the manufactured good under monopoly conditions stands to obtain the greater share of the gains from trade, rivalry over these potential gains could inhibit the countries from trading freely.
2.  If there are several groups in manufacturing, a solution with bidirectional trade in manufacturing is possible, with each country producing the sole good in some groups and exchanging part of the output for goods in the other groups. There would be no *intra-industry* trade, however, automobiles being exchanged for shoes but not for other kinds of automobiles.

Thus, the predicted pattern of trade between identical economies in which preferences are invariant over individuals is quite different from that in which preferences are diverse, even when all other features (such as economies of scale properties) are the same. In particular, only diversity of preference leads to intra-industry trade. It might seem, at first glance, that there is some kind of paradox in the idea that diversity of preferences leads to gains from trade due to economies of scale when identical preferences do not, at least in the perfect competition case. There is no paradox, however; diversity of preferences always causes a loss of economies of scale as compared with identical preferences, and the gains from trade arise from reduction of these losses. In the identical preferences case, the existence of a perfect competition equilibrium implies that there are no economies of scale lost even in isolation and thus nothing to gain from trade in the absence of comparative advantage or some other difference between the two economies.

### Size differences and false comparative advantage

Consider now the case of two countries that are identical in all respects except size, so that country 1 has $k$ times the resources of country 2 and $k$ times the population, the latter being distributed identically in both countries with respect to incomes and preferences.

By contrast with the case of economies of the same size, the pre-trade configurations of the two countries will not be the same. Because of the scale economies in manufacturing the larger country (which we will take to be country 1) will, in general, have greater product variety, will certainly have a lower equilibrium price for manufactures relative to agriculture, will have a higher per capita income, and will devote proportionally more resources to manufacturing than the smaller country because the elasticity of substitution in consumption between manufactures and agriculture must be greater than unity. Thus, the consumption and production patterns will differ between the two countries. More importantly, the larger country will have an apparent comparative advantage in manufacturing since the price of its manufactures relative to agricultural prices will be lower than in the smaller country. This is a false comparative advantage, however, since in any post-trade equilibrium each good will be produced in one country only at an average resource cost which is the same whichever country produces the good.

If the countries are trading freely and costlessly, with a perfect monopolistic competition equilibrium in manufacturing, the per capita incomes of the two countries will be identical and independent of the relative proportions in which resources are divided between manufacturing and agriculture in either country. Since the distribution of incomes and preferences is the same in both countries, the per capita consumption of all goods will be the same in both, so that total consumption of each good in country 1 will be $k$ times the consumption of the same good in country 2. If $Q$ denotes the consumption of each manufactured good in country 2 and $X$ its consumption of the outside good (agriculture), the quantities for country 1 will be $kQ$ and $kX$, respectively.

Proceeding as in the identical country case, the trade balances for the two countries, when there is a single group in manufacturing, are given by

$$T_1 = k(\bar{V} - X) - (n_1 C((1 + k)Q) - p(n_1 - kn_2)Q) \tag{9a}$$

and

$$T_2 = (\bar{V} - X) - (n_2 C((1 + k)Q) - p(n_1 - kn_2)Q) \tag{9b}$$

from which balanced trade with $T_1 = T_2 = 0$ then requires that

$$(n_1 - kn_2)(C((1 + k)Q) - (1 + k)pQ) = 0 \tag{10}$$

The balance equation is satisfied if price equals average cost ($= C((1 + k)Q/(1 + k)Q)$ or if $n_1 = kn_2$. As in the identical country case, it can be argued that the only long-run stable solution is the latter.

If manufacturing consists of more than one commodity group, the same type of arguments as given for the countries of identical size can be used to show that the number of goods within each group will be divided between country 1 and country 2 in such a way that country 1 produces $k$ times as many goods in that group as country 2.

Thus, the pattern of trade between countries which are identical in all respects but size will have the following properties:

1.  The countries will exchange only manufactured products and will exchange products within the same group, each good being produced in one country only.
2.  Within each product group, the number of products produced in each country will be proportional to its size. The smaller country will import more than half the products in each group, the quantity of each being less than half the total output, and will export less than half the products but in quantities more than half their total output.
3.  Each country will supply its own home market with agriculture and other outside goods.
4.  The per capita incomes of the two countries will be the same after trade and thus the smaller country will reap the greatest per capita gains from trade, since its pre-trade per capita income is lower than that of the larger country.

**True comparative advantage**
The simplest case illustrating the effect of true comparative advantage is one in which country 1 (for example) requires either more resources per unit of agricultural output or less resources per unit of manufacturing output, than does country 2 for the same levels of output. Country 1 then has a comparative advantage in manufacturing both before and after trade, arising from an absolute advantage in manufacturing or an absolute disadvantage in agriculture.

Consider first the case in which country 1 has an absolute disadvantage in agriculture. If the countries are otherwise identical, country 1 will have a lower per capita income in the pre-trade situation, a comparative advantage in manufacturing, and a higher proportion of resources engaged in manufacturing than does country 2. After trade, the equilibrium situation will be such that

(a)   no agriculture will be produced in country 1 unless country 2 is already devoting all its resources to agriculture, and

(b)   if manufacturing is produced in both countries, each good will be produced entirely in one country.

The equilibrium trade pattern will depend on the importance of agriculture relative to manufacturing in the world consumption pattern. If manufacturing goods represent more than half of total consumption (which can be taken as characteristic of industrialized economies), then the combined consumption of agricultural goods can be supplied by country 2 without using all that country's resources. In this case there will be unidirectional trade in agriculture combined with bidirectional trade in manufactures. Country 2 will export both agricultural and manufactured products and import only manufactured products. As in the previous cases, goods from each product group will be produced in each country. Since the countries are identical except for costs in agriculture, which become moot since no agriculture is produced in country 1, the income levels and consumptions of every good will be the same in both countries. It is easy to show that the number of goods in each group which are produced in the two countries are then related by the formula

$$n_1/n_2 = 1/(2m - 1) \tag{11}$$

where $m$ is the proportion of total expenditure which is spent on manufactures, this proportion being the same for both countries.

If $m < \frac{1}{2}$ (the developing country case), country 2 will specialize in agriculture and country 1 in manufacturing, giving the traditional pattern of an exchange of agricultural products for manufactures. Country 1 will need to produce some agriculture even at its high domestic cost, the exchange rate equating the price of agricultural products in the two countries. Country 2's trade gains occur because the exchange rate will give it manufactures at less than their local cost of production for the same levels of output.

Now consider the case in which the comparative advantage arises from an absolute advantage in manufacturing in country 1. This advantage is assumed to be constant across all manufacturing so that any good produced in the same quantity in both countries will have the same relative resource costs in the two countries. If manufactured goods account for the major part of total consumption expenditures (the industrialized country case), both countries will produce manufactures but each good will be produced in only one country, as before. The exchange rate necessary to equalize equilibrium prices for equivalent goods in the two countries will make country 1's agriculture non-competitive with imports from country 2. Thus, country 2 will produce agriculture for both markets, together with some of the manufactures in every group. The trade pattern will be essentially the same as when country 1 has an absolute disadvantage in agriculture, but post-trade incomes will not be the same in both countries (being lower in country 2) and thus the consumption patterns need not be identical.

If the greater share of consumption expenditure is on agricultural products, only country 1 will produce manufactures. Country 2 will export agricultural products and import manufactures, supplying part (but not all) of country 1's consumption of agricultural products. Country 1 gains from trade because of the economies of scale in its expanded manufacturing, country 2 because of both these economies of scale and the greater productivity of manufacturing in country 1. The gains are greater for country 2 because its pre-trade income is lower than that of country 1, but post-trade incomes are the same.

If country 1 has an absolute advantage in both manufacturing and agriculture, but a greater relative advantage (and thus a comparative advantage) in manufacturing, the situation is equivalent to one in which country 1 has an absolute advantage in manufacturing only but a higher ratio of resources to population than country 2. Incomes will be higher in country 1 both before and after trade, but the general pattern of trade will be the same as in the comparative advantage cases already studied. If manufactured goods predominate in consumption, country 1 will import all its agriculture but there will be bidirectional trade in manufactures, while if agricultural goods predominate there will be a simple exchange of agricultural products for manufactures with no manufacturing in country 2.

Even when there is a true comparative advantage situation, therefore, there will be intra-industry trade in manufacturing if agriculture accounts for a minority share of total expenditure, corresponding to the industrialized economy case.

## A Heckscher–Ohlin analysis

It has been assumed in the analysis up to this point that 'resources' are either a single homogeneous resource or a fixed-proportions bundle of resources, used in the same proportions in both manufacturing and agriculture, and that there are no factor ratio effects within the countries or between them. It is not difficult to modify the analysis to take account of differing factor intensities between manufacturing and agriculture and differing factor endowment ratios between the two countries.

For simplicity, we will confine the analysis to a two-factor model in labor and capital, with capital-intensive manufacturing and labor-intensive agriculture, 'land' being either irrelevant or abundant in both countries. It is assumed, as usual, that there are no factor reversals and that the factor endowment ratios of the two countries are not so different as to lead to complete specialization after trade – especially appropriate here since we are primarily interested in trade between similar economies. It is further assumed that the factor intensities of all manufactured goods are the same, so that factor ratio effects are uniform over all manufactures.

If country 1 is relatively capital-abundant in its endowments, the trade equilibrium will be such that country 1 produces a higher ratio of manufacturing output to agriculture than does country 2. If the countries are similar enough in other respects to give approximately the same ratio of manufactures to agriculture in consumption, country 1 will be a net exporter of manufactured goods and a net importer of agricultural products.

The trade pattern will not, however, be the simple traditional one of country 1 exporting only manufactures and country 2 exporting only agriculture. Although there will be unidirectional trade in agriculture, with country 2 the only exporter, there will be bidirectional trade in manufactures since each good will be produced in only one country. Country 2 will export both manufactures and agricultural products but will produce fewer manufactured goods than country 1 and thus will be a net importer of manufactures even though it exports such products. As compared with the traditional Heckscher – Ohlin model, the model presented here will differ in the following respects:

1. The existence of reciprocal trade in manufacturing.
2. The greater volume of trade owing to this reciprocal trade.
3. Considerable trade in goods (manufactures) for which the equilibrium factor ratios are identical in the two countries.

The basic Heckscher–Ohlin theorem, that each country's exports will be intensive in its relatively abundant factor, still holds if the factor intensities are calculated as a weighted average of exports. But note that for countries having factor endowment ratios which are not too dissimilar, the 'Heckscher–Ohlin' component in the overall trade patterns may be almost swamped by the reciprocal trade in manufacturing.

If the factor intensities vary between groups in manufacturing, or even vary over products within a group, but the effects of these variations are small relative to the economies of scale effects for individual products, the trade pattern will be essentially the same as that described above except that the countries may specialize in product groups rather than trade products within the same group.

**The effects of protection**
In the traditional analysis, where trade in any industry is unidirectional, protection by either country in a two-country two-sector model reduces trade in both

sectors and expands the protected sector relative to the export sector in the protecting country. A prohibitive tariff on the sector in which the country has a comparative disadvantage will eliminate all trade. In this model, protection of manufacturing may reduce the manufacturing sector relative to agriculture while protection of agriculture may have little effect on total trade in manufacturing but will change its pattern.

Consider first the identical country case in which free trade gives reciprocal trade in manufacturing but no trade in agriculture. If country 1 imposes a prohibitive tariff on manufacturing (and only the prohibitive tariff case will be discussed here), it may still be possible that it can export manufactures to country 2. If $n_1$ is the number of products that country 1 exports, while $n_2$ is the number of products that are not traded and are thus produced for home consumption only by both countries, it can be shown that the balance equation has the form

$$n_1(C(2Q) - 2pQ) = 0$$

where it is assumed that the consumption of each good is the same in both countries. Although this equation can be satisfied by price equal to average cost (the perfect monopolistic equilibrium condition) for all values of $n_1$, the same arguments as used previously can be used to show that the only stable equilibrium solution is when $n_1 = 0$, that is, when there is no trade in manufacturing, reciprocal or unidirectional, and thus no trade at all. The countries are then in their pre-trade configuration, with higher average costs in manufacturing and thus higher prices for manufactured products than under free trade. Since the elasticity of substitution between manufacturing and agricultural products (in consumption) has been taken to be greater than unity, the manufacturing sector will be smaller under protection than under free trade. It is actually agriculture which is the potential gainer from protection of manufacturing and even agriculture may lose if the income effects from the lowered real income outweigh the substitution effects.

If there are many groups in manufacturing, and only one group is protected, it can be shown that the long-run stable solution is such that there is no trade within the protected group but that the reciprocal intra-industry trade within other groups is unaffected except to the extent that the income effects due to the loss of scale economies within one group and the substitution effects due to the higher prices of the protected group, which work in opposite directions, change the total quantities of the goods and perhaps the equilibrium number of goods. The manufacturing sector will shrink (slightly, at least) as the single-group case.

In the comparative advantage cases, the free trade structure differs from that of the traditional model in the existence of bidirectional trade in manufacturing, so that protection of manufacturing might occur in the country with a comparative advantage in manufacturing or in the country with the comparative disadvantage, giving different outcomes. Furthermore, protection of agriculture by the agricultural importing country does not necessarily eliminate all trade.

Consider first the case in which manufactured goods account for the greater part of total consumption, so that manufactures are produced by both countries even when one has a comparative advantage in the manufacturing sector. If country 1 has the advantage in manufacturing, it will produce only manufactures and import all its agriculture, while country 2 will export some manufactures as well as agriculture. If country 2 protects manufacturing we obtain a traditional kind of result with zero trade and in which manufacturing expands in country 2 (the protecting country) while agriculture expands in country 1. If it is country 1 that protects its manufacturing, however, the bidirectional trade in that sector will vanish and the classic pattern of exporting manufactures in exchange for agriculture will emerge. Since country 1 cannot supply enough manufactures to satisfy both markets fully, country 2 will still produce some manufactures for its domestic market and there will be a combination of relative price and quantity adjustments within manufacturing together with a change in the terms of trade so that country 2's residual manufacturing can compete with imports. Finally, it is possible that country 1 may choose to protect agriculture, in which it has a comparative disadvantage. In this case the comparative advantage considerations become moot and the countries will behave much as in the identical country case, with bidirectional trade in manufacturing and each good produced in only one country. In all cases there is, of course, a loss of potential gains from trade – a loss of only the comparative advantage gains if country 1 protects agriculture, a loss of only economies of scale gains if country 1 protects manufacturing, and a loss of both kinds of gains if country 2 protects its manufacturing.

If agricultural products account for the major share of total consumption, the free trade structure will be a simple exchange of manufacturing exports by country 1 for agricultural imports. Country 2 will produce no manufacturing and there will be no bidirectional trade in that industry, but country 1 will produce some agriculture. There are only two possibilities for protection: either country 1 protects agriculture or country 2 protects manufacturing. In both cases, the outcomes are as before: if country 2 protects manufacturing, trade will cease, while if country 1 protects agriculture the identical country pattern will arise, with bidirectional trade in manufactures.

## Conclusion

When preferences are diverse within each economy and manufactured goods can be varied continuously in specification, the most competitive market structure within the manufacturing sector, both in autarky and in trade, will be that of perfect monopolistic competition. Such a structure will necessarily lead to a high degree of intra-industry trade in manufactures, encompassing exchange of goods within each product class but not exchange of goods which are totally identical. This intra-industry trade will certainly occur when the economies are absolutely identical in all respects and can persist under conditions of comparative advantage. However, a sufficiently great difference in comparative advantage, either because of technological or factor endowment differences, can eliminate the two-way trade in manufactures. Thus, intra-industry trade not only may occur between similar economies; it is most likely to occur between such economies and the volume may be much higher than trade based on comparative advantage. Although some kinds of protection will eliminate intra-industry trade, protection of the agricultural sector by the country with a comparative disadvantage in agriculture may even increase two-way trade in manufactures.

## Notes

1. Originally published in the *Journal of International Economics,* **10** (1980), 151–75.
2. See EEC trade statistics, for example, or discussions by Balassa 1966, 1975, Davies 1975, Dreze 1961, Grubel and Lloyd 1971, Linder 1961 and Truman 1972.
3. See previous references, plus Davies 1977, Finger 1975 and Gray 1973, 1977, for some representative studies.
4. Grubel 1970.
5. Linder 1961.
6. For example, from Grubel 1970: 'If there are substantial static economies of scale in the production of differentiated products, international trade between countries with very similar resource endowments and tastes is likely to give rise to significant welfare gains which conventional theory would have failed to predict.'
7. Gray 1973, 1977.
8. Davies 1977.
9. Lancaster 1979.
10. 'Perfect' monopolistic competition is not a form of imperfect competition, but market imperfections can give rise to 'imperfect' monopolistic competition.
11. As discussed in Lancaster 1966, 1971.
12. The author's early work on the characteristics approach emphasized combinable goods.
13. This was called the 'optimal good' in the author's first sketch of this analysis, Lancaster 1975.
14. Later work by the author has shown that the fundamental properties of the model are preserved without strict uniformity. See Lancaster 1979a.
15. See Lancaster 1979b.
16. That is, goods are brought into common measure by using cost or resource units relative to a base output level.
17. This key property is examined in some detail in Lancaster 1979a, where it is shown to be robust with respect to limited variations away from uniformity and uniform density.
18. It is assumed, except where specified to the contrary, that there is a single scarce resource which is mobile between agriculture and manufacturing. This could, of course, be an aggregate bundle of resources used in the same proportions everywhere.
19. But if manufactures alone constitute a sufficiently large proportion of total consumption so that one country alone cannot supply the total market even when specialized, manufactures will be produced in both countries and there will be some intra-industry trade. See below.
20. The comments of the previous note apply here also.

# 3   Protection and product differentiation[1]

**Introduction**

This paper is devoted to some initial exploration of the relationship between protection, product differentiation, and product variety – in particular, the way in which the degree of product differentiation or variety is changed by tariffs or other protective measures.

Note that a distinction is being made here between product differentiation and product variety, a distinction that is not usually drawn. The reason is that, in a trade context, we need to keep track of two measures involving numbers of products: the number of products produced by the industry in a particular country, and the number of products available to the consumers in that country. The two numbers are the same in an isolated economy, but obviously need not be the same when there is trade. Since the term 'product differentiation' is an active term, it will be used to denote the number of distinct products produced by the relevant industry, a number that is the result of active decision making by its existing and potential member firms. The passive term 'product variety' will be used to describe the number of different products available to the consumers in a given country.

A study of the effect of protection on product differentiation and/or product variety presumes, of course, that the degree of product differentiation is endogenously determined and in such a way as to be capable of being affected by trade restrictions. Some models of monopolistic competition and product differentiation used in the growing recent work on trade in differentiated products have been simplified to answer questions of a different kind, and are not suitable for use here. Differentiated-product trade models by Dixit and Norman 1980, Helpman 1981, Krugman 1979, 1980, for example, are so structured that the number of different products produced in each country is predetermined by the parameters of the system. Trade increases the degree of product variety because the number of products available in the world is the sum of the number produced in each country (no two firms will produce the same product, so there is no duplication after trade), and costless free trade makes all of these available in every country. Indeed, since outputs are constant and there are no increased scale economies, the gains from trade in the Krugman and Dixit–Norman models are due to the increased product variety, the utility functions being structured so that $1/n$ units of each of $n$ goods gives more utility than $1/(n-1)$ units of each of $n-1$ goods. Neither the degree of product differentiation nor the degree of product variety is affected by the level of protection – the number of products produced by the local industry is always the same, whether there is trade or not, and the number of products available to the consumer is always the same (the world total) so long as there is *any* trade, although the products will not all be available on equal terms.

## The model

The context in which the effect of protection on variety will be examined here is a version of the model of monopolistic competition which was developed earlier by the author (Lancaster 1979, 1980). This model resembles other analyses of monopolistic competition modified for the investigation of problems in international trade in that it is based on a two-sector economy, the output of one sector being a single homogeneous numeraire good produced under constant returns to scale and that of the other being a heterogeneous mix of product differentiates each of which is produced under some kind of economies of scale. The product-differentiated sector is modeled in the neo-Hotelling tradition, that is, the degree of substitutability between any two products is related to some measure of the distance between them in a space of product characteristics. Such an approach might be contrasted with the neo-Chamberlinian approach of such a model as that of Dixit and Stiglitz 1977, in which all goods are equal substitutes for each other and the degree of substitutability is a parameter of the system, not one of the endogenous variables.

Consumers are assumed to have separable utility functions, with one subutility a function of the amount of the homogeneous good, and the other a function of the amount and characteristics of the differentiated product. There are assumed to be only two relevant characteristics for the differentiated product, so that its characteristics specification can be defined along a one-dimensional spectrum. Each consumer has some point on the spectrum which is his 'most preferred specification', the particular way in which he would choose to have the characteristics combined if he were ordering the product custom-made. The consumer has also a 'compensating function', $h(v)$, where $v$ is the distance along the spectrum between his most preferred specification and the specification of some good actually available, such that he would be indifferent between the available good at price $P$ and his most preferred good at price $h(v)P$. Obviously, $h(v)$ is an increasing function of $v$ and $h(0) = 1$.

The utility function is formulated in constant elasticity of substitution form as

$$U(q, v, y) = (\alpha q^{\rho} h(v)^{-\rho} + (1 - \alpha) y^{\rho})^{1/\rho} \tag{1}$$

where $q$ is the quantity of the differentiated goods available, $v$ the distance between its specification and the most preferred specification of the consumer, and $y$ is the quantity of the homogeneous numeraire good.

The individual's demand function for the given product differentiate can easily be shown to be

$$q(P, v, I) = \frac{I}{\left(1 + Ah(v)^{\sigma-1} P^{\sigma-1}\right)P} \tag{2}$$

where $\sigma = 1/1(1 - \rho)$ is the elasticity of substitution,[2] $P$ the price of the differentiated product in terms of the homogeneous product, and $I$ the income in units of the homogeneous good.

The economy is taken to be populated with individuals whose preferences are identical except as to their most preferred specifications, and these preferences to possess a uniformity such that individual demand is, as it is written above, a function of price, income and the *relative* specifications of the consumer's most preferred good and the available good, and independent of the *absolute* position on the spectrum. The population distribution is taken to be such that most preferred specifications are distributed continuously over the spectrum with constant density and income is assumed to be distributed uniformly.

Since we shall be confining our attention to cases in which there are some economies of scale in the differentiated industry, the number of goods actually produced will be finite. These goods will each be defined by the position of their product specification on the spectrum. In general, a consumer will not find his most preferred specification among those of the goods actually available, and he must choose one of the latter. There will be two goods which are closest to his most preferred, one in each direction along the spectrum. If the goods sell at prices $P$, $P'$ and are situated at distances $v$, $v'$, the consumer will choose the unprimed good if $h(v)P < h(v')P'$ and the primed good if the inequality is reversed.

Aggregate market demand for a good selling at price $P$, with the next good on the spectrum at distance $D$ and selling a price $P'$ in one direction, and at distance $D'$ and price $P''$ in the other, is determined in the following way:

(i)   The total market for the good is made up of two half-markets, one in each direction. The half-markets are determined independently, so we can confine our attention to one only.

(ii)  The half-market is made up of all the individuals who choose the target good rather than the neighboring one, that is, all individuals with most preferred specifications out to a distance $u$, where $u$ satisfies the *dividing condition*:

$$h(u)P = h(D - u)P' \tag{3}$$

(iii) Each of the individuals in the market has a demand for the product given by the expression (2) set out previously, which is a function of $v$, the individual's spectral position relative to the good. Thus the aggregate demand in the half market is a function of $P$, $P'$ and $D$ given by

$$Q(P,P',D) = \int_0^u q(P,v)dv \qquad (4)$$

where $u = u(P, P', D)$ is given by the dividing condition (3) above.

The demand function has the following properties which are relevant to the later analysis:

(a)   Using subscripts to represent partial derivatives:

$Q_P < 0, Q_{P'} > 0, Q_D > 0$

as expected.

(b)   The elasticity of demand $E(P, P', D)$ is not a constant as in some other models of monopolistic competition such as Dixit and Stiglitz 1977, but is a variable. Changes in the elasticity (and thus in the ratio of price to marginal revenue) form an important mechanism in attaining equilibrium. The properties of the elasticity function are given by:

$$E_P > 0, E_{P'} < 0, E_D < 0$$

In particular, $E \to \infty$ as $D \to 0$ – goods become perfect substitutes as their specifications converge.

On the production side, firms are assumed to have the same cost functions for all specifications within the product-differentiated industry. For simplicity this cost function is taken to be determined by a constant marginal cost plus a fixed cost.

In order to provide numerical results with which to back up the various stories which will be given to describe the effects of protection on product differentiation and variety, a special model is used which satisfies all the assumptions of the more general analysis. To obtain this specific model, details of which are given in the appendix,

(a)   the compensating function was assumed to have the quadratic form[3] $h(v)$ = $1 + v^2$

(b)  the elasticity of substitution in (2) was taken to have the value $\sigma = 2$. In addition, numerical values were chosen for the marginal and fixed costs in production and for the constant A in expression (2).

The particular form chosen for the compensating function not only satisfies all the criteria, but permits integration of the demand function (4), to give

$$Q(P, P', D) = \frac{k}{4P^2} \arctan \frac{2P^{1/2}\left( P'\left(PP'D^2 - (P-P')^2\right)^{1/2} - P'D\right)}{(P-P')^2(1+4P)^{1/2}} \qquad (5)$$

with an explicit, but complicated expression, for the elasticity $E(P, P', D)$, details of which are given in the Appendix. Unfortunately, although explicit expressions for $Q, E$ can be found, solutions of the various equilibrium equations can only be found by numerical methods.

**The reference situation**
Consider first an isolated economy with an industry group conforming to the model as detailed. Within the product-differentiated industry, each firm has two variables at its disposal, the specification of its product (the mix of characteristics) and the price of the product. Assuming perfect information, costless adjustments, free and willing entry, and no collusion, the equilibrium of the product-differentiated industry will be taken to be the zero-profit Nash equilibrium in which each firm takes the specification and price of the other firms as given. The equilibrium will, of course, be such that marginal cost and marginal revenue are equal for each firm and that price and average cost are also equal. A zero-profit Nash equilibrium will not necessarily exist,[4] but it does exist under the conditions of the model being used here – in particular, because of the uniform distribution of consumers over the spectrum and the assumed absence of boundary effects. With this uniformity of distribution and the assumed uniformity of preferences, the demand conditions for any product depend only on prices and the *relative* positions of goods on the spectrum, but not on *absolute* spectral locations. Thus the Nash equilibrium is such that the equilibrium values for the individual firms (price, quantity, profit) will be identical except for specification, and furthermore, that the specifications of the various goods produced will be evenly spaced along the spectrum.
    The above equilibrium is fully characterized by the price, output and profit for any one firm, since these will be the same for all firms, and by the spacing between adjacent goods along the spectrum. In fact, only two values – price and spacing – are sufficient for a specific model, the remaining values being derivative. We shall normally use the inverse of the spacing, defined as the degree

of product differentiation or degree of product variety (according as whether the spacing is that between products produced in the country, or all products available), rather than the inter-good spacing itself. For the specific model used for illustration in this paper, the equilibrium solution values can be obtained by numerical methods. Since the absolute numbers have meaning only relative to the arbitrarily chosen units of the model, they will be utilized only for reference in discussing what happens to the same economy under different trade regimes. Thus we shall give equilibrium values for all the variables (prices, quantities, degree of product differentiation) as indexes to base 100 relative to the solution values for the reference situation, which we shall take initially to be the economy in isolation.

Now consider costless free trade between two identical economies, each exactly like the economy described above. Since there are no comparative advantage effects, there will be no trade in the homogeneous outside good even if it is tradeable (and not leisure, for example). Trade will consist solely of differentiated products, each country producing half the total number of different goods and supplying consumers in both countries. Under free trade with zero transport costs and identical cost and demand conditions at home and abroad, the equilibrium values for the representative firm will be the same as those for a firm in a single isolated country having twice the population density of the country used as reference.

What should our expectations be as to the relationship between the equilibrium in isolation and the configuration resulting from free trade? The initial effect of opening trade between absolutely identical countries will be that there are now two firms producing each product, so we can expect one of the two firms to be forced out.[5] The main difference from the pre-trade situation will then be in the quantity produced by each firm, since it is the expanded market open to the single surviving firm that provides the driving force toward the new equilibrium as well as much of the gains from trade. But we would not generally expect that the trade solution would simply be one in which the number of products remained the same as before, with the number of firms in each country halved but their outputs doubled. Consider an initial post-trade situation in which half the original firms in each country have left the industry and each surviving firm has a market of double the size but with other parameters (in particular, elasticity of demand) unchanged.[6] At the original price the firm can sell twice the quantity at the same marginal revenue as before, which will still equal the marginal cost (this having been assumed constant). But average cost is declining with output, so that these firms will be making positive profits and thus new firms will enter and the number of products will increase.

Thus the free trade equilibrium, when fully established, can be expected to be such that each country has more than half the number of firms that existed in isolation, but necessarily less than the original number. Price will be lower after trade, since it is equal to average cost which will certainly have fallen. Table 3.1 shows the actual solution values for the model, relative to the autarky values, and the expectations are seen to be fulfilled. The center column labelled 'intermediate' refers to the situation after the first impact (when one of the two firms producing each product is assumed to be forced out), but before the new round of entries and changes in products. Note that this intermediate situation is put in for reference only – a real scenario might never include such a stage, since firms may commence by varying their products immediately after the opening of trade rather than competing head-on by price wars, exits, then some re-entries. The figure 'excess profit' is the percentage by which the excess of revenue over variable cost exceeds the fixed cost.

*Table 3.1   The effects of trade*

|  | Autarky | Free trade (Intermediate) | Free trade (Final) |
|---|---|---|---|
| Price (local good) | 100 | 100 | 93.3 |
| Price (import) | – | 100 | 99.4 |
| Product variety | 100 | 100 | 159.7 |
| Number of local firms | 100 | 50 | 79.9 |
| Output per firm | 100 | 200 | 138.4 |
| Excess profit (%) | 0 | 101 | 0 |

Note that free trade *increases* the degree of product variety available to consumers, although it *reduces* the degree of product differentiation in each country. The gains from trade come partly from the greater degree of product variety and partly from the lower price per product. When there is variable product specification, trade improves the distribution of welfare as well as its average level, since greater variety means more consumers can find a good closer to their most preferred specification.

**Symmetric trade restrictions**
To consider the effect of tariffs and protection on product differentiation, let us commence with the simplest case to analyze, that of the completely symmetric case in which two identical countries impose identical non-prohibitive tariffs on each other's imports.

Before proceeding further, however, we need to consider the effect of different simplifying assumptions concerning the relative arrangement of goods on the spectrum in the two countries. As in the free trade case, the final equilibrium will be such that each country will produce half the total number of different goods. In the free trade case, however, it did not matter which goods were produced in which country since the equilibrium configurations were the same in all markets. In this case, it is obvious that the equilibrium configuration for a home good will be different from that for an import because of the effects of trade restrictions. Since the equilibrium for a single market depends on the equilibria in the adjacent markets, the world equilibrium will depend on the arrangement of goods. For example, consider two different arrangements which are both symmetrical:[7]

(a)   In which the products of the two countries alternate in specification as we move along the spectrum, so that every home good has an imported good as its immediate neighbor on each side. (There is a Japanese car closely similar to every American car.)

(b)   In which one country makes all the goods on the right half of the spectrum and the other makes all those on the left. (Japan makes all the small cars and the United States all the large cars, for example.)

We shall refer to (a) as the 'interleaved case', (b) as the 'split case'. The two cases will lead to quite different world equilibria, since each market is surrounded by dissimilar markets in the interleaved case (home goods surrounded by imports, and imports by home goods) and by similar goods (home goods surrounded by other home goods, imports by other imports) in the split case. If we ignore the boundary effects in the split case, both cases can give simple symmetric solutions defined by two equilibria, one for the home market which will apply to all home markets in both countries, and one for the export market which will also apply universally. In both cases, the solution will be such that:

(i)     The number of firms is the same in each country, each firm selling in both the local and export markets.

(ii)    The price, quantity, and elasticity of demand are the same for foreign sales at home as for home sales abroad.

(iii)   the price, quantity, and elasticity of demand are the same in the local markets of both the home and foreign producers.

(iv)    Total sales and total profit (from combined local sales and exports) are the same for all firms in both countries.

Consider first the interleaved case. Denote the constant marginal cost assumed in the model by $m$ and the revenue, marginal revenue and price in the market for the home good by $R$, $MR$, and $P$, respectively. Primes will denote equivalent values for the market for imports. Denote the distance between adjacent goods by $D$, which will be constant along the spectrum because of the assumption that home and foreign goods alternate.

In any of the home markets, the demand conditions and thus the marginal revenue will be determined by the product price $(P)$, the price of adjacent goods ($P'$, the same in both directions), and the inter-good distance ($D$ in both directions). The same will be true of the market for imports, with the roles of $P$, $P'$ interchanged. Thus we can write the net revenues (revenue less variable cost – linear in quantity and thus assignable between markets) from home sales and from exports as $NR(P, P', D)$ and $NR'(P', P, D)$, respectively, with the same relationships between functions and arguments for $MR$, $MR'$. The profit $\pi(P, P', D)$ is given by

$$\pi(P, P', D) = NR(P, P', D) + NR'(P', P, D) - FC \qquad (6)$$

where $FC$ is the fixed cost.

If we take the tariff to be a specific one of value $t$, then the Nash equilibrium for the system, given the number of firms (and thus the value of $D$), will be the solution to the pair of equations:

$$MR(P, P', D) = m \qquad (7)$$
$$MR'(P', P, D) = m + t$$

provided the non-arbitrage condition $P' \leq P + t$ is satisfied. The profit $\pi$ then becomes a function of $D$ only, with the equilibrium value of $D$ found by the condition $\pi = 0$.

For the split case, the home market has other home markets adjacent to it, so that the net and marginal revenues are functions of $P$ and $D$ alone. Similarly the net and marginal revenues in the import markets are functions of $P'$, $D$ alone. Thus the Nash equilibria for the home and import markets are determined independently, given $D$ (which must be the same for both types of markets since every good is sold in a home market in one country and an import market in the other), the system being as follows:

$$MR(P, D) = m \qquad (8)$$
$$MR'(P', D) = m + t$$
$$\pi(P, P', D) = 0$$

Although it will be argued later that the interleaved case represents the final equilibrium situation in a world of full information and costless adjustment, the split case has a more clear-cut solution, and will be analyzed first.

Suppose, in particular, that the free trade equilibrium happened to result in this configuration and then consider the effect of adding the specific tariff $t$, a move reciprocated by the other country. Take the short-term temporary equilibrium to be that in which no firms have yet entered or exited following the trade restrictions, but each firm sells in the home and export markets at prices which equate marginal revenue and marginal cost (including tariff, where relevant). The Nash equilibrium for the home markets will be unchanged, since marginal revenue is independent of the import market price, the spacing between adjacent goods has not yet changed, and marginal cost is unchanged.

Thus the home market price will be the same as under free trade and the profit on the home market will be unchanged. But the profit on export sales will necessarily fall because of the tariff, so that total profit will fall (to less than zero) and firms will exit. Thus the final equilibrium will be with fewer firms (and products) than under free trade. The price of the home product will be slightly higher (since reducing the number of home goods will lower the elasticity of demand for each and increase the markup of price over marginal cost), and the price of the import considerably higher because of the same effect plus the tariff effect. The story is illustrated, for the model being used, in Table 3.2. Note that the reference situation is now the free trade equilibrium.

*Table 3.2   The split case*

|  | Free trade | Restricted trade (Intermediate) | (Final) |
|---|---|---|---|
| Price (local good) | 100 | 100 | 100.7 |
| Price (import) | 100 | 119.4 | 119.9 |
| Product variety | 100 | 100 | 98.0 |
| Number of firms | 100 | 50 | 98 |
| Excess profit (%) | 0 | −4.4 | 0 |

In this case, as in all the symmetric cases, the degree of product differentiation (number of local firms) will always be half the number of different goods, as with free trade. Thus the degree of product variety and the number of firms will always stand in the same relationship to their free trade levels, and only the degree of product variety need be traced.

There are no ambiguities in the solution of the split case, since profit per firm will necessarily fall when a tariff is imposed and the number of firms (and thus of products) will be reduced. Formal comparative static analysis can be used to show that the sign of $dD/dt$ is unambiguously positive.

The interleaved case is more complex, since the home and import markets are adjacent and intimately related instead of being separable. Assume that the initial free trade structure is one of alternating home and imported goods, then consider the effect of equal specific tariffs introduced by the two countries. The very first effect will be that the firms will be out of equilibrium in their export markets, the marginal cost of selling in which has risen by the amount of the tariff, so the export price will be raised. From the point of view of the other country, the (consumer) price of imports will rise – but import and home markets are adjacent on the spectrum so that there will be substitution in favor of home goods. Since this is happening in all markets in both countries, the price of home goods will rise. In the initial stage (with the same firms as under free trade) the price of both home and imported goods will rise. It is clear that the firms will each make less profit on their exports, but more profit on their home sales, than in the free trade position. Does this mean that firms gain or lose from the tariff? In the specific model being used here, the firms gain – increased home market profits outweigh decreased export market profits, as shown by the figures in the center column of table 3.3.

*Table 3.3   The interleaved case*

|  | Free trade | Restricted trade (Intermediate) | (Final) |
| --- | --- | --- | --- |
| Price (local good) | 100 | 105.2 | 103 |
| Price (import) | 100 | 112.6 | 110.3 |
| Product variety | 100 | 100 | 112.6 |
| Excess profit (%) | 0 | 23.3 | 0 |
| Home firms' market share (%) | 50 | 74.9 | 81.2 |

As the table shows, the pre-entry pre-exit effect of the tariff is to give positive profits to the existing firms. These profits will then induce entry so that the number of firms (and the number of products) is larger with protection than with tariffs. This is the opposite result from that found in the split case. There is a perfectly reasonable explanation for the existence of positive profits at the intermediate stage of the interleaved case (as compared with the negative profits in the split case): since the immediate competitors for every home good are imports in the interleaved case, protection reduces that competition and increases the monopoly power and thus the profits in the home market. Although the effect of the tariff is necessarily to reduce profits in the export market, this loss can be outweighed by the home market gains. In the split case, on the other hand, the immediate competitors of home goods are other home goods, so that protection brings no home market gains from increased monopoly power to outweigh reduced export profits.

The increased degree of product variety may seem paradoxical when restricted trade is compared with autarky and with free trade. Since the equilibrium number of products is less under autarky than under free trade, it might seem that restricted trade should give an intermediate result – fewer products than with free trade but more than in isolation – rather than a result in the opposite direction from autarky. The outcome is less paradoxical, however, when it is noted that the number of *firms* (degree of product differentiation) does have this intermediate property, being 13% more than under free trade but 10% fewer than in isolation.

While the number of firms converges to the autarky level as the tariff converges to the prohibitive level, the degree of variety shows a discontinuity. What happens is as follows: the higher the tariff, the smaller the import sales (home sales are 81% for the model) so that, although the number of products available to consumers is twice the number produced at home, the half that are imported have very small markets because of the high price due to the tariff. As the tariff approaches the prohibitive level, the number of firms approaches the autarky level while the product variety approaches twice the autarky level, but with half the products having minute sales. At the prohibitive tariff, these minute sales become zero and the number of goods available in either country collapses to the autarky value.[8] The effect of protection on product differentiation and product variety depends, as shown above, on the relationship between arrangements of products on the spectrum in the two countries. In the split case, the degree of product differentiation falls as a result of tariffs; in the interleaved case, it rises. But the arrangement of the goods on the spectrum could itself be endogenously determined, and if so, there should be a clear choice between the two cases. There has been some considerable recent study of the problems of predicting patterns from entry in spatial and quasi-spatial models of competition, and the subject is a difficult one.[9] One criterion that has considerable merit is to assume that a final equilibrium will be that configuration which contains the largest number of firms possible that can all be sustained without loss, a kind of 'minimum entropy' property. For any other zero-profit configuration, there is some reorganization of the firms and product specifications such that at least one firm can make a positive profit. The author has referred elsewhere to the possibility of 'innovative entry' which can arise in such a case (see Lancaster 1982), so that the long-run full information full flexibility equilibrium should be such that no innovative entry is possible. As between the split and interleaved case, only the interleaved case possesses this property, since there are clearly profits to be made by rearrangement from the split configuration.

Thus the conclusion for the case of symmetric tariff protection is that the interleaved case is the appropriate one, and thus that protection leads to *increased* product differentiation and product variety.

It should be noted that protection has distribution effects (meaning distribution with respect to a consumer's location on the spectrum) resulting from the change in the product mix which will tend to pull in two different directions:

1. Insofar as there is an increase in the degree of product variety, distribution is more even – the average distance between consumers' most preferred goods and the goods actually provided by the market is reduced.

2. Because of the direct effect of the tariff, however, consumers whose most preferred goods are close in specification to the imported good will be worse off (higher prices) relative to consumers close to the home products, making the distribution less even.

In the split case, or under any circumstances in which the degree of product variety is reduced by the tariff, the distributional effects will all be in the direction of increasing the unevenness of the welfare distribution.

## Asymmetric protection

In order to study the effects of unilateral tariff protection, we shall change the context somewhat from the above symmetrical case to that of a small country in a large world. We shall assume that the home country does not export the product-differentiated industry's output, but that there is an industry abroad which does sell products of this group in the home market. The industry abroad has the same marginal cost as the home industry (this is a gold standard world), but not necessarily the same fixed costs, and it reacts passively to home country tariffs.

Take the initial situation to be that in which there is no tariff, the home market being shared equally between home goods and imports,[10] where this is taken to mean that home and foreign products alternate on the spectrum and sell at the same prices. For the model under consideration, this implies an equilibrium at the same values as autarky except that only half the goods are produced by the home firms. Measurements of the properties of other situations will be taken with reference to this situation as base.

Now consider the effect of a tariff which, for convenience, we will take to be a specific tariff of level $t$, as in the analysis of the symmetric cases. Since the foreign supplier has the same marginal cost ($m$) as the domestic industry, the effect of the tariff on the foreign firms is to make their effective marginal cost equal to $m + t$ for sales in the home market. The effect of the tariff will be a consequence of the foreign firms' adjustment to equate marginal revenue in the home market with the new marginal cost in that market. Since the pre-tariff marginal revenue is less than the new marginal cost, the initial post-tariff change will cause a rise in the price of the foreign good on the home market. The market widths for imports will fall as some consumers with most preferred specifications lying in between the domestic and foreign goods shift from the latter to the relatively cheaper domestic products. But the expanded size of the market for the home goods will reduce their elasticity of demand and the price of domestic goods will rise to re-equate marginal revenue with marginal cost. Both prices will rise, but the foreign price more (since the foreign marginal cost has risen relative to the domestic), and the sales of the foreign models will drop while those of the domestic models will expand. Since both price and quantity of the domestic model increase, zero profits change into positive profits. With the specifications of goods unchanged, the post-tariff, pre-entry equilibrium will be related to the pre-tariff situation as shown in the center column of Table 3.4. As before, the values given are those for the numerical solution of the specific model being used to illustrate the events.

*Table 3.4  The asymmetric case*

|  | Free trade | Post-tariff trade | |
|  |  | (Pre-entry) | (Post-entry) |
| --- | --- | --- | --- |
| Price (local good) | 100 | 104.2 | 97.6 |
| Price (import) | 100 | 112.6 | 104.6 |
| Product variety | 100 | 100 | 129.2 |
| Excess profit (%) | 0 | 44 | 0 |
| Home firms' market share (%) | 50 | 67.1 | 73.4 |

The existence of positive profits will attract new domestic firms. We shall assume that the rest of the world is large, so that foreign firms will continue to sell in the home market so long as revenue more than covers variable cost plus tariffs. Somewhat more heroically, we shall also assume that the imports remain interleaved with the home goods. Since the spacing between the home firms will change as a result of new entry, this implies that the specifications of imports also change – even though it is being assumed that the country is too small to cause restructuring of foreign industry. Such a situation might arise when (a) the rest of the world is very large and produces a wide range of products and (b) the only kinds of these products that will be imported are those having specifications midway between those of home goods, since these will always be the most profitable.

As a result of entry, there is an increase in the degree of product differentiation and product variety. Since the goods are now closer to each other on the spectrum, the elasticity of demand rises so that price moves closer to marginal cost in the home good market, and closer to marginal cost plus tariff in the import market. Thus the prices of both local goods and imports will fall relative to the post-tariff pre-entry stage, and the price of home goods will be less than under free trade.

The final equilibrium, as shown in the last column of Table 3.4, has the following characteristics:

1.  The degree of product differentiation and product variety is increased by the tariff, as in the symmetric case.
2.  The price of the home good is pushed *down* as a result of protection.

It may seem paradoxical that there are more firms selling at a lower price than before while profit per firm remains the same as before the tariff (zero). However, although the firms are closer together, their markets are actually wider because the foreign firms' market areas have been reduced by their relatively higher prices due to the tariff. In the model analyzed, it can be shown that, although there are 29.2% more firms, the output per firm is 14.5% higher than before the tariff. The larger output means lower average cost and thus a lower price at which profit is zero. Although tariffs could be used in the small country case to lower the price of local goods, the prices of imports necessarily rise. The rise in import prices is less than the tariff, however, since price is closer to marginal revenue than under free trade and marginal revenue in the import market has risen by only the amount of the tariff.[11] Thus, if the tariff revenues were returned to the purchasers of imports (in such a way as still left them treating the market price as the relevant decision variable), the purchasers of both home goods and imports would be better off as a result of the tariff. In addition, there is a gain due to the increased product variety.

Thus a small country which is powerless to gain from tariffs under conditions of perfect competition can gain from protection under monopolistic competition. This gain occurs only if the imports are closely related to the home goods, as in the assumed interleaved relationship above. Had the relationship between imports and home goods been like the split case studied earlier, there would be no interactions and no gains from the tariff.

**How general are the results?**
The analysis which has been given has consisted of plausible stories backed up by the results generated for a specific (if highly representative) model. To obtain some idea of the extent to which these results can be generalized, it is necessary to look at the formal comparative statics, commencing with the symmetric case. Starting from a zero-profit equilibrium, increased profit per firm will lead to new entry and decreased profit to exits, so it is sufficient to fix the number of firms and examine the effect of the tariff on profit levels – the rest of the story then follows.

Define $NR(P, P')$ as the 'net revenue' or revenue less assigned variable cost from home market sales, and $NR'(P', P)$ as the net revenue from export sales, given by:

$$NR(P, P') = (P - m)Q(P, P') \tag{9}$$
$$NR'(P', P) = (P' - m - t)Q'(P', P')$$

Since the firms will choose $P$ to maximize $NR$ and $P'$ to maximize $NR'$, the first order conditions for maximization will take the form

$$NR_1 = Q + (P - m)Q_1 \tag{10}$$
$$NR'_1 = Q' + (P' - m - t)Q'_1$$

where subscript 1 indicates the partial derivative with respect to the own price. Subscript 2, used below, will indicate cross-price derivatives. The effect of a small tariff change on the equilibrium position will be:

$$\frac{dP}{dt} = -\frac{Q'_1 NR_{12}}{NR_{11}NR'_{11} - NR_{12}NR'_{12}} \tag{11}$$

$$\frac{dP'}{dt} = \frac{Q'_1 NR_{11}}{NR_{11}NR'_{11} - NR_{12}NR'_{12}} \tag{12}$$

The denominator in (11) and (12) is positive if the direct effects outweigh the cross effects, a standard condition for stability of equilibrium which will be assumed to hold here. Since $NR_{11} < 0$ is also a stability condition and $Q'_1$ is essentially negative, we have $dP'/dt > 0$ unambiguously – the unsurprising result that the consumer price of the imported good will rise as a result of the tariff.

The effect of the tariff on the equilibrium price of the home good is less certain, since it depends on the sign of the cross effect $NR_{12}$. Noting that $NR = (P - m)$ $Q(P, P')$, we have

$$NR_{12} = Q_2 + (P - m)Q_{12} \tag{13}$$

where $Q_2 \geq 0$ and, in general, $Q_{12} < 0$, so that $NR_{12}$ may have any sign, as may $dP/dt$ in consequence. If the cross effects vanish, then $dP/dt = 0$, of course.

With the number of firms fixed, the profit per firm is the sum of the net revenues from the home and foreign markets less the fixed cost:

$$\pi = NR(P, P') + NR'(P', P) - FC$$

so that

$$\frac{d\pi}{dt} = NR_1 \frac{dP}{dt} + NR_2 \frac{dP'}{dt} + NR'_1 \frac{dP'}{dt} + NR'_2 \frac{dP}{dt} + \frac{\partial NR'}{\partial t} \tag{14}$$

$$= NR_2 \frac{dP'}{dt} + NR'_2 \frac{dP}{dt} - Q' \tag{15}$$

since $NR_1$, $NR'_1 = 0$ ($P$, $P'$ being the net revenue maximizing prices in the home and foreign markets) and $\partial NR'/\partial t = -Q'$.

If the cross effects are zero, so that $NR_2$, $NR'_2$ vanish, then profits necessarily fall when the tariff is increased, so that the new final equilibrium will have fewer firms than before the tariff rose. This corresponds to the 'split case' of the previous discussions. If the cross effects are not zero, however, then the effect of the tariff on profit is no longer unambiguous since $NR_2$, $NR'_2$, $dP'/dt$ are all positive, $-Q'$ is negative, and $dP/dt$ can be positive or negative.

Thus, although the result given previously, that profits initially rise from the effect of the tariff in the 'interleaved' case, is certainly true for the specific model analyzed, and the model itself has features that would be generally accepted as representative, the result cannot be regarded as truly general. It seems possible that tariffs might reduce the degree of product variety for some functional forms and some parameter values.

In the asymmetric case, the circumstances set out had certain special features, an important one of which was that the home produced goods were not sold abroad. As a result, the increased monopoly power in the home market due to the tariff on imports gave a relatively large increase in profits. The larger the proportion of the home good sold abroad, the smaller the effect on profits due to this effect and thus the less the increase in the degree of product differentiation. Thus the no-export assumption gives a much stronger effect than when there are exports, and might thus be regarded as a special case.

## Conclusions

It has been shown in this paper that, when there is monopolistic competition and a product-differentiated industry which operates in both trading partners, the degree of product differentiation (number of different products produced by the home industry) and the degree of product variety (number of different products available to the home consumers) are both affected by the existence and level of intra-industry trade, and both will, in general, be changed by protection.

Although trade increases the degree of product variety, trade restrictions do not necessarily reduce it. On the contrary, in both the large-country case (symmetric trade between two identical countries) and the small-country case (where the rest of the world does not react), the degree of product variety is *increased* as a result of the imposition of tariffs, at least for the specific model studied.

The reason for this result is basically the same in both the small- and large-country cases. With intra-industry trade in a monopolistic competition setting, imports are close but imperfect substitutes for home goods. Tariffs lower their competitiveness, so that the local firms have more monopoly power (lower elasticity of demand) and their profits rise. But excess profits then induce entry and thus more firms and more products.

Because of the interactive but imperfectly competitive markets for home products and imports, a small country which imports goods in the same product-differentiated group as it makes locally can *gain* by imposing a tariff, something impossible with perfectly competitive markets. This possibility exists only when there are imports which are relatively close substitutes for local goods.

## Appendix

The appendix sets out the features and properties of the special model on which the numerical solutions given in the text are based. The model conforms in all respects to the general model analyzed in Lancaster 1979, but has specific functional forms for the compensating function of the consumer and the cost functions of firms, as well as specific numerical values for the system parameters. The compensating function has the specific form:

$$h(v) = 1 + v^2 \tag{16}$$

On the basis of this compensating function, a consumer whose most preferred good is at distance $u$ from the available good will be indifferent between buying that good and the adjacent available good (at distance $D$ from the first available good) when the price of the target good ($P$) and that of the adjacent good ($P'$) are related as follows:

$$P = \frac{1 + (D-u)^2}{1 + u^2} \tag{17}$$

For the above compensating function and the assumed value of the elasticity of substitution ($\sigma = 2$), the demand function for the individual at distance $v$ from the available good has the form:

$$q(P,v) = \frac{1}{P\left[1 + AP\left(1 + v^2\right)\right]} \tag{18}$$

where $A$ is a constant expressing the importance of the group good in the total utility function. The value $A = 4$ will be assumed for all the succeeding analysis, a convenient number that implies expenditure on the product differentiated group is 20% of total expenditure when $P = 1$, that is, when the price of the group good is equal to that of the homogeneous outside good used as numeraire. It is convenient to write (18) in the form:

$$q(P,v) = \frac{k}{4P^2(a^2 + v^2)} \tag{19}$$

where $a^2 = (1 + 4P)/4P$ and is a function of $P$ but not of $v$.

*Note*
$q$ as used above is the per capita demand for an individual with unit income. It is also used for the total demand at a point, and for other income levels. In these cases, the basic $q$ is multiplied by a factor $k$ representing the population density and/or per capita income.

For a uniform density $k$, aggregate demand for a half-market of width $u$ is given by:

$$Q(P,u) = k\int_0^u q(P,v)\,dv$$

$$= \frac{k}{4P^2}\int_0^u \frac{dv}{a^2 + v^2}$$

$$= \frac{k}{4P^2}\arctan\frac{u}{a} \tag{20}$$

Solving for $u$ as a function of $P$, $P'$ and $D$ in (17), we can obtain an explicit expression for $Q$ as a function of $P$, $P'$, $D$. This expression (21) is reproduced in the main text as equation (5):

$$Q(P,P',D) = \frac{k}{4P^2}\arctan\frac{2P^{1/2}\left(P'\left(PP'D^2 - (P-P')^2\right)^{1/2} - P'D\right)}{(P-P')^2(1+4P)^{1/2}} \tag{21}$$

To determine the elasticity of demand $E$, we note that

$$\frac{dQ}{dP} = q(P,u) + \int_0^u \frac{\partial q(P,v)}{\partial P}\,dv \tag{22}$$

From the dividing condition (17), the effect of $P$ on $u$, given $D$ and $P'$, can be shown to be

$$\frac{du}{dP} = -\frac{1}{2}\frac{1+u^2}{(P-P')u+P'D} \tag{23}$$

For an equilibrium configuration in the uniform case, goods are uniformly spaced along the spectrum and have the same prices, so that $P' = P$. Since adjacent goods have equal prices, the dividing consumer is at the midpoint between adjacent goods, so that $u = D/2$ and (23) becomes

$$\frac{du}{dP} = \frac{1}{P}\frac{D^2+4}{8D} \tag{24}$$

Differentiation of $q(P,v)$ from (18) with respect to $P$ gives:

$$\frac{\partial q}{\partial P} = \frac{2k}{P^2}\frac{b^2+v^2}{\left(a^2+v^2\right)^2} \tag{25}$$

*Table 3.5   Numerical solution values*

| Variable | Autarky | Free trade | Protection (Symmetrical) | (Asymmetrical) |
|---|---|---|---|---|
| $P$ | 0.625 | 0.573 | 0.590 | 0.610 |
| $P'$ | n.a | 0.573 | 0.632 | 0.654 |
| $D$ | 0.535 | 0.394 | 0.350 | 0.414 |
| $Q_L$ | 12.00 | 10.40 | 13.80 | 13.80 |
| $Q_I$ | – | 10.40 | 3.200 | 5.000 |

where $b^2 = (1 + 8P)/8P$.

By direct integration of (25) with respect to $v$ we obtain

$$\int_0^u \frac{\partial q}{\partial P}\,dv = -\frac{1}{a^2P^2}\left(\frac{\left(b^2-a^2\right)u}{a^2+u^2} + \frac{b^2+a^2}{2a^3}\arctan\frac{u}{a}\right) \tag{26}$$

The elasticity $E(P, P', D) = -PdQ/Qdp$ can be obtained as an explicit but complicated expression by combining (18), (21), (22) and (25). The elasticity properties given in the main text can be show to hold by investigating these various components of $E$ taken separately.

The numerical solutions used to illustrate the scenarios described in the text were based on the above demand model with $k$ (the population–income density) put equal to 50 and a cost function for all firms with a marginal cost of 0.5 and a fixed cost of 3.0. The actual numerical solution values for key variables at different equilibrium configurations are given in Table 5, where $Q_L$ is the quantity of the home good sold on the local market, and $Q_I$ is the quantity of imports sold locally. In the symmetric case, the latter is also equal to the export sales of the home firms.

**Notes**

1. This paper was presented at a conference on monopolistic competition and trade at Geneva in 1982, and published in the conference volume Kierzkowski 1984.
2. The monopolistic competition equilibrium is stable only if $\sigma > 1$.
3. The general quadratic form $1 + bv^2$ satisfies all the requirements of the compensating function, as shown in Lancaster 1979, Appendix A. The choice of $b$ ( $= 1$ here) sets the scale on the spectrum. When a good is at unit distance from the consumer's most preferred good, it is valued half as much as a unit of most preferred good. This 'psychic' measure is valid in this model because of the assumption that consumers' preferences are identical in every way except for their choice of most preferred good.
4. Preliminary studies by the author suggest that the analysis of monopolistic competition with non-uniform preference distributions may differ considerably from the analysis of the uniform case.
5. There are, of course, many scenarios for the process of attaining equilibrium. The one set out here is simple and illustrates the forces operating.
6. In the uniform density case with uniform preferences, increasing the density by a factor of $k$ merely changes the marginal and average quantities by $k$, leaving all elasticity relationships unchanged.
7. There are, of course, many other arrangements, including many other symmetrical ones. The two chosen represent the most and the least interactive structures.
8. It would be possible to devise some index of product variety that gives less weight to goods consumed in smaller quantities, and which converges to the autarky level as the tariff reaches the prohibitive rate.
9. See, for example, Eaton and Lipsey 1976, Prescott and Visscher 1977.
10. There may be, in addition, a very large range of imported product differentiates which are on a portion of the spectrum where no home goods are produced – this is what we might expect when this is a very small country. It will be assumed that our interest is confined to the region in which home goods compete, and that tariffs are imposed only on goods in this region.
11. The argument here would not hold completely if the marginal cost curve were rising.

# 4 Multi-product defensive monopoly in an open economy[1]

## Introduction

The general context of this paper is that of an industry in which continuous variations of product specification are possible and in which these specifications can be defined in terms of measurable product characteristics and represented as points on a spectrum in characteristics space, in a manner discussed in depth elsewhere.[2] There is perfect information and equal access to resources and technology so that no cost or information advantages exist for one firm over potential rivals. There are no inter-product economies in production, so the multi-product firm has no cost advantages over a collection of single-product firms, but does have the ability to coordinate prices and product specifications. In effect, the multi-product firm analyzed here is functionally identical to an irrevocable cartel with centralized direction.

## Demand

The analysis will be carried out in terms of a two-characteristics model in which the characteristics proportions can be represented on a one-dimensional line spectrum, as for a good group with different sour – sweet ratios or sports cars with different speed – comfort ratios. It can also be applied more or less directly to pure locational variation. In any case, it will be assumed that each individual consumer has a given location or a most preferred characteristics combination represented by a definite point on the spectrum, and that his/her interest in other products diminishes with distance away from the most preferred choice. In spatial models, this diminution of desirability with distance can be treated as a transport cost. In the characteristics model it can, if one wishes, be regarded as a 'psychic transport cost'.

The individual's demand function for a good which is the only good available in this group, is located on the spectrum at distance $v$ from his most preferred good, and sells at a price $p$ in terms of an aggregate 'outside good' representing all goods not in the group, will have the form $q(p, v)$.

The sensitivity of $q(p, v)$ to $v$ is determined by two things:

1. The importance to the individual of differences in location on the spectrum.

*51*

2. The substitutability of outside goods for goods in the group. If there is zero outside substitutability, then $q_v$ may be zero even though the spectral distance counts.

When distance counts and there is some degree of substitutability between group goods and outside goods, $q_v$ will be strictly negative. This will be taken to be the normal case.

When two goods in the group are both available, an individual will choose the one that gives him the best value per dollar, buying the closer if both have the same price, the cheaper if both are at the same distance (in opposite directions, of course, or they would not be different), otherwise weighing distance from his most preferred specification against price. The size of the market for the goods at price $p$ will thus depend on both $p$ and $P$, the price of the adjacent good, as well as on $s$, the distance between neighboring goods.

The analysis here will be restricted to the uniform market, the special case in which it is assumed that

1. An individual's view of a particular good depends on the position of the good on the spectrum *relative* to the position of his most preferred good, and not on the absolute position of either.
2. Individual demands are identical except as to their most preferred specifications, and individuals need be identified only by their most preferred goods.
3. The population and income density of individuals having the same most preferred good is the same everywhere on the spectrum.
4. End of spectrum effects can be ignored.

The uniform market leads to symmetrical situations with events described by the minimum number of parameters, and the analysis can be confined to cases in which the adjacent goods in both directions are at the same distance and sell at the same price. The aggregate demand for the target good can be written as $Q(p, P, s)$, with $p$ the price of the good itself and $P$, $s$ the prices and distances of both neighboring products. The profit for a single product firm can then be written as

$$\pi(p, P, s) = pQ(p, P, s) - C(Q(p, P, s))$$

It is important to note that the analysis is that of a two-sector economy, although the emphasis is on the differentiated-product sector. The other sector is assumed to produce a good (which may be a composite), the 'outside good' from the viewpoint of the differentiated-product sector, which is produced under constant returns to scale in a competitive market. All prices (including input prices) are measured in terms of this good, and it is assumed that the outside good is internationally traded and preserves its numeraire status in the open economy.

## Benchmark configurations

There are two market structures that provide reference patterns for comparison with other configurations. These are the traditional monopolistic competition or zero-profit non-collusive Nash equilibrium of single-product firms with free entry, and 'full group monopoly', the equilibrium of a single multi-product firm having an institutionally guaranteed monopoly over all products (actual or potential) within the group.

Over a closed economy, it is assumed that the cost functions for all products in the differentiated group are identical. Since the demand functions depend only on the relative positions of goods on the spectrum, any non-collusive Nash equilibrium will be completely symmetrical with products evenly spaced over the spectrum all selling at the same price. This equilibrium will be fully described by the price-spacing pair $(p^*, s^*)$, determined by the conditions

$$\pi(p^*, p^*, s) = \max_p \pi(p, p^*, s)$$

$$\pi\,(p^*, p^*, s^*) = 0$$

By 'full monopoly' is meant a firm which is the only producer of goods within the group and faces no potential entrant into the group, whatever its behavior. Such a monopoly (or cartel) can coordinate the prices and locations of the individual goods so as to maximize overall profit. Since there are assumed to be no inter-product economies, the only advantage of the multi-product monopoly is this power to coordinate.

It is obvious before proceeding further that the monopoly equilibrium in the uniform distribution case will be such that all products are sold at the same price and spaced evenly along the spectrum, so the equilibrium can be described by a single price-spacing pair $(p_m, s_m)$ just as in the monopolistic competition case.

The maximand in the monopoly case must be considered carefully. Whereas the single-product firm will maximize profit from the production and sale of its one product, the monopolist will choose the price and number of products to maximize overall profit, not profit per individual product. This may call for few products at a large profit per product, or many products at lower profits per product. Since the number of products is proportional to $1/s$, the inverse of the spacing, the monopolist can be considered to maximize the profit density per unit spectrum given by

$$z(p, s) = {}^1\!/_s \pi(p, p, s)$$

where $\pi(p, p, s)$ is the profit per product when each is sold at price $p$ and the products are uniformly spaced at distance $s$. The full monopoly solution will be some price-spacing pair $(p_m, s_m)$ such that

$$z(p_m, s_m) = \max_{p,s}(^1/_s \pi(p, p, s))$$

In general, we shall have $p_m > p^*$ and $s_m < s^*$.

### Entry and the multi-product firm

Consider a situation in which there is an incumbent multi-product firm in the industry and a potential entrant, initially taken to be a single-product firm, which must choose both the product specification and the price for its good. The potential entrant is assumed to have the same access of information, technology, and inputs as the incumbent, and so will have the same costs.

It is obvious that the most desirable way to enter would be to find an empty region, a portion of the spectrum in which neighboring goods are so distant that they can be neglected. But such a region would be equally profitable for the incumbent, so empty sector entry can be ruled out except in a dynamic and evolving industry in which new entrants can find such sectors before the incumbent is able to cover the market.

We shall be concerned primarily with the mature incumbent who has been able to move into the desired strategic configuration prior to being assailed by potential entrants. Such a firm will have adopted either the full monopoly equilibrium configuration $(p_m, s_m)$, or a configuration appropriate to some other defensive strategy. In the uniform market case, it is obvious that any rational defensive configuration will be characterized by uniform prices and a uniform spacing between goods, since a potential entry is free to choose the point or points of entry. The most profitable price-spacing combination which still inhibits entry will be the same in one portion of the spectrum as in another. Thus the mature multi-product incumbent will produce goods with specifications at some uniform spacing $s_i$ and will sell all at the same price $p_i$.

With the incumbent thus configured, the potential entrant has two basic choices as to the entry strategy:

1. *Face-to-face entry.* The entrant produces and sells a good which is identical to one of the goods being produced and sold by the incumbent. Since the costs of the incumbent and entrant are identical, the post-entry equilibrium will be symmetrical between the two firms. The best feasible symmetrical outcome for the entrant will be the implicit collusion solution, the two firms splitting the market.

2. *Interstitial entry.* The entrant produces and sells a new product which is located at a point on the spectrum between two of the goods produced by the incumbent. The entrant's price is given by

$$\arg \max_{p} \pi(p, p_i, s_i/2)$$

It has been shown elsewhere that interstitial entry dominates face-to-face entry where firms have the same costs,[3] because $Q(p, p, s/2) \geq Q(p, p, s)/2$ for all $p, s$. A potential entrant can always do better by entering with a new good positioned on the spectrum between two of the incumbent's goods than by producing a good identical with one of the incumbent's and splitting the market. To inhibit entry, it is sufficient for the incumbent to adopt a configuration which makes interstitial entry, the potential rival's best strategy, unprofitable in every part of the spectrum.

**Results for the closed economy**
The closed economy analysis gives two important results in addition to the above proposition as to the dominance of interstitial entry:

1. If a monopolistic competition equilibrium (or any zero-profit Nash equilibrium with at least two firms) is possible, a sustainable defensive monopoly position is also possible, with prices and degree of product variety such that no other firm will choose to enter the incumbent will make positive profits.
   It can be shown that the monopolistic competition price $p^*$ combined with a spacing slightly greater than the monopolist competition equilibrium value $s^*$ is a sustainable defensive strategy, although not necessarily the optimal one.
2. The optimal multi-product sustainable defensive strategy is shown to be the solution to

$$\max_{P,s} z(P, s) = \pi(P, P, s)/s$$

subject to

$$\max_{P} \pi(p, P, s/2) \leq 0$$

The propositions show that, in a closed economy in which all firms face identical costs, it is almost always possible for an incumbent in an industry with continuous product variability to so choose prices and the degree of product variety as to draw positive profits indefinitely without attracting new firms into the industry.

## The open economy

To open up the economy into a two-country world, it will be assumed that the 'outside good' (outside to the differentiated group, not the economy) is freely traded or tradeable and can be used as a universal numeraire. Local input prices and thus local costs are measured in terms of the numeraire, so that variations in the terms of trade or exchange rates, as well as productivity differentials, are reflected in these costs. It will be assumed that the cost differentials are homogeneous across countries (fixed and variable costs differ in the same proportions), so that costs abroad can be written in the form $rC(Q)$ where $C(Q)$ is the home cost function, all in terms of the numeraire.

It will be assumed that the demand for differentiated products is a world demand. This demand is initially supplied by the home industry alone. The purpose of this paper is to investigate the extent to which the home industry can maintain its initial world monopoly in the face of potential competition from abroad *without government intervention*, and how its behavior will change in the face of potential competition. The emphasis is on free trade competition with negligible transport costs, in which a potential entrant competes with the incumbent for part of the world economy in exactly the same way a potential entrant would compete in a closed economy, except that the overseas competitor's costs may differ from those of the incumbent.

## Free trade competition

This is analogous to the closed country case except that the potential competitor's costs may differ from those of the incumbent. The cost differences have been assumed homogeneous and thus measurable in terms of the single relative cost parameter $r$, the incumbent's cost level being at $r = 1$. All costs and prices in both countries are measured in terms of the numeraire good.

When costs differ between the incumbent and the potential entrant, the analysis of entry is greatly changed from that in the equal cost case. If the potential entrant has higher costs than the incumbent, face-to-face entry is irrelevant and only interstitial entry need be considered. If the entrant has lower costs than the incumbent, the entrant can enter face-to-face at a lower price than the incumbent, a price that can be sustained indefinitely by the entrant but not the incumbent. It may seem that the entrant is then capable of gaining the whole market for the entry good,[4] and not merely half of it. But this fails to take account of the potential counter-strategies in a product-differentiated market. As in the well known analysis of the Hotelling case,[5] the incumbent can vary his specification slightly to regain that part of the original market between his new position and the nearest adjacent good, plus its split of the part of the market between itself and the entrant.

The entrant will have that part of the market on the other side from the incumbent's new position (this will be at least half the original market) plus its split of the market between the two goods, which will be more than half because of its lower price.

Suppose the incumbent's original configuration was the price-spacing pair $(P, s)$ and the potential entrant was able to sell at price $p < P$. The total sales of the target good by the incumbent would be $Q(P, P, s)$ originally, while the entrant would be able to sustain sales of $Q(p, P, s) > Q(P, P, s)$ if the incumbent failed to react, so that its sales would be zero. But if the incumbent varied its product to a point on the spectrum at a small distance $d$ from its original position, it would have total sales in two half-markets given by

$$\tfrac{1}{2}(Q(P, P, s - d) + Q(P, p, d))$$

while the entrant's total sales would now be

$$\tfrac{1}{2}(Q(p, P, s) + Q(p, P, d))$$

The smaller is $d$, the larger the incumbent's sales and the smaller the entrant's so long as the above configuration holds. But if $d$ is too small relative to the price differential, even consumers on the side of the incumbent good *away* from the entrant good will find the entrant good cheap enough to counterbalance the slightly large divergence from the consumer's preferred specification, and the incumbent will lose the whole market. The minimum value of $d$ is an increasing function of the price differential. Taking all functions to be continuous and well behaved, the following result can be stated:

**Proposition I**   *For face-to-face entry at price p into a market with configu-ration (P, s), where $p \leq P$, the maximum sustainable sales for the entrant after reaction by the incumbent will be given by a function of the form*

$$\phi(p, P, s) = \tfrac{1}{2}Q(p, P, s) + h(p, P, s)$$

*where $h(p, P, s) \leq 0$, is decreasing in p for $p < P$, and $\rightarrow 0$ as $p \rightarrow P$.*

As in the closed economy, interstitial entry is possible in the open economy. The maximum sales for an interstitial entrant (at a mid-point between incumbent goods) will be $Q(p, P, s/2)$, where $p$ is the entrant price and $(P, s)$ the incumbent configuration. For interstitial entry it is possible to have $p > P$, but this case is not of much interest. Since $Q$ is strictly concave[6] in $s$, it is easily shown that

$$Q(p, P, s/2) > Q(p, P, s)/2$$

in general. However, this is not sufficient to show the dominance of interstitial entry over face-to-face entry in the case where the entrant has lower costs. From Proposition I, the maximum face-to-face sales quantity for the entrant $\rightarrow Q(p, P, s)/2$ as $p \rightarrow P$, while the excess of interstitial sales $Q(p, P, s/2)$ over $Q(p, P, s)/2$ depends on the concavity properties of preferences and is strictly positive even for $p = P$. Thus interstitial entry will be better for firms with costs only slightly below those of the incumbent, while face-to-face entry will be better for firms with large cost advantages.

Since the defensive incumbent monopolist must adopt a strategy which makes both face-to-face and interstitial entry unprofitable, choice of an optimal defensive strategy is a two-constraint problem.

**Proposition II**   *The optimal sustainable defensive strategy for an incumbent facing one or more potential entrants is to choose the price-spacing pair $(P_d, s_d)$ which is the solution to the problem*

$$\max_{P,s} \left( z(P,s) = \frac{PQ(P,P,s) - C(Q(P,P,s))}{s} \right)$$

*subject to*

$$\max_{p} (p\phi(p, P, s) - rC(\phi(p, P, s))) \leq 0$$

$$\max_{p} (pQ(p, P, s/2) - rC(Q(p, P, s/2))) \leq 0$$

*where r is the smallest cost parameter among possible entrants.*

In general, the second (interstitial entry) constraint will be binding for larger values of $r$, the face-to-face constraint for smaller values of $r$. For sufficiently low values of $r$, it is clear that the incumbent cannot sustain its monopoly position since there is no $(P, s)$ satisfying the constraints which gives a non-negative value for $z(P, s)$. For values of $r$ sufficiently close to unity, a sustainable defensive strategy will exist, in general.

**Proposition III**   *A sustainable defensive strategy is possible in an open economy facing lower cost competition from abroad whenever a monopolistic competition equilibrium is possible for the closed economy, provided the cost advantage is not too large.*

Denote by $(P^*, s^*)$ the monopolistic competition equilibrium for the economy when closed. Then $z(P^*, s^*) = 0$ and is increasing in $s^*$. For $r$ sufficiently close to 1, interstitial entry dominates face-to-face entry. But the latter is strictly losing for $r = 1$, and is only breakeven for some $r_0 < 1$. Because $z(P, s)$ is increasing in $s$, there is some $\varepsilon$ such that $z(P^*, s^* = \varepsilon) > 0$ and entry is deterred for all $r \geq \hat{r}(\varepsilon)$, where $r_0 < \hat{r}(\varepsilon) < 1$. Note that this does not give an *optimal* defensive strategy; it merely establishes a feasible defensive strategy which will apply to all cases in which the overseas cost advantage is not too large.

## A simulation

Models of the processes described above which possess acceptable properties do not lend themselves to analytical solutions, so it seems useful to stimulate the processes by giving numerical solutions for models with appropriate properties. It can be shown that the class of demand functions of the form

$$Q(p, P, s) = kp^{-(a + bc)}P^{bc}s^c \quad [a > 1, b > 0, 1 > c > 0]$$

can be derived from acceptable (although not totally ideal) premises. For such a function and its implied primitives, it can be shown that the function $\phi$ of Proposition I has the form

$$\phi(p, P, s) = (1 + 2^c(1 - (p/P)^b)^c)Q(p, P, s)/2$$

Note that $\phi(p, P, s) \to Q(p, P, s)/2$ as $p \to P$ from below.

The specific numerical example used for the simulations is obtained by inserting the values $k = 1$, $a = 2$, $b = 1$, $c = 0.5$ in the above model. The cost function is assumed to have the simple form of constant marginal cost plus a fixed cost, in particular $C(Q) = r(1 + Q)$, where $r$ is the relative cost parameter ( $= 1$ for the incumbent). The benchmark values for the closed economy are:

Monopolistic competition: $p^* = 1.67$, $s^* = 17.36$
Full monopoly: $p_m = 2$, $s_m = 64$, $z(p_m, s_m) = 0.0156$
Defensive monopoly: $p_d = 1.84$, $s_d = 31.45$, $z(p_d, s_d) = 0.0124$

Table 4.1 sets out selected numerical results for the optimal defensive posture of an incumbent in an open economy facing different levels of relative foreign costs. The solutions have been normalized to base 100, relative to the values for an incumbent firm in a full monopoly situation. Note that the system has not been solved for the face-to-face constraint in the narrow range of cost differentials for which that form of entry would dominate interstitial entry and for which a sustainable defensive strategy is possible.

The general picture from the simulation is that, for the model used, a multi-product incumbent could inhibit both foreign and home entry even when foreign firms had a cost advantage up to about 10%. For a cost advantage of 12% or more, however, the foreign firm could not be denied entry and the incumbent could not survive without tariff protection. Over the range for which it can be successfully used, the incumbent's defense strategy is to simultaneously lower prices and increase variety.

*Table 4.1   Optimal defensive posture in face of foreign costs*

| Cost ratio of potential entrant | Defensive price | Defensive spacing | Profit to incumbent | Comment |
|---|---|---|---|---|
| | | (full monopoly value = 100) | | |
| < 0.88 | – | – | Loss only | See 1 |
| 0.88 – 0.91 | (84–86) | (28–33) | (9.6–35.1) | See 2 |
| 0.92 | 86.5 | 34.5 | 42.2 | |
| 0.94 | 87.7 | 37.9 | 54.5 | |
| 0.96 | 88.9 | 41.5 | 64.6 | |
| 0.98 | 90 | 45.4 | 72.9 | |
| 1.00 | 91.1 | 49.6 | 79.7 | |
| 1.05 | (93.9) | (61.5) | (91.3) | |
| 1.10 | (96.5) | (75.5) | (97.4) | See 3 |
| 1.15 | (99) | (91.9) | (99.8) | |
| ≥1.172 | (100) | (100) | (100) | See 4 |

*Notes*
1.  For an entrant cost ratio less than 0.88, the incumbent cannot prevent even interstitial entry, the least favorable in this range. In this relative cost range, the incumbent is doomed! (In the real world he will lobby for protection.)
2.  In this cost ratio range, face-to-face entry dominates interstitial. The incumbent could defend against interstitial entry with the price and spacing figures in parentheses, but defense against face-to-face entry would be less profitable. Thus the incumbent's position becomes untenable somewhere in this range.
3.  For cost ratios above 1.0, the figures in parentheses are relevant only if the firm has a full monopoly at home, but no protection from abroad. Otherwise it is the potential home entrants with cost ratios of 1.0 which dominate the scene and the defensive posture at 1.0 (which is the sustainable defensive configuration for the closed economy) holds for all higher levels of foreign costs.
4.  An incumbent with a monopoly at home is fully protected from competition abroad once foreign cost levels reach 1.172. No defensive posture is required and the full monopoly solution holds.

Note that, even if the incumbent has a guaranteed monopoly of home production and foreign costs are actually *higher*, it does not possess full monopoly power. Just as the firm may successfully defend against entry from lower-cost foreign competition, it can be threatened with competition from higher-cost foreign firms. In the example given, the incumbent with the home production monopoly has a *de facto* full world monopoly only if foreign costs are more than 17.2% higher than home costs.

### Notes
1. Originally presented at a conference on *International Trade under Imperfect Competition* at the University of Sussex in September 1984.
2. See Lancaster 1979.
3. See Lancaster 1984.
4. Because of the lower price, the entrant's sales will encroach on the markets of the adjacent goods.
5. In a simple location model with linear transport costs of $t$ per mile, we would have $d_{min} = (P - p)/t$. In characteristics space, the exact relationship depends on the shapes of the preference functions, but is always increasing the price differential.
6. See Lancaster 1979. This strict concavity, rather than linearity, is an important difference between analysis in characteristics space using preferences and the pure spatial analysis.

# 5   The 'product variety' case for protection[1]

## Introduction

To make an acceptable case for divergence from free trade requires proof of
the existence of a potential for *inherent* market failure or distortion, followed
by proof that this same failure or distortion can be fully corrected by an appropriate tariff, and that no other policy can do better. This paper makes such a
case, using just such a sequence of arguments, for industries producing differentiated products subject to economies of scale when consumer tastes are
diverse.

It will be shown that there is potential for market failure under free trade for
industries of the above kind, in the sense that they may be unprofitable although
the economy would gain from their operation, and the market failure can be
fully overcome by an appropriate degree of protection which results both in the
realization of the potential social gain and makes it profitable for the industry
to function. There are two essential features of this case:

1. The industry must produce a differentiated product in a context of preference
   diversity *and* must possess some degree of scale economies. Both features
   must be present or there is no market failure and no case for protection.
2. The tariff must give *partial* protection only. A prohibitive tariff nullifies the
   case for protection, which is based on increasing product variety by having
   imports and local products both available.

While it has seemed a reasonable conjecture from intuitive arguments that
there might exist a case for tariffs based on the potential gain from product variety,
and although the author had published computer simulation results in 1984 which
confirmed this conjecture,[2] the models chosen did not lend themselves to
analytical solutions and no clear proof of the existence of this case was provided.

The present paper is the outcome of a search for the simplest acceptable model
of an open economy in which it is possible to give a clear proof of the existence
of the 'product variety' case for protection.

The arguments given here do not depend on terms of trade effects, or on oligopolistic or large market effects.[3] They are not arguments in favor of temporary
protection policies designed to foster R & D or have other effects which will
improve competitiveness in the long run (modern variations on the infant
industry argument),[4] but arguments in favor of continuing partial protection.
Nor are they arguments for second-best countering of distortions with other
distortions[5], although there is some element of similarity to those cases. Here

the tariff policy achieves the first-best configuration, not just a second-best. This is because the optimum cannot be attained under the combination of product differentiation, variety in tastes (or a taste for variety), and scale economies, without intervention.[6]

## The model

We are in a small open economy which consumes two goods, one homogeneous and perfectly divisible, the other a differentiated product in discrete units. The latter will be referred to as a manufacture, for convenience in terminology. Both types of good are available freely on a large world market under conditions unaffected by our own behavior or policies. The differentiated product is viewed by consumers as a bundle of characteristics, so product specifications can be represented by locations in characteristics space. The world supply of the differentiated good is available in only a finite number of varieties, distributed uniformly at spacing $2S$ over the characteristics spectrum, all selling in the world market at price $m$ in terms of the world price of the homogeneous good taken as numeraire. The price is determined by the structure of world manufacturing, in the market for which our economy's demand is insignificantly small.

### Consumer preferences

Domestic consumers have preferences which are all identical except as to each individual's view of the *most preferred* or *ideal* specification of the manufacture. The distribution of ideal specifications is taken to be uniform over the range of tastes covered by the domestic population. All consumers have the same *compensating* or 'psychic transport cost' function which determines how the potential utility of a differentiated product declines as the distance between its specification and the consumer's ideal increases.

Since it is assumed that the manufactured good is available, for technical reasons, only in relatively large discrete units, consumption by an individual is either 0 or 1 unit. If more than one variety of the good is available, the consumer will consume one unit of one of the goods, at most.

Consumers are identified by the parameter $x$, which is the 'location' of the consumer (that is, of his ideal specification) on a spectrum of characteristics. Preferences are taken to be representable by a utility function of the form:

$$u(x) - q(x) + j\phi(v)$$

where $q(x)$ is the quantity consumed of the homogeneous good, $j$ is 0 or 1 according as the manufacture is consumed or not, and $v$ is the distance in characteristics space between the 'locations' of the consumer and the manufacture he consumes.

The subutility function $\phi(v)$ determines how the utility of a discrete unit of the manufactured good changes with distance between its specification and the ideal specification of the consumer. It will be assumed to possess the following two properties:

1. $\phi(v)$ is strictly decreasing in $v$.
2. $\phi(v)$ is concave in $v$ over the relevant range.

If the first property did not hold, differentiation of the product would have no significance for the market since consumers would be insensitive to specification variations and would treat the products as homogeneous. The concavity property (which need not be strict) assumes rather more about reactions to differences in specification – in particular, that the effect of distance increases as products differ more and more from the ideal.

The form $\phi(v) = A\,(1 - \gamma v^{\beta})$, $\beta \geq 1$, $\gamma > 0$, satisfies the requirements of the model here for $v \leq \gamma^{-1/\beta}$ and is used (with $\beta = 2$) in the numerical example presented later. A bell-shaped $\phi$, concave for some distance out from $v = 0$ and then convex, might be more realistic, with the effect of distance increasing as products diverge from the ideal but then decreasing again when products are so far from the ideal that the minor distinctions become irrelevant. A function of the form

$$\phi(v) = \frac{A}{\left(1 + \gamma v^2\right)^{\beta}} \qquad 0 \leq \beta \leq 1$$

has this shape and exactly fits the specifications in Lancaster 1979, while the classic bell curve $e^{-\gamma v^2}$ has all the properties appropriate for a $\phi$-function. We simply assume that all relevant choices involve the region over which the functions are concave.

The homogeneous good is a stand-in for 'all other goods' with $q$ assumed to be large relative to $\phi$, so the assumption of constant marginal utility for this good is not unreasonable.

Consumers are assumed to be uniformly distributed over the spectrum, meaning that the density of consumers having any given specification as their ideal is the same for all specifications. The density will be denoted by $\alpha$.

### The economy
The domestic economy has a fixed amount of a single resource, units being chosen to give a unit input–output coefficient for the homogeneous good. The economy can produce both the homogeneous good and the differentiated manufactured good with this resource, the latter at a constant marginal resource cost of $c$, which is also the cost in terms of world currency units. To produce any quantity of

the manufactured good to any one specification may incur a fixed *flow* cost of $F$ so long as the good is produced. The same fixed cost must be incurred for every distinct specification of good produced. There are major differences in analysis and results between cases in which there are economies of scale ($F > 0$) and those in which there are none ($F = 0$).

It is assumed that the only role of government is to improve welfare by appropriate choices of tariffs, taxes, and subsidies. All net revenues are returned to consumers, or extracted from them, if negative.

## The market for manufactures

If there is no local production of manufactures, only imports are available. These are assumed to be located evenly on the spectrum at spacing $2S$ and sell at a local price $P$ (the world price $m$ plus applicable tariffs). A consumer with ideal specification at distance $v$ ($0 \leq v \leq S$) from that of the nearest import will buy a unit of that import provided that $\phi(v) \geq P$ and his income is at least $P$. It will be assumed that all incomes are greater than $P$ and $\phi(S) \geq P$ in all cases, so that even the consumer with ideal furthest from an import will buy it.

Now consider the possibility of local manufacture. Given the symmetric situation, it is obvious that, if there is a market for local manufacture at all, there is a market for a local producer with product located at the midpoint between each adjacent pair of imported goods, at distance $S$ from each. The structure of the local industry then depends on whether or not there are economies of scale.

### Economies of scale present

Our primary interest in this paper is in the case in which there are economies of scale ($F > 0$ in this model), so we shall take this case first. The economies of scale are here specific to a particular model or product variant, so it will cost more to produce $n$ units to each of two specifications than to produce $2n$ to a single specification. Local industry, if it operates at all, will produce goods to only a finite number of different specifications, and it will not be optimal for any firm to produce to the same specification as another.

The analysis in this paper will be confined to the simple case in which the size of the market relative to the economies of scale is such that one local firm, at most, can find it profitable to operate in each segment.[7] This will necessarily locate itself midway between the specification points of adjacent imports, at the segment center. Such a firm competes only with the two neighboring imports, which have fixed price and specification. There are no oligopolistic interactions and thus a well-defined demand function for the product of the local firm at the given import price $P$. The firm will act as a local monopolist and maximize profit in terms of this demand function and its own costs, to give an equilibrium price $p(P)$ and equilibrium profit $\pi(P)$.

*Scale economies absent*

If there are no economies of scale in local production ($F = 0$), the whole analysis is changed and appropriate results cannot be obtained merely by letting $F \to 0$ in the previous case. The two fundamental changes are:

1. There is no 'natural monopoly' effect and free entry will give competitive firms all selling at price $c$.
2. Since there is no difference in cost between producing $n$ units of good to a single specification and producing one unit each of goods with $n$ different specifications, and since a consumer will always prefer a good having his ideal specification to any other at the same price $c$, local firms will offer goods to custom specification.

*Market division*

If there are economies of scale, a consumer's choice is between the locally produced good at price $p$ and the import good at price $P$, with the two goods differing in specification by distance $S$. A consumer whose ideal is at distance $v$ from the specification of the local good will choose it over the import if

$$\phi(v) - p \geq \phi(S - v) - P$$

The marginal consumer, on the boundary between the import and local markets, is at distance $w$ from the center of the latter, where

$$\phi(w) - p = \phi(S - w) - P \tag{1}$$

This is the *dividing condition* for the markets in the scale economies case, determining the widths of the two markets as a function of their prices.

Note that the relevant dividing condition here is that for a market in an indivisible good, and differs from that in the market for an infinitely divisible good.[8] Here the consumer cannot compare marginal dollars spent but must compare product utilities less full prices for each good.

If economies of scale are absent, competition will ensure that the consumer can always find a local firm willing to produce to his ideal specification at price $c$. His choice is between this and an import at price $P$ which is not to his ideal specification (unless he is located at 0 or $2S$). Suppose the consumer's ideal specification is at distance $S - v$ from that of the import. Then the consumer will buy the local product if

$$\phi(0) - c \geq \phi(S - v) - P$$

In this case the half market $[0, S]$ is divided between consumers in $[0, S - w]$ who buy the import, and those in $[S - w, S]$ who will buy a custom-produced local product. The value of $w$ will be given by the dividing condition for this case

$$\phi(0) - c = \phi(S - w) - P \tag{2}$$

Since consumers buy only one unit, the demands for all the manufactured goods are directly proportional to the widths of their markets. The demand for the local manufacture is $2\alpha w$, where $w$ is given by the relevant dividing condition (1) or (2), depending on whether there are scale economies or not.

### Equilibrium of the firm
In the absence of economies of scale, firms will be competitive and sell custom products at price $c$, as already pointed out. With economies of scale, however, there is a 'natural monopoly' effect, so that each local firm is a quasi-monopolist even with free entry. The analysis which follows is for the firm under economies of scale.

Using (1), the effect of price on the firm's market width is given by

$$\frac{dw}{dp} = \frac{1}{\phi'(w) + \phi'(S - w)} \tag{3}$$

so that

$$\pi = 2\alpha(p - c)w - F$$

$$\frac{d\pi}{dp} = 2\alpha\left(w + \frac{p - c}{\phi'(w) + \phi'(S - w)}\right)$$

The profit-maximizing price $\hat{p}$ and equilibrium market width $\hat{w}$, if they exist, are given by the equation pair

$$\hat{p} - c = -(\phi'(\hat{w}) + \phi'(S - \hat{w}))\hat{w} \quad \text{(from } d\pi/dp = 0\text{)} \tag{4}$$
$$\hat{p} - P = \phi(\hat{w}) - \phi(S - \hat{w}) \quad \text{(from (1))} \tag{5}$$

To examine the existence of such solutions, note that (4) and (5) together imply

$$\phi(\hat{w}) - \phi(S - \hat{w}) + \hat{w}\phi'(\hat{w}) + \hat{w}\phi'(S - \hat{w}) = c - P \tag{6}$$

Denote the left-hand side of the equation by $\hat{\Psi}(\hat{w})$. Now $\Psi$ is continuous, $\Psi$ $(0) > 0$, and $\Psi\,(S) < 0$, so there is a solution with $\hat{w} \in [0, S]$ if

$$\hat{\Psi}(0) \geq c - P \geq \hat{\Psi}(S)$$

Solutions will exist for both $c < m$ and $c > m$, provided $|\,c - m\,|$ is not too large relative to the properties of $\phi$.

Although there may be a potential market for a local manufacture if $\hat{\Psi}(0) > c - P$, no firm will enter this market unless there is a non-negative profit. Using (4), the maximum profit depends on $P$ and is

$$\hat{\pi}(P) = -2\alpha(\phi'(\hat{w}) + \phi'(S - \hat{w}))\hat{w}^2 - F \tag{7}$$

There will be a local manufacturing industry in the economies of scale case only if $P$ is such that $\hat{\pi}(P) \geq 0$.

## The gain from variety

**Proposition I**    *If consumers are sensitive to differences in product specification and have diverse tastes, there is a pure variety gain in welfare when the number of different products is increased. This gain may, however, be partly or wholly offset by an efficiency loss. Nevertheless, even if local manufacturing costs are high relative to imports, there may still be a net welfare gain from local production because the potential gain from variety is sufficient to outweigh the efficiency loss.*

*Proof*
Consider the distribution of welfare associated with the distribution of one unit of the imported good per individual together with some distribution of the homogeneous good over individuals. This is the reference distribution. The individual at position $x$ on the spectrum (measured from the location of the nearest import) will have utility $u(x)$, given by

$$\hat{u}(x) = q(x) + \phi(x) \tag{8}$$

for $0 \leq x \leq S$.

Now suppose the individual is supplied with a local good, at distance $S$ from the import, instead of the import. His subutility from the manufactured good will now be $\phi(S - x)$ which will be, in general, different from $\phi(x)$. Let $q'(x)$ be the amount of homogeneous good just sufficient to give the individual the original utility level $\hat{u}(x)$. Write

$$\Delta q(x) = q(x) - q'(x) = \phi(S - x) - \phi(x) \tag{9}$$

Then $\Delta q(x)$ measures the amount of homogeneous good that the individual at $x$ could give up and still remain at the original utility level when he replaces a manufactured good at distance $x$ by one at distance $S - x$.

If the situation changes from one in which only the import good is available (with specifications spaced at $2S$) to one in which both the import and a local good are available, the latter at distance $S$ from the former, a consumer can now be supplied with either the import or the local good, whichever brings the highest subutility. Then, for consumers in the half segment $[0, S]$

$$\Delta q(x) = \min (0, \phi(S - x) - \phi(x)) \ge 0 \tag{10}$$

Provided $\phi$ is strictly decreasing (consumers are sensitive to product differences), $\Delta q(x) = 0$ for $x \le \frac{1}{2}S$ and $\Delta q(x) > 0$ for $x > \frac{1}{2}S$. Thus an increase in product variety due to the availability of a second good in each segment represents a Pareto improvement, since $\Delta q(x) > 0$ for some $x$ and $\ge 0$ for all $x$, and the surplus homogeneous good can then be distributed to make everyone better off.

If the import is replaced by the local product for all consumers in the interval $[S - w, S + w]$, where $w \le \frac{1}{2}S$, the aggregate gain over the segment $[0, 2S]$ is given by $2\alpha\Delta J(w)$, where

$$\begin{aligned} \Delta J(w) &= \int_0^S \Delta q(x) dx \\ &= \int_{S-w}^S \big(\phi(S - x) - \phi(x)\big) dx \\ &= \int_0^w \big(\phi(v) - \phi(S - v)\big) dv \end{aligned} \tag{11}$$

after an appropriate change of variable.

The value of $2\alpha\Delta J(w)$ measures the *gross* surplus available for redistribution and for covering any changes in resource use due to replacement of some imports by local production. This is the *pure variety gain*.

It is obvious that $\Delta J(w) > 0$ for any $w > 0$ provided consumers are sensitive to differences in product specification ($\phi' < 0$). This sensitivity is sufficient to give a pure variety gain when the number of products is increased, proving the first statement in the proposition.

If the resource cost of producing the local manufactures is exactly equal to the previous resource cost of purchasing the displaced imports, the gross gain from variety is also the net gain. If the two costs are not equal, however, then there is an *efficiency* gain or loss. The *net gain from variety* is the combination of the pure variety gain and the efficiency gain or loss. For the model we are analyzing, the total resource cost of the displaced imports is $2\alpha mw$, while that of the local replacement is $2\alpha cw - F$, so that the increase in resource costs per segment from local production of a single good in that segment is given by

$$2\alpha(c - m)w - F$$

Denote the net variety gain by $X(w)$. This is the *excess* homogeneous good left over after ensuring that all consumers reach their initial welfare levels $\hat{u}(x)$ and all changes in resource cost have been covered. If positive, it can be distributed to make all consumers better off than in the initial situation and thus give an unambiguous Pareto improvement. The value of $X(w)$ is given by

$$X(w) = 2\alpha(\Delta J(w) - (c - m)w) - F \tag{12}$$

This is the value of the net variety gain when local production of a single good per segment replaces imports for consumers located in the interval $[S - w, S + w]$.

If consumers are sensitive to product differences then $\phi' < 0$ and $\Delta J(w) > 0$, so that there exists a range of parameters for which $X(w) > 0$ for some $w$ even through $c > m$. This proves the second statement given in the proposition.

*Size of the variety gain*
The size of the pure variety gain for given $w$ is measured by $\Delta J(w)$ and depends on the rate of decline in value to the consumer when distance from the ideal specification increases. The greater the effect of distance, the larger the variety gain. Using the property that $\phi$ is strictly decreasing, we can place upper and lower limits on $\Delta J(w)$:

$$(\phi(0) - \phi(S))\, w > \Delta J(w) > (\phi(w) - \phi(S - w))w \tag{13}$$

(for $0 < w \leq \tfrac{1}{2}S$).
Since

$$\frac{dJ(w)}{dw} = \phi(w) - \phi(S - w)$$
$$\frac{d^2 J(w)}{dw^2} = \phi'(w) + \phi'(S - w) < 0$$

$J(w)$ is symmetrical about $w = \tfrac{1}{2}S$ and has a maximum at this value. However $\tfrac{1}{2}S$ is not, in general, the value of $w$ which optimizes the *net* gain $X(w)$.

For the maximum net gain we have

$$\frac{dX(w)}{dw} = 2\alpha\big(\phi(w) - \phi(S-w) - (c-m)\big) \tag{14}$$

so the optimal choice will be $w^*$, which satisfies

$$\begin{aligned}
\phi(w^*) - \phi(S-w^*) &= & c-m & \quad\text{if }\; 0 \le w^* \le S \\
w^* = 0 & & \text{if} & \quad \phi(0) - \phi(S) \le c-m \\
w^* = S & & \text{if} & \quad \phi(0) - \phi(S) \le -(c-m)
\end{aligned} \tag{15}$$

While a solution $w^* = 0$ implies that $X(w) \le 0$ for all $w$, and thus that it is not optimal to produce locally, a solution $w^* > 0$ does not imply that $X(w) > 0$ and thus that there should be local production, since the fixed cost $F$ must also be considered. The value of $w^*$ is, of course, independent of $F$.

*No economies of scale*
The analysis above has assumed that local production, if it exists, will produce to a finite number of specifications. This is appropriate for the economies of scale case with $F > 0$. But if $F = 0$, every consumer in an interval of width $w$ can be supplied with his ideal good for precisely the same resource cost as supplying every consumer with the same good.

In the absence of scale economies, therefore, every consumer receiving the local product can obtain his ideal good and thus attain a subutility level $\phi(0)$, so that (9) is replaced by

$$\Delta q_0(x) = \phi(0) - \phi(x) \tag{16}$$

The subscript 0 will be used to distinguish the no scale economies values from those for the scale economies cases.

The pure variety gain is given by

$$\Delta J_0(w) = w\phi(0) - \int_{S-w}^{S} \phi(v)dv$$

$$\ge \big(\phi(0) - \phi(S-w)\big)w \tag{17}$$

In this case, provided $\phi' < 0$, there is a pure variety gain for all values of $w$ including $w = S$, since the local good is differentiated to the maximum possible extent over its market range.

The net variety gain is given by

$$X_0(w) = 2\alpha\left(w\phi(0) - \int_{S-w}^{S} \phi(v)dv - (c-m)w\right) \tag{18}$$

The condition for optimal variety (optimal choice of $w_0$) when there are no scale economies is given by

$$
\begin{aligned}
\phi(0) - \phi(S - w_0^*) &= c - m \\
w_0^* = 0 &\quad if \quad c - m \geq \phi(0) - \phi(S) \\
w_0^* = S &\quad if \quad m \geq c
\end{aligned}
\tag{19}
$$

*Remarks*
1. There is nothing in this proposition as to the operation of the economy under market conditions, or as to whether any potential gain from variety will actually be realized within a market system. These issues are addressed in subsequent analysis and propositions.
2. The analysis holds for any initial distribution, provided everyone receives a unit of the manufactured good.
3. If the marginal cost of local manufacture is sufficiently low relative to the import cost so that $m - c \geq \phi(0) - \phi(S)$ *and* $(m - c)S \geq F > 0$, there is an efficiency gain from producing locally and then it will not be optimal to import at all. The variety gain is then obtained efficiently by having the local industry produce to the specification of the replaced import as well. There is a large range of parameter values in which $m > c$ but it is still optimal to import, however, because $F$ is high.
4. If there are no economies of scale, there is an efficiency *and* a variety gain whenever $m \geq c$, so it will *never* be desirable to import if the local manufacturing cost is lower.
5. With low marginal cost for local manufacture but high fixed cost, it would be possible to have $m - c \geq \phi(0) - \phi(S)$ *but* have $(m - c)S < F$. Although it would be optimal to have local production supply the whole market if it supplied any in this case, it is not optimal to start a local industry and thus all manufactures should be imported.

## When free trade is optimal
**Proposition II** *Any potential welfare gain from local production will be fully realized by operation of the market under free trade when either*
1. *there is potential gain from variety but there are no economies of scale in local manufacturing production, or*
2. *there is no potential gain from variety because local consumers are insensitive to product differences.*

*Proof of statement 1*
From the dividing condition for the no-scale economies case (2), the market width $w_0(P)$ for local manufacturing when $P$ is the consumer price for imports is the solution of

$$\phi(0) - \phi(S - w_0(P)) = c - P \qquad (20)$$

From the optimality condition (19), the welfare-maximizing value for $w_0$ is given by

$$\phi(0) - \phi(S - w_0^*) = c - m \qquad (21)$$

It follows that $w_0(m) = w_0^*$. That is, the optimum is achieved for the no-scale economies case under market conditions $P = m$ and thus when the tariff is zero.

*Proof of statement 2*
If $\phi(v)$ is constant, so that consumers are insensitive to differences in product specification, any welfare gain is a pure efficiency gain. The division of the consumers into segments then becomes irrelevant, so we are interested in the maximum social gain, measured by

$$nX^* = -2\alpha n(c - m)S - F$$

where $n$ is the total number of segments and $2\alpha nS$ is the total population.

In this case consumers will consider all manufactured goods the same and buy the cheapest, so that either $p \leq m$ and the local industry will have the whole market, or $p > m$ and imports will have the whole market. The local industry will function if and only if $c < m$. Provided $nX^* \geq 0$ at least one firm can charge price $p = m$ and make no loss. Thus the market will generate local production under free trade whenever there is a potential social gain from such production.

**Market failure under free trade**
**Proposition III**    *If there are scale economies in local production and consumers are sensitive to differences in product specification, it is possible to have market failure under free trade in the sense that local production is socially desirable but unprofitable. This is not a pathological case, but can occur under very reasonable assumptions if the system parameters lie within a certain range.*

*The problem*
If there is free trade, so that imports are sold internally at the world price $m$, and there are scale economies, the maximum profit for a local firm will be $\hat{\pi}(m)$ given by (7). The corresponding market width $\hat{w}$ satisfies:

$$\phi(\hat{w}) - \phi(S - \hat{w}) + \hat{w}\phi'(\hat{w}) + \hat{w}\phi'(S - \hat{w}) = c - m$$

from (6).

There will be market failure under free trade if

1. $\hat{\pi}(m) < 0$, so that local firms will not enter.
2. $X(w) > 0$ for some $w$, so that there is a welfare gain from having local industry.

The possible existence of such failure cannot be asserted. It requires to be proved, since both $\hat{\pi}(m)$ and $X(w)$ depend on the same system parameters in a rather similar way.

*Proof of the proposition*
Consider the firm's optimal values $\hat{p}$, $\hat{w}$. From the dividing condition (1)

$$\phi\hat{w} - \phi(S - \hat{w}) = \hat{p} - m = (\hat{p} - c) + (c - m)$$

while profit is given by

$$\hat{\pi} = 2\alpha(\hat{p} - c)\hat{w} - F$$

so that

$$(c - m) = \phi(\hat{w}) - \phi(S - \hat{w}) - \frac{\hat{\pi} + F}{2\alpha\hat{w}} \tag{22}$$

Now, provided $\phi' < 0$

$$
\begin{aligned}
X(\hat{w}) &= 2\alpha(\Delta J(\hat{w}) - (c - m)\hat{w}) - F && \text{(from (12))} \\
&= 2\alpha(\Delta J(\hat{w}) - [\phi(\hat{w}) - \phi(S - \hat{w})]\hat{w}) + \hat{\pi} && \text{(using (22))} \\
&> \hat{\pi} && \text{(from (13))}
\end{aligned}
$$

Condition (15) for the welfare-maximizing choice of $w$ is never satisfied at $\hat{w}$ because $\hat{p} > c$, so that $X(w^*) > X(\hat{w})$ and the inequality max $X > \hat{\pi}$ is strengthened. Thus the potential welfare gain from local production is always larger than the potential profit of the local firms, a result that is related to the well known proposition that a non-discriminating monopolist cannot capture the whole consumer surplus. Market failure occurs if max $X > 0$ but $\hat{\pi} < 0$, and is always possible for an appropriate range of parameters. Since $X - \hat{\pi}$ is independent of $F$, while $\hat{\pi}$ is not, there is always a value of $F$ which will give market failure.

*Remarks*
1. Market failure requires that there be *both* gain from variety and economies of scale in the local industry. Proposition II showed that there would be no failure if either condition was absent.
2. Market failure can occur with local marginal cost higher *or* lower than imports. A low value of $c$ relative to $m$ can give market failure if $F$ is large enough, and failure can also occur with a low value of $F$ if $c$ is high relative to $m$.
3. The scope for market failure increases with the gain from variety, which in turn increases with the degree of sensitivity of consumers to specification differences (properties of $\phi$) and with the degree of specification difference between available imports (the size of $S$).

**The optimal industry-creating tariff**
**Proposition IV** *If there is market failure in the sense of Proposition III, where welfare-maximizing local production fails to occur because no firm can operate except at a loss, the potential welfare gain can be fully realized by the operation of the market under an appropriate partially protective tariff. In particular there exists a tariff level under which the operation of the market generates both the socially optimal level of local production and non-negative profits for local firms, provided there is indeed a net welfare gain from some level of local production. The post-tariff equilibrium is first-best, not second-best, and is not an infant industry tariff since the market failure reappears if the tariff is removed.*

*Determination of the tariff*
Choose $\tau^*$ to satisfy

$$\tau^* = -(\phi'(w^*) + \phi'(S - w^*))w^* \tag{23}$$

where $w^*$ is given by

$$\phi(w^*) - \phi(S - w^*) = c - m \tag{24}$$

We shall show that

1. Welfare is maximized by a division of the market between local production and imports in the ratio $w^*/(S - w^*)$.
2. At a price $m + \tau^*$ for the import, the price $p^*$ for the local good at which the market will be divided in the above ratio is the profit-maximizing price for the local firm.

3. The profit $\pi^*$ generated at price $p^*$ is non-negative if the net welfare gain from local production is non-negative, and thus the industry will operate if it is socially optimal for it to do so.

*Proof*
The optimality of the half-market width $w^*$ follows immediately, since (24) is identical with the optimal condition (15).

From (5), the price $p^*$ at which the market divides in the ratio $w^*/(S - w^*)$ is given by

$$p^* - (m + \tau^*) = \phi(w^*) - \phi(S - w^*) = c - m$$

so that

$$p^* - c = \tau^*$$
$$-(\phi'(w^*) + \phi'(S - w^*))w^* \qquad \text{(From (23))}$$

But this last relationship is the condition that $p^*$ be profit-maximizing, from (4).

We now need to show that it will indeed be profitable for the local firm to operate if there is a welfare gain from local production. An upper limit on the welfare gain is derived as follows:

$$\begin{aligned} X^* &= 2\alpha(\Delta J - (c - m)w^*) - F \\ &< 2\alpha[(\phi(0) - \phi(S))w^* \\ &\quad - (\phi(w^*) - \phi(S - w^*))w^*] - F \qquad \text{(From (13) and (24))} \\ &< 2\alpha w^*[(\phi(0) - \phi(w^*)) \\ &\quad + (\phi(S - w^*) - \phi(S))] - F \\ &< -2\alpha(w^*)^2 (\phi'(w^*) + \phi'(S)) - F \qquad (25) \end{aligned}$$

where the last step follows from the assumption that $\phi$ is concave.[9] Note that it is sufficient for $\phi$ to be concave over the range $[0, S]$.

Now consider the profit of the local firm

$$\begin{aligned} \pi^* &= 2\alpha(p^* - c)w^* - F \\ &= -2\alpha(\phi'(w^*) + \phi'(S - w^*))(w^*)^2 - F \\ &\geq -2\alpha(\phi'(w^*) + \phi'(S))(w^*)^2 - F \qquad \text{(Concavity of } \phi) \\ &> X^* \qquad \text{(From (25))} \\ &\qquad (26) \end{aligned}$$

Thus $\pi^* > 0$ if $X^* \geq 0$ and the local firms will certainly operate under the protection of the tariff $\tau^*$ if there is a social gain from their doing so. Note that the strictness of the inequality is derived from (13) which depends only on the property $\phi' < 0$, and not on concavity. Weak concavity is used to complete the chain of argument. Thus a linear decreasing $\phi$ would be sufficient to give the result.

*Remarks*
1. If the tariff is removed, the equilibrium reverts to what it would be at free trade and any potential market failure will reappear. (A dynamic analysis in which the 'fixed' cost is a one-shot *capital cost* rather than a flow might reach different conclusions, but this must be left for later research.)
2. It is clear from the proof that it is possible to have $\pi^* > 0$ and $X^* < 0$, in which case $\tau^*$ is industry-creating but not socially desirable. The tariff $\tau^*$ is desirable only if $X^* > 0$.
3. From (23) it is necessarily true that $\tau^* \geq 0$. There is no inverse case for a negative tariff if imports are high-cost relative to local production.
4. It can never be desirable to protect high-cost local industry by a *prohibitive* tariff, since the gain from variety – the source of the potential welfare improvement – is then eliminated.
5. The optimum can also be achieved via the market by a *subsidy* on local production equal to the amount of $\tau^*$ per unit. It is easily shown that this will give the firm a profit-maximizing price $p'$ such that $w(p') = w^*$ and $\hat{\pi}(p') = \pi^*$, so the previous analysis then holds. Consumers pay less for both imports and local goods but pay taxes, instead of paying more for both goods and receiving tariff proceeds, the net result being the same.
6. There is a *non-market* way of achieving the optimum, by direct command to the local producer to sell at marginal cost $c$ while paying a lump sum subsidy of $F$. This is clearly inferior to the tariff policy since it attains no better result but replaces incentive by coercion.
7. If there is no market failure and the local industry operates, it may still be optimal to impose a distortion-correcting tariff in order to achieve the welfare-maximizing division between imports and local production, since the tariff $\tau^*$ induces the regular market forces to make the welfare-maximizing division between imports and local production. This result is closely related to the Lerner proposition[10] that optimality can be achieved with universal monopoly, under appropriate conditions, if the degree of monopoly is the same for all firms. The optimality condition in the present case $(P - m = p^* - c)$ is analogous to the Lerner condition.
8. The concavity property for $\phi$ over the range $[0, S]$ is clearly sufficient but not necessary to prove that $\pi^* \geq X^*$. It does not seem that there is any simple statement of the necessary and sufficient condition in economically meaningful terms.

## Distributional effects of the tariff
Consider the effect on the welfare distribution of a movement from free trade with market failure to an economy operating under an optimum tariff. At the

arbitrarily given free trade distribution of 'money' income $y(x)$ (= $q(x) + m$), the post-tariff gains and losses in any half-segment, prior to any redistributions, are as follows:

1. *Import buyers* All those who continue to buy imports after imposition of the tariff lose the amount of the tariff $\tau^*$, which appears as an increase in the price paid by consumers. Since they bought the same goods under free trade and the goods are not divisible, there is no other change. These are the consumers located in the interval $[0, S - w^*]$.
2. *Buyers of local goods* Those who switch from the import to the local good do not necessarily gain relative to their initial position. Although their choice reveals a gain relative to buying the import at the *post*-tariff price, there may be a loss relative to buying the import at the *pre*-tariff price. The consumer in the interval $[S - w^*, S]$ has a gain (loss if negative) given by

$$\Delta y(x) = \phi(S - x) - \phi(x) - p^* + m$$

Since $p^* > c$, the dividing condition determining $w^*$ implies that $\Delta y(S - w^*) < 0$. The gain/loss boundary is distance $w'$ from the local good, where $\Delta y(S - w')$ = 0. It is possible that there is no $w' > 0$ and thus no clear pre-distribution gainers, as in the numerical example given later.

In the post-tariff situation, there are two 'funds' available for redistribution, the tariff proceeds and the profits of the local firms. Obviously, the combined losses of the import buyers are exactly equal to the tariff proceeds. For the buyers of the local products, it is easily shown that the aggregate gains

$$\int_{S-w^*}^{S} \Delta y(x)dx$$

are equal to $X^* - \pi^*$ and thus necessarily negative. Then the difference between $\pi^*$ and the aggregate loss is $X^*$. Since the tariff is welfare-increasing (or the optimum tariff would be zero), this difference is positive, so that the pre-redistribution losses of the buyers of local goods are more than covered by the profits of the local firms. Thus everyone can be made better off by an appropriate redistribution.

Note that, as in all problems involving a finite number of goods and continuously varied preferences, 'appropriate' welfare redistributions require that compensation for each consumer be determined by the location of his ideal specification. In this model, import buyers as a class can be treated equally, but local goods buyers cannot be. Thus it is not feasible in practice to properly compensate each buyer of local goods, so as to make $\Delta y(x) = 0$ for all $x \in [S - w^*, S]$. Uniform monetary compensation over the class will under-compensate some and overcompensate others.

Since the profits of the firms in the model arise from the assumed fact that the spacing between imports is smaller than twice the break-even market size per firm, they are pure rents and a 'license' fee of $\pi^*$ - $\varepsilon$ can be charged for permission to produce locally, with no distorting effect. This would be more than sufficient to compensate the buyers of local goods on average, but does not solve the distribution problem.

## A simple numerical example

Consider the case in which $\phi(v) = 1 - v^2$, $\alpha = \frac{1}{2}$. This satisfies all the basic assumptions of the model provided $m + S \leq 1$ and $|c - m| < S$. For simplicity write $\delta = (c - m)/S$. Then

$$
\begin{aligned}
\phi(v) - \phi(S - v) &= S(S - 2v) \\
\Delta J(w) &= Sw(S - w) \\
X(w) &= Sw(S - w) - Sw\delta - F \\
w^* &= \tfrac{1}{2}(S - \delta) \\
X^* &= X(w^*) = \tfrac{1}{4}S(S - \delta)^2 - F
\end{aligned}
$$

From the equilibrium conditions of the firm, with import price $m + \tau$:

$$
\begin{aligned}
\hat{w}(\tau) &= \tfrac{1}{4}(S - \delta + \tau/S) \\
\hat{p}(\tau) - c &= 2S\hat{w}(\tau) \\
\hat{\pi}(P) &= \tfrac{1}{8}S(S - \delta + t)^2 - F
\end{aligned}
$$

where $t = \tau/S$.

Write variables as functions of the tariff. Then

$$
X(\tau) = X(w(\tau)) = \tfrac{1}{4}S(S - \delta + t)(\tfrac{3}{4}(S - \delta) - \tfrac{1}{4}t) - F
$$

*Market failure*
Under free trade:

$$
\begin{aligned}
X(0) &= \tfrac{3}{16}S(S - \delta)^2 - F \\
\hat{\pi}(0) &= \tfrac{1}{8}S(S - \delta)^2 - F
\end{aligned}
$$

so that $X^* > X(0) > \hat{\pi}(0)$, Proposition III is satisfied and there is market failure if $F$ lies in the range $\tfrac{1}{4}S(S - \delta)^2 > F > \tfrac{1}{8}S(S - \delta)^2$.

Note that for $F$ between $\frac{3}{16}S(S-\delta)^2$ and $\frac{1}{4}S(S-\delta)^2$, $X(0) \leq 0$ but $X^* > 0$. There would be no social gain if firms did operate at the free trade market width $w(0)$, but there would be a potential gain at the optimal market division $w^*$.

Market failure requires appropriate relationships between parameters, which can be satisfied by various combinations of $F$ and $\delta$. The relationship $F = \frac{3}{16}S(S-\delta)^2$ gives market failure and includes the following combinations (for $S = 1$):

$$\delta = 0.2, \, F = 0.12; \, \delta = 0, \, F = 0.1875; \, \delta = -0.2, \, F = 0.27$$

so failure can occur with local marginal costs higher than, lower than, or the same as the cost of imports.

*The optimum tariff*
the optimum tariff is given by

$$\tau^* = S(S-\delta)$$

so that

$$
\begin{aligned}
\hat{w}(\tau^*) &= \tfrac{1}{2}(S-\delta) = w^* \\
p(w^*) &= Sc + S(S-\delta) \\
\hat{\pi}(\tau^*) &= \tfrac{1}{2}S(S-\delta)^2 = F \\
&> X^*
\end{aligned}
$$

and Proposition IV is satisfied.

Thus if $F = \frac{3}{16}S(S-\delta)^2$, $\hat{\pi}(m) = -\frac{1}{16}S(S-\delta)^2 < 0$ but $X^* = \frac{1}{16}S(S-\delta)^2$ so there is market failure. Imposing a tariff of $S(S-\delta)$ gives $\pi^* = \frac{5}{16}S(S-\delta)^2 > 0$ and $X^* = \frac{1}{16}S(S-\delta)^2$ so that the optimum is achieved by the regular operation of the local industry under the protection of the tariff.

*Distribution*
Prior to redistribution of either the tariff proceeds or the local firm's profit, the effect of the optimum tariff on the various consumers is as follows:

1.  Those who buy the imports lose $\tau^*$. Collectively their loss is

$$(S - w^*)\tau^* = \tfrac{1}{2}S(S-\delta)(S+\delta)$$

These losses can be covered by the tariff proceeds, to which they are equal.
2.  Those who buy the local good gain

$$\phi(v) - \phi(S - v) - p(\tau^*) + m = -2Sv$$

where $v$ is the distance from the local good. Their aggregate gain is $-\frac{1}{4}S(S - \delta)^2$, always negative as shown previously. Note that the gain/loss boundary $w'$ is here $0$ – all buyers of the local good lose in the absence of redistribution. However the losses can be more than covered by redistribution of profits, which are $\frac{1}{2}S(S - \delta)^2 - F$, since $F < \frac{1}{4}S(S - \delta)^2$ (otherwise the optimum tariff is zero).

Two special tariff values might be noted:

- The break-even tariff ($\hat{\pi}(\tau) = 0$) at $\tau_{\pi=0} = 2\sqrt{(2FS)} - S^2 + S\delta$. It can be shown that $X(\tau_{\pi=0}) < 0$ for $F > 2S(S - \delta)^2$. If $F$ is in this range, there is an industry-creating tariff, but it reduces welfare.
- The prohibitive tariff ($\hat{w}(\tau) = S$) at $\tau_{w=S} = S(3S + \delta)$. Then $X(\tau_{w=S}) = -\frac{1}{2}S^2\delta < 0$ and there is a welfare loss.

## World Equilibrium

To show that the analysis presented in the paper has applicability and relevance and is not confined to pathological, disequilibrium, or short-run cases, we shall demonstrate that the local and rest-of-the-world (ROW) configurations are not inconsistent, and can coexist as long-run equilibria of their respective economies in an open world economy. We shall consider only the case in which there is a potential gain from the tariff.

As in any small open economy model, there must be some difference between the local economy and the rest of the world to generate any interesting results at all. Size is certainly one of these here, since the local demand for each imported manufacture is taken to be negligible relative to ROW demand. There are no comparative advantage effects here since a single homogeneous input is assumed and the technology must be universal in the long run. So, apart from size, the only differences are in individual preferences and/or their distribution.

It is of the essence of the model that local manufacturing uses a different technique from ROW manufacturing, so the world technology must contain at least these two techniques. Let the ROW technique be given by $(k, K)$ (a constant marginal cost $k$ and fixed cost $K$). Then $c > k$ and $F < K$, since neither can be dominant.

For world equilibrium, we need to show that there are reasonable and realistic conditions under which both of the following configurations are consistent:

1. In the absence of a tariff, ROW manufacturing has an equilibrium configuration using the technique $(k, K)$ but local economy does not produce any manufactures with either technique.
2. With the tariff, local manufacturing uses technique $(c, F)$ and produces to a specification intermediate between imported manufactures, but ROW neither produces this good nor imports it from the local economy.

### The ROW economy

The ROW economy is assumed to be qualitatively similar to the local economy, with uniformly distributed consumers having utility functions of the general form as in the local economy. The subutility of ROW consumers for the manufactured good, denoted by $\psi$, is assumed to have the same *qualitative* properties as the local subutility function $\phi$, but otherwise may be different. ROW consumers are assumed to be distributed uniformly over the spectrum with density $\beta$. The price $m$ and product spacing $2S$ for ROW manufactures are taken to be the zero-profit Nash values and thus represent long-run equilibrium.

Since the technique $(k, K)$ is chosen for ROW manufacturing over the technique $(c, F)$, we must have

$$c - k > \frac{K - F}{2\beta S} \tag{27}$$

This condition is always satisfied for a sufficiently large value of $\beta$.

It is also necessary to show that no firm in ROW can gain by using the technique $(c, F)$ and goods more closely spaced than $2S$. A *sufficient* condition of this is that the consumer whose ideal good is midway between goods produced by the $(k, K)$ technique would not be willing to pay the marginal cost $c$ to have a good to his own specification rather than one at distance $S$ and price $m$. This will be true if $c > m$ and

$$\psi(0) - \psi(S) \leq c - m \tag{28}$$

This condition also guarantees that there is no demand from ROW for the output of local manufacturing in a post-tariff situation.

### The local economy

To be consistent with ROW, it must be uneconomical for local firms to produce with the $(k, K)$ technique. Thus

$$c - k \leq \frac{K - F}{2\alpha S} \tag{29}$$

which is derived similarly to (27) and is consistent with it if $\alpha$ is small compared with $\beta$. This in turn is consistent with the requirement that the local market for any product be negligible compared with that in ROW.

Since there is gain from the tariff, there must be a social gain from supplying some consumers with the local good using the $(c, F)$ technique. That is, there must be consumers whose welfare gain exceeds the difference between the import price and the local marginal cost. This must certainly be true for consumers with the most to gain – those having ideal goods midpoint between available imports:

$$\phi(0) - \phi(S) > c - m \tag{30}$$

This can be consistent with (28) since $\psi$ and $\phi$ are different.

*Consistency conditions*
Consistency between the assumed ROW equilibrium and pre- and post-tariff equilibria of the local economy requires that:

1. The density of consumers must be much higher in ROW than in the local economy ($\beta \gg \alpha$). This is implicit in the treatment of the local economy as 'small' relative to the world economy.
2. The relationship

$$\phi(0) - \phi(S) > \psi(0) - \psi(S)$$

which is a necessary condition for the joint satisfaction of (28) and (30). That is, preferences in the local economy differ from those in ROW in a particular way – consumers in the local economy are *more sensitive* to variations in product characteristics than those in the ROW.

The first condition presents no problems. The second requires that the local small economy has consumers who feel more intensely about the differences among some range of products than does the rest of the world. Does this case have real applicability?

The answer would seem to be, yes. It can be argued that cultural differences lead to many cases in which one society is sensitive to differences among a certain group of products which the rest of the world finds rather similar. French consumers would surely be in this position relative to a world in which 'Cheddar' and 'Swiss' provided sufficient diversity in cheese, and there are plenty of other examples covering goods as varied as rice, bicycles, and whisky.

**Concluding remarks**
The analysis here shows that there can be a case for the use of *partial* tariff protection to obtain a first-best welfare outcome for a small open economy whose

policies have no strategic or monopolistic effects on world markets. While not a special case – the underlying conditions, namely a differentiable product, diversity of preferences, and some type of scale economies, perhaps quite small – are common enough, it is a *restricted* case in the sense that it holds only over a range of parameter relationships.

There are two aspects of the analysis that are of primary importance in assessing its practical relevance, *generality* and *applicability*. We shall conclude by considering these in turn.

### Generality

Although the results given here have been based on a relatively simple model, it seems a reasonable conjecture that they hold much more generally. It is not difficult to generalize Proposition I, that there is a potential gain from variety if consumers are sensitive to product differences, and Proposition II, optimality of free trade in the absence of either economies of scale or a gain from variety. Proposition III, the possibility of market failure under free trade when there is a potential gain from variety and economies of scale, holds because local firms cannot capture all the surplus, a well-known proposition of considerable generality.

Proposition IV, that an appropriate tariff can always fully compensate for market failure (and which is the central proposition of the paper), depends on specific properties of the model to a greater extent than the other propositions. It is proved by showing that there exists a tariff level which

- makes it profitable for local firms to produce if there is a social gain from their doing so, even though it is unprofitable for them to produce under free trade.
- Results in a market price for local manufactures which gives optimal allocation between imports and local production, thus ensuring that the potential social gain is achieved.

It is easy to show that, in general, either of these results can be achieved independently by a tariff chosen for that specific purpose. The crux of the matter is to prove the existence of a single tariff which does both. The proof here draws upon the assumed concavity of the subutility from the differentiated good as a function of the degree of difference between that good and the consumer's ideal. While this is a reasonable assumption, and is certainly stronger than needed, the degree of generality of the proposition remains somewhat unclear.

### Applicability

It is clear enough that, given prices and specifications for goods available from the rest of the world, there are acceptable combinations of preference and cost parameters within the small open economy for which the case for tariff protection holds. The analysis can be said to have general applicability in the sense that no pathological conditions are imposed on the local economy.

However, although it is traditional in small open economy models to take the rest of the world (ROW) as arbitrarily given, and although interesting results require that *something* differs between the local economy and ROW, a convincing case for applicability can only be made by showing that the differences between ROW and the local economy are themselves reasonable. This case has been made in the preceding section.

**Notes**
1. Originally published in the *Journal of International Economics*, **31** (1991), 1–26.
2. See Lancaster 1984, reprinted as Chapter 3 in this volume.
3. For arguments in favor of protection for such cases, see Brander and Spencer 1984, Eaton and Grossman 1986, Dixit 1984 and Cheng 1988.
4. Flam and Helpman 1987, for example.
5. See Bhagwati 1971 and Corden 1974.
6. See Lancaster 1979, Chapter 7.
7. This is to avoid the complexities of the analysis of market structures in which firms face more than one kind of rival. For such analysis see Lancaster 1990.
8. The divisible case is analyzed fully in Lancaster 1979.
9. If $f(x)$ is concave decreasing and $a < b$ then

$$-(b-a)f'(a) \le f(a) - f(b) \le -(b-a)f'(b)$$

# 6   The Heckscher–Ohlin trade model[1]

The particular approach to the general theory of international trade which was first made by Heckscher[2] and which was developed, and first published in English, by Ohlin[3] has now become part of the basic structure of the theory. In a sense it has replaced the classical and neoclassical method of approach, in which comparative costs provided the starting point for the theory of international trade, and its *raison d'être*.

There is, of course, no real conflict between the Heckscher–Ohlin approach and that by way of comparative costs. Comparative costs, properly stated, emerge from the Heckscher–Ohlin model, and this model, in fact, goes behind comparative costs and establishes them as due to something more fundamental – differences in factor endowments.

As far as the theory of commodity trade is concerned, virtually all of the traditional structure of analysis could be carried out in terms of some elaboration of the comparative costs approach, such as the assumption of different, given, transformation functions for the trading countries. But the Heckscher–Ohlin model provided, for the first time, an analysis that was capable of integrating the factor markets into international trade theory in a satisfactory way, and much of its impact has been in this field. To a body of international trade theory which consisted primarily of propositions about the relative prices (or the results of certain relationships between the prices) of *goods*, there was now added a series of propositions about the relative prices of factors, culminating in the recent discussions concerning 'factor price equalization'.[4]

In its simplest (and, in many ways, most revealing) form, the Heckscher–Ohlin model concerns itself with a world which consists of a group of countries which use identical factors to produce identical goods by the use of identical production functions, these production functions having the property of constant returns to scale. These assumptions are necessary (but not sufficient) to result in the equalization of factor prices throughout the world.

Now the factor price equalization theorem, and so, by implication, the simple form of the Heckscher–Ohlin model, has been sharply criticized[5] for the specialized nature of these assumptions. In particular, the assumptions of identical production functions and of constant returns to scale have been attacked as 'unrealistic'.

It is, of course, quite true that the Heckscher–Ohlin model, even in its more developed form, and certainly it its simpler form, is unrealistic. So are a great many models, in the physical, as well as the social sciences. Nevertheless, the

Heckscher–Ohlin model occupies the very center of international trade theory, for reasons unconnected with its realism and, indeed, strengthened by the very properties which have been subject to so much criticism.

In constructing a body of international trade theory, the first step must be to show why trade takes place at all, as a voluntary activity of both sides, and this problem was dealt with by Ricardo and Mill in a manner that, broadly speaking, satisfied economists for several decades. In essence, Ricardian theory found the reason for trade in differences between countries, primarily differences of technique, skill, factors or all combined.

Given that trade depends, in a loose way, on differences, a good scientific enquirer would ask the question, 'What is the *minimum* difference between countries which would be sufficient to explain the existence of trade?'

This question does not seem to have been asked, let alone answered, until Heckscher, but the Heckscher–Ohlin model provides the complete answer, that the minimum difference necessary is a difference in the relative endowment of factors between countries. Once the matter is seen in this light, as a problem of determining the minimum difference necessary for trade, the apparent vices of the Heckscher–Ohlin model are seen, in this context, to be virtues. The identity of production functions eliminates differences in knowledge and technique, the constant returns to scale eliminate differences in size, so that only one difference remains, a difference in proportions between qualitatively identical factors.

A second broad question to which the Heckscher–Ohlin model provides a satisfactory answer is that concerning the 'future of trade' (in the rather abstract sense). In other words, since the ordinary comparative costs approach relied on accidents to explain the difference which initiated trade, accidents such as differences in knowledge or skill, there was a reasonable presumption that international trade could ultimately cease to exist: Portugal could learn to make cloth as cheaply (in terms of wine) as England.

In the Heckscher–Ohlin model it follows clearly that international trade would continue even if there were perfect transmission of knowledge and techniques and absolute freedom for the costless migration of factors. For the identity of techniques is part of the model in any case, and factor price equalization shows that there would be no incentive for factor endowments to become uniform, so resulting in the cessation of trade.

The Heckscher–Ohlin model, therefore, deserves a place at the center of international trade theory. It is, in fact, *the* simple model of international trade when things are reduced to most elemental terms (not necessarily the most elementary terms), just as the two-commodity indifference curve is *the* simple model of consumer behavior. It is for this reason that an attempt has been made in the present paper to express the character and fundamental properties of the model in reasonably simple geometric terms, using the Edgeworth box diagram as a basis.

No new conclusions are reached in the analysis,[6] and the method is derived from the extension of a construction devised by Rybczynski.[7] The only claim made for the paper is that it brings out the properties of the model in a reasonably neat and concise fashion, houses them under the one roof, and uses the geometrical technique in circumstances which simplify, rather than complicate, the matter in hand. The geometrical method chosen is capable of extension to a considerable degree, but the use here is confined to elucidating the more basic properties of the simple Heckscher–Ohlin model.

**The Edgeworth box diagram**
The particular type of geometric device which is usually known as the Edgeworth box diagram, or the Edgeworth–Bowley box diagram, has been described many times in the literature and the brief description given here is inserted in the interests of autonomy. There are, however, some properties of the diagram which are essential for the succeeding analysis, and these need emphasis.

The Edgeworth box is a device for illustrating the allocation of two resources, each fixed in total amount, between two types of use. It can be used to show the interrelationships between no less than twelve economic variables in terms of a plane diagram, provided that the relationships are of a certain kind.

Figure 6.1 shows the particular version of the diagram that will be used in the Heckscher–Ohlin model. The rectangle $ABCD$ represents an economy with fixed total resources of two factors (called labor and capital, for convenience) the total quantities of labor and capital being represented by $AC$ (or $BD$) and $AD$ (or $BC$), respectively. There are two 'industries', producing two goods, $A$ and $B$, the quantities of labor and capital used in the production of $A$ being measured, for any point inside the box, by the vertical distance from $AD$, and the horizontal distance from $AC$, respectively. Then the vertical distance of the point from $BC$ and its horizontal distance from $BD$ give the quantities of the two factors used in the production of $B$. Any point inside the box, therefore, represents some allocation of the two factors between the two industries.

The actual outputs of $A$ and $B$ do not appear directly on the diagram, but are read off from isoquant lines which join factor quantities producing the same quantity of output. The isoquants $A = 1$ and $B = 1$ are shown in Figure 6.1. All the production functions with which this paper is concerned are homogeneous, that is, with the property that all the isoquants are geometrically similar and can be obtained from one another by uniform radial expansion or contraction relative to the origin. The unit isoquant thus defines the production function completely, except for the scale of output.

In perfect competition, which will be assumed henceforth, the allocation of factors must be such that the ratio between the marginal productivities of the two factors in the production of $A$ is equal to the ratio between their marginal

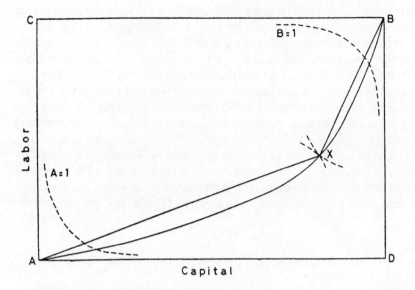

*Figure 6.1   The Edgeworth box diagram*

productivities in the production of *B*. The ratio in question is given by the slope of the isoquants, so that the condition is that the allocations must be such as to give points at which the *A*- and *B*-isoquants are tangential.

Points which satisfy this condition, such as *X* in Figure 6.1, lie along a locus which is termed the 'contract line'. If the isoquants are smooth, continuous, and convex to the origin, the contract line will be smooth and continuous, will pass through *A* and *B*, and will (in the case being considered here) lie wholly to one side or the other of the diagonal *AB*.

On which side of the diagonal the contract line lies depends on the relative factor intensities of the two production functions. If *A* is always the more capital-intensive industry, then, at the same relative prices for the factors in both industries (i.e. along the contract line), the ratio of capital to labor will be higher in *A* than in *B*. That is, the contract line will lie to the south-east of the diagonal *AB*, as in the diagram.

For the case in which *A* is the more capital-intensive industry at one set of factor prices, and the more labor-intensive at another, see below.

### Properties of a ray through the origin
Consider the corner of the Edgeworth diagram in which the *A* origin lies and consider any ray *AX* through *A*. Then, due to the homogeneity property, *AX* cuts all *A*-isoquants at the same angle so that $MPL_A/MPC_A$ is constant along *AX*, where

$MPL_A$, $MPC_A$ represent the marginal productivities of labor and capital in the production of $A$, their ratio being the tangent to the isoquant.

If there are constant returns to scale, then, if the ratio of labor to capital is kept constant, production is proportional to the quantity of either factor. Along $AX$, the factor ratio is constant, and the distance $AX'$ is proportional to the factor quantities at the point $X'$. Therefore, the production of $A$ at any point $X'$ along $AX$ is proportional to the distance $AX'$. Note that this proportionality holds only for points along the *same* ray; there is no common linear measure between point on different rays.

Finally – and this is the property which is the key to much of the succeeding analysis -- the *absolute* values of the marginal productivities of the factors are constant along $AX$, if there are constant returns to scale. For, since the production functions are homogeneous of the first degree, Euler's identity holds, so that

$$A = L_A \cdot MPL_A + C_A \cdot MPC_A$$

where $A$ = production of $A$, $L_A$, $C_A$ = labor, capital used in production of $A$.

$$\frac{A}{L_A} = MPL_A \left( 1 + \frac{C_A}{L_A} \frac{MPC_A}{MPL_A} \right)$$

Also, since, as has just been demonstrated, the ratio of output to the input of either factor is constant along $AX$, and the expression inside the bracket on the right-hand side above is also constant along $AX$, $MPL_A$, the only other quantity in the equation, must also be constant along $AX$. It follows that $MPC_A$ is constant as well.

All the above properties hold, of course, for the $B$-isoquants relative to a ray $BX$ through the point $B$.

### Determination of price

Since the points along the contract line represent equilibrium points under conditions of perfect competition, the payments to the factors must be the same in both industries. That is,

$$p_A \cdot MPL_A = p_B \cdot MPL_B$$
$$p_A \cdot MPC_A = p_B \cdot MPC_B$$

whence

$$\frac{p_A}{p_B} = \frac{MPL_B}{MPL_A} = \frac{MPC_B}{MPC_A}$$

This property is of extreme importance for the analysis which follows.

## A simple Heckscher–Ohlin model

The defining assumptions of the simple Heckscher–Ohlin model are as follows:

1. All countries produce the same two commodities, using the same two factors, using processes defined by the same two production functions.
2. The production functions for both goods involve the use of both factors, are homogeneous, convex, and with constant returns to scale.
3. The production functions are such that the relative factor intensities are the same at all factor prices which are the same in both industries. That is, the labor-intensive good remains the labor-intensive good.[8]
4. There is perfect competition in all markets and full employment of resources.
5. There are no transport or similar costs, and no tariffs or other trade barriers.
6. The relative endowments of the two factors vary from country to country.
7. Consumer preferences are identical in all countries.[9]

Since each country has a fixed endowment of factors, and produces two goods, it can be represented by an Edgeworth box diagram similar to that of Figure 6.1. Furthermore, any pair of countries can be represented by a pair of Edgeworth box diagrams, drawn to the same scale and located with equivalent edges parallel.

In Figure 6.2, *ACBD* and *A'C'B'D'* represent such a pair of diagrams, corresponding to two countries I and II. These are drawn so that *A*, *A'* represent the origins for the *A*-isoquants, *B*, *B'* the origins for the *B*-isoquants, *AC*, *A'C'* the endowments of labor, and *AD*, *AD'* the endowments of capital, in the two countries. As the figure is drawn *AD > A'D'*, *AC < A'C'*, so that country I has more capital and less labor than country II.

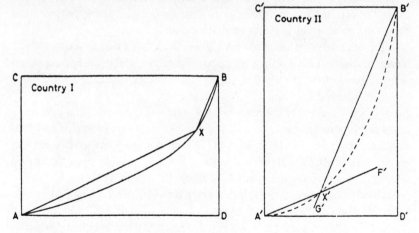

*Figure 6.2    Box diagrams for two countries*

Now let $X$ be some point on the contract curve of country I. In $A'C'B'D'$ (i.e. country II), draw $A'F'$ so that it is parallel to $AX$ in $ACBD$, that is, so that $\angle D'A'F' = \angle DAX$, and draw $B'G'$ so that it is parallel to $BX$ in $ACBD$. Let $A'F'$ and $B'G'$ intersect in $X'$. Then follows a remarkable and neat theorem which may be called the *Theorem of Corresponding Points*, to the effect that $X$ and $X'$ form a pair of points such that

(i)   If $X$ is on the contract line for country I, then $X'$ is on the contract line for country II.
(ii)  The marginal productivities of both factors, in both industries, are the same at $X'$ as at $X$.
(iii) The commodity price ratio at $X'$ is the same as at $X$.
(iv)  The proportions in which the two goods are produced at $X'$ will differ from the proportions in which they are produced at $X$, the proportions being such that each country produces more, relatively, of the good which is most intensive in its abundant factor, the supplies of both factors being exactly used up in both countries.

This theorem sums up, very concisely, the important properties of the simple Heckscher–Ohlin model. Free trade equilibrium will occur with both countries 'at' corresponding points, since such a pair of points satisfies the internal conditions of equilibrium in each country (from (i)) and represents the same terms of trade in both countries (from (iii)). Trade *will* take place since both countries have the same tastes but produce the two goods in different proportions at any given price level (from (iii) and (vi)). Finally, at whatever pair of corresponding points trade equilibrium takes place, factor prices will be equal in both countries (from (ii)). It also follows, from (iv), that each country will export the good which is intensive in its abundant factor.

Although the formulation has been given in terms of two countries only, it is clear that it is equally true of any number of countries which satisfy the assumptions of the model.[10]

*Proof of the Theorem of Corresponding Points*
Since the production functions are identical for both countries, the set of $A$-isoquants spreading out from $A'$ in $A'C'B'D'$ are the same as the set spreading out from $A$ in $ACBD$. Therefore, since $\angle D'A'X' = \angle DAX$, those properties relevant to the $A$-isoquants which hold along $AX$ also hold along $A'X'$.

Similarly, those properties relevant to the $B$-isoquants which hold along $BX$, hold also along $B'X'$.

From the previous section it follows, therefore, that the marginal productivities of labor and capital in the production of $A$ are the same along $A'X'$ as along

$AX$, and that the marginal productivities of labor and capital in the production of $B$ are the same along $B'X'$ as along $BX$.

Since $X$, $X'$ lie, respectively, on both $AX$, $BX$ and $A'X'$, $B'X'$, the marginal productivities of labor and capital, in the production of both $A$ and $B$, are the same at $X'$ as at $X$.

In particular,

(a)  Since $X$ lies on the contract line of country I, the ratio between the marginal productivities of labor and capital, in country I, is the same in the production of $B$ as of $A$. The same equality holds, therefore, in country II, so that $X'$ lies on the contract line in country II.

(b)  Part (ii) of the theorem (the equality of marginal productivities) follows immediately from the properties of rays through the origin.

(c)  Since the commodity price ratio in country I is given by the ratio of the marginal productivity of a factor in one industry to that in the other, and both these marginal productivities are the same at $X'$ as at $X$, it follows that the commodity price ratio is the same at $X'$ as at $X$.

The proof of part (iv) of the theorem (which may seem the most intuitively obvious part) is simple enough, but requires some additional manipulation. Taking the two diagrams as in Figure 6.2, apply $A'C'B'D'$ to $ACBD$ so that $D'$ coincides with $D$, $D'A'$ lies along $DA$, and $D'B'$ lies along $DB$. The result is shown in Figure 6.3.

Since the original diagrams had the properties $AD > A'D'$ and $BD < B'D'$, it is clear that, when $A'C'B'D'$ is applied to $ACBD$, $A$ will lie to the left of $A'$, so that $AX$ will lie above $A'X'$, and $B$ will lie below $B'$, so that $BX$ will lie below $B'X'$, giving the configuration shown in Figure 6.3.

Referring to the figure,

$$AX = AP + PN + NX$$

Since $PN$ is parallel to $A'X'$ and $NX'$ is, at most, vertical, it follows that $PN \geq A'X'$. Hence,

$$AX \geq AP + NX + A'X'$$
$$> A'X'$$

But, from the previous section, the production of $A$ at the point $X$ in country I is proportional to $AX$, and the production of $A$ at the point $X'$ in country II is proportional to $A'X'$. Since $AX$, $A'X'$ are directly comparable, it follows that the production of $A$ is greater in country I than in country II. Similarly, it can be shown that the production of $B$ is less in country I than in country II, by

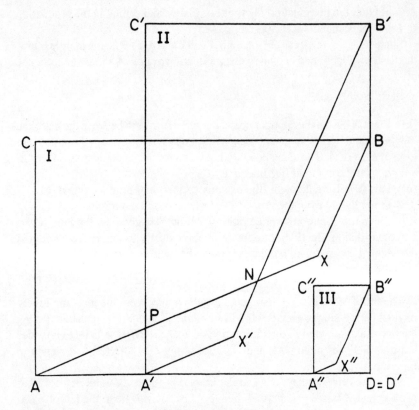

*Figure 6.3    Box diagrams for three countries*

comparing *B'X'* with *BX*. Hence it follows that the production of *A*, relative to the production of *B*, is greater in country I than in country II.

Now, as was pointed out earlier, in reference to Figure 6.1, the model has been built up with *A* as the relatively capital-intensive good. Since it has also been assumed that country I is the country relatively abundant in capital, the above proof can be generalized into the statement that each country produces relatively more of the good intensive in its abundant factor.

The scale has not yet been taken into account, however. In Figures 6.2 and 6.3, it has been assumed that each country has absolutely more of one factor, and absolutely less of the other, than the other country. Consider a third country, country III, which is similar to country II, but smaller in all respects – a shrunken version of country II. Such a country is shown as the box *A"C"B"D* in Figure 6.3.

Since country III is similar in all respects except scale to country II, and there are no scale effects in production, all *ratios* in country III are equal to the equivalent ratios in country II. In particular, the ratio of production of *A* to *B* is the same in III as in II, and therefore less than the ratio in I. This proves part (iv) of the theorem for the case when the countries are not of the same 'size'.

**Specialization and migration**
In the preceding analysis it was assumed, in the construction that defines the corresponding points in the two countries, that the lines $A'F'$ and $B'G'$ in country II do, in fact, intersect inside the box. This case is the one usually discussed, because it is, in many ways, the more significant.

It can, and will be shown, however, that there are points on the contract curve of either country which have no corresponding points in the other country, and that it is possible for there to be no corresponding points between the two economies.

Consider Figure 6.4 which is, basically, the same as Figure 6.2. To the point $X$ in country I there corresponds the point $X'$ in country II. Now examine what happens as the point $X$ moves down country I's contract curve in a south-westerly direction. As this happens, $X'$, the corresponding point to $X$, moves in the same direction along country II's contract curve, with $A'X'$ keeping parallel to $AX$ and $B'X'$ to $BX$. Eventually a point ($R$) will be reached in country I where $\angle DBR$ in I is equal to $\angle D'B'A'$ in II. That is, the corresponding point to $R$ will be $A'$. Since $AC/AD < A'C'/A'D'$, $R$ will lie well inside the box $ACBD$. Clearly, the points on the segment $AR$ of I's contract curve have no corresponding points on II's contract line.

Similarly, by moving $X'$ in a north-easterly direction along the contract line of country II, a point will be reached ($T'$), at which $\angle D'A'T' = \angle DAB$ which

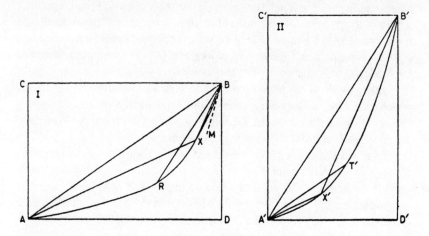

*Figure 6.4   Box diagrams and contract curves*

corresponds to the point $B$ on the contract line of country I, so that the segment $T'B'$ of II's contract line has no corresponding points on I's contract line.

Hence, provided the relative factor endowments of the two countries differ at all (i.e. $AC/AD \neq A'C'/A'D'$), there will be points, in the segments $AR$ and $T'B'$, which lie on the contract curve of one country, but have no corresponding points on the contract curve of the other.

Now consider what would happen if the divergence in the relative factor endowments between the two countries increased. Suppose that the ratio of capital to labor in country II decreased, so that $A'D'$ declined relative to $A'C'$. Then the angle $D'B'A'$ would become smaller and, since $\angle DBR = \angle D'B'A'$, $R$ would move along I's contract curve towards $B$. Eventually, when the factor proportions in II were such that the angle $D'B'A'$ was just equal to the angle $DBM$ (the tangent to I's contract line at $B$), $R$ would coincide with $B$. Then, since $\angle D'B'T'$, which must be equal to $\angle DBM$, would be equal to $\angle D'B'A'$, $T'$ would coincide with $A'$. At these factor proportions, the segments of the two contract curves, $RXB$ and $A'X'T'$ on which the corresponding points lie, would have contracted into the two corresponding points $A'$ and $B$.

Now the angle $DBM$ must be greater than zero for, if it were not, it would imply that there existed a marginal reallocation of resources at $B$ in which labor would be given up to industry $A$ by industry $B$ with no capital in exchange. Thus, since $\angle DBM > 0$, there exists some ratio of labor to capital in country II (such that $\angle D'B'A' = \angle DBM$) for which there are no corresponding points between the two economies.

Consider the commodity price ratios on the segments of the contract line which have no corresponding points in the other country. In Figure 6.4, $T'$ in II is the corresponding point to $B$ in I. Now any point on the segment $T'B'$ in II represents a ratio of the price of $A$ to the price of $B$ (since it represents the production of more $A$ relative to $B$) higher than at the point $T'$, and so higher than at the point $B$, or any other point in I. Similarly, points along $AR$ in I represent a higher price for $B$ relative to $A$ than any points in country II.

In other words, if the price ratio in trade leads to a point in one country to which there is no corresponding point in the other country, the second country will always specialize in production, using the whole of its resources to produce the good most intensive in its more abundant factor.

Factor prices need also to be considered. At the point $T'$ in II, factor prices are the same as at the point $B$ in I (since these are corresponding points). Any point in the segment $T'B'$ of II represents a higher ratio of labor to capital in both industries (and thus a lower price for labor) than at $T'$, so that, if trade results in a situation in which country II is producing at a point along $T'B'$ (so that country I is specializing), the wage of labor will be lower, and the return to capital higher, than in country I.

That is, if trade results in specialization by one country, the wage of that country's more abundant factor will be lower, and the wage of its less abundant factor higher, than in the other country. Consequently, if there is free migration of factors, such migration will continue until the relative factor proportions are such that the two countries have just one pair of corresponding points (e.g. *B*, *A'* in Figure 6.4). Then, since factor prices will be equalized, there will be no further incentive for migration.

### The equivalence between countries in trade and a single economy
Although it is not a difficult matter to show the equivalence between a pair of countries engaged in trade and a single economy, under certain assumptions, it is quite interesting to have this demonstrated in a simple geometric fashion. What will be shown is that, over the range of commodity price ratios represented by the set of corresponding points, a pair of countries, with the properties which have been analyzed in this paper, is exactly equivalent to a single country whose endowment of labor and capital is equal to the sum of the endowments of the two individual countries.

Let *ACBD*, *A'C'B'D'*, represent the two countries. Apply *A'C'B'D'* to *ACBD* so that *A'* coincides with *B*, *A'C'* lies along *DB* produced, and *A'D'* lies along *CB* produced. Produce *AD* to meet *B'D'* produced in *N*, and produce *AC* to meet *B'C'* produced in *M*. The construction is shown in Figure 6.5.

Since *AM* = *AC* + *CM* = *AC* + *A'C'*, *AM* represents a quantity of labor equal to the combined labor resources of the two countries, and *AN*, similarly, represents the combined capital resources of the two countries. Then, since there exists (in *ACBD*) a series of isoquants spreading out from *A* and (in *A'C'B'D'*) a series of *B*-isoquants spreading out from *B'*, the rectangle *AMB'N* is the Edgeworth diagram of an economy whose factor resources are equal to the sums of the factor resources of the two countries.

Let *X*, *X'* be corresponding points in *ACBD*, *A'C'B'D'*. Let *AX* produced meet *B'X'* produced in *X"*. Then *X"* has the properties which are common to *X* and *X'* (i.e. the same factor and commodity prices) and must lie on the contract line of the combined economy.

Also, since *X*, *X'* are corresponding points, *BX* is parallel to *X'X"*, and *A'X'* is parallel to *XX"*. Thus *XBX'X"* is a parallelogram, so that *XX"* = *A'X'* and *BX* = *X'X"*. Now the production of *A* in the combined economy is given by *AX"* but this is equal to *AX* plus *A'X'*, that is to the sum of the quantities of *A* produced by the two countries. Similarly the production of *B* in the combined economy is equal to the sum of the quantities of *B* produced by the two countries.

Over the range for which corresponding points exist in the two countries, therefore, they are, in trade, exactly equivalent to a single country with factor endowments equal to the sum of the endowments in the two countries.

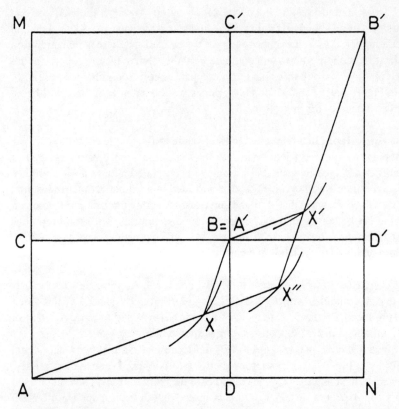

*Figure 6.5   Equivalence of two countries*

### The case of changing relative factor intensities

The model has, so far, been based on the assumption that the relative factor intensities of the two production functions remained the same at all factor prices. That this assumption is not always valid, and some of the other possibilities and their results have been pointed out by Lerner.[11]

Suppose that representative isoquants for the two production functions are drawn on the same diagram, relative to the same origin. Since the production functions are homogeneous of the first degree, all isoquants of the same production function have the same shape, so that any isoquant from one function may be compared with any isoquant from the other. Let there be chosen a pair which cross at least once, which must be the case if the two production functions are not identical.

If, as in Figure 6.6, the isoquants do not cross more than once, then points on the two isoquants which have parallel tangents (i.e. the same factor price ratios), such as *A* and *B* in the diagram, are always such that the slope of *OA*

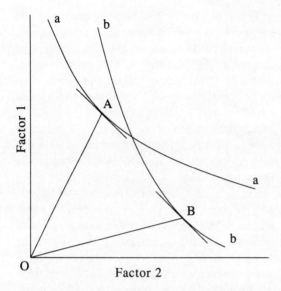

*Figure 6.6   Single intersection of isoquants*

(the ratio of factor 1 to factor 2 in the production of *A*) is greater than the slope of *OB* (the ratio of factor 1 to factor 2 in the production of *B*), so that *A* is always more intensive in factor 1.

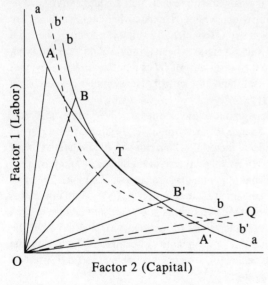

*Figure 6.7   Multiple intersection of isoquants*

If, however, as in Figure 6.7, the isoquants cross more than once (as *aa* and *b'b'*) or are tangential (as *aa*, *bb*), then for two pairs of points with parallel tangents, such as *A*, *B* and *A'*, *B'*, at opposite ends of the isoquants, *OA* has a steeper slope than *OB*, but *OA'* has a more shallow slope than *OB'*. At a low price for factor 1 relative to factor 2, therefore, *A* is relatively more intensive in factor 1 than is *B* but, at a high price for factor 1 relative to factor 2, the relative factor intensities of *A* and *B* are reversed.

The first case, that of a single intersection of the isoquants, is generally accepted as the usual case, one industry being always more intensive in one particular factor than the other. As will become apparent from the analysis to follow, all cases of trade between two countries with factor endowments which are not very widely different can be treated as falling within this case – the analysis of this has been the concern of the preceding sections of the paper. Nevertheless, the other case, in which the relative factor intensities change, presents analytical points of very great interest, and the remaining analysis will be concerned with them.

There is an infinity of possible ways in which the relative factor intensities may vary between one end of the scale of relative factor prices and the other. One set of these has, however, particular analytical significance and acts as a guide-post for analysis of other cases. This set of cases is that in which there exists perfect symmetry in the production functions for both goods.

Consider the situation depicted in Figure 6.7, in which the curvature of one isoquant is greater than that of the other. Due to the homogeneity property, it is always possible to choose a pair of isoquants which are tangential, such as *aa* and *bb*. Then the case of perfect symmetry exists when both isoquants are symmetrical about the tangent ray *OT* (which, by suitable choice of the scale along one of the axes can always be made to lie at an angle of 45° to each axis), so the part of the diagram to the north-west of *OT* is a mirror image of the part lying to the south-east, *OT* itself being the mirror. The symmetrical case is, in fact, the one depicted in Figure 6.7.

Take any pair of points *B*, *B'* on one of the isoquants in the symmetrical case, such that $\angle BOT = \angle B'OT$. Then *B*, *B'* are symmetrically situated with respect to *OT*. It follows that the ratio of factor 1 (which can be called labor) to factor 2 (capital) represented by point *B* is the inverse of the factor ratio represented by the point *B'*. Also, for reasons of symmetry, the tangent at *B* makes the same angle with the axis 1 as the tangent at *B'* does with the axis 2, so that the ratios of the marginal productivities of the two factors at *B* and *B'* are inverse to each other. Finally, again from considerations of symmetry, *OB* = *OB'*, and the quantity of labor used at *B* is equal to the quantity of capital used at *B'*, and the quantity of capital used at *B* is equal to the quantity of labour used at *B'*, in terms of the actual scale of the diagram.

*Properties of inverse rays through the origin*

In the symmetrical case, rays such as $OB$, $OB'$ above, where the angle between one ray and one axis is equal to the angle between the other ray and the other axis (so that the line of symmetry bisects the angle between the rays), may be referred to as inverse rays and have the following properties:

(i)   The ratio of labor to capital along one ray is the inverse of that along the other ray.
(ii)  The ratio of the marginal productivity of labor to the marginal productivity of capital along one ray is the inverse of that along the other.
(iii) Equal distances along the two rays represent equal levels of output of the commodity.
(iv)  The marginal productivity of labor along one ray is equal to the marginal productivity of capital along the other.

(i), (ii) and (iii) follow directly from the symmetry considerations and have already been deduced. To demonstrate (iv), consider two points at which inverse rays cut the same isoquant, such as $B$, $B'$ in Figure 6.7. Denoting values at one of the points by primes, values at the other by unprimed symbols, it follows from Euler's theorem that, since both points lie on the same isoquant,

$$L_A \cdot MPL_A + C_A \cdot MPC_A = L'_A \cdot MPL'_A + C'_A \cdot MPC'_A$$

$$L_A \cdot MPL_A \left(1 + \frac{C_A}{L_A}\frac{MPC_A}{MPL_A}\right) = C'_A \cdot MPC'_A \left(\frac{L'_A}{C'_A}\frac{MPL'_A}{MPC'_A} + 1\right)$$

From (i) and (ii) above, the expressions in brackets must be equal. Also, from the symmetry properties, $L_A = C'_A$, so that

$$MPL_A = MPC'_A$$

Since this holds for two points along the inverse rays, it must hold for all points along the rays since, as given earlier, $MPL_A$, $MPC'_A$ are constant along the respective rays.

*The Edgeworth box diagram for the symmetrical case*

Consider any Edgeworth box, such as $ACBD$ in Figure 6.8, and consider possible points on the contract line of such a box. Such points will be defined by points of intersection (such as $X_1$, $X_2$) of rays through the $A$ and $B$ origins which are such as to cut the $A$ and $B$ isoquants, respectively, at points where the tangents are parallel. Let $\phi$, $\theta$ be the angles whose tangents represent the ratio of labor to capital in the production of $A$ and $B$. Then, in Figure 6.8, $\phi_1 = \angle DAX_1$, $\theta_1 = \angle CBX_1$, and $\phi_2 = \angle DAX_2$, $\theta_2 = \angle CBX_2$.

When the isoquants are drawn from the same origin, as in Figure 6.7, the angles $\phi$ and $\theta$ are given by $\angle COA$ and $\angle COB$, or by $\angle COA'$ and $\angle COB'$. Now, if $\propto$ is the angle whose tangent represents the endowed ratio of labor to capital in the economy ($\propto = \angle DAB$ in Figure 6.8), then, of all pairs of points, one from each isoquant, at which the tangents are parallel.

(a)   those pairs for which $\phi < \propto < \theta$ will define a point on the contract line, and this contract line will lie to the south-east of the diagonal in the box diagram,

(b)   those pairs for which $\phi > \propto > \theta$ will define a point on the contact line, and this contract line will lie to the north-west of the diagonal,

(c)   that pair of coincident points for which $\phi = \theta = \propto$ will define an infinity of points lying along the diagonal which will also be the contract line,

(d)   those pairs of points for which $\phi, \theta > \propto$ or $\phi, \theta < \propto$ will not define points on the contract line of any box whose factor endowment ratio is represented by $\propto$.

All these considerations follow directly from an observation of the geometry of Figure 6.8 in conjunction with that of Figure 6.7. Imagine an economy whose endowed ratio of labor to capital increases from zero to infinity, so that

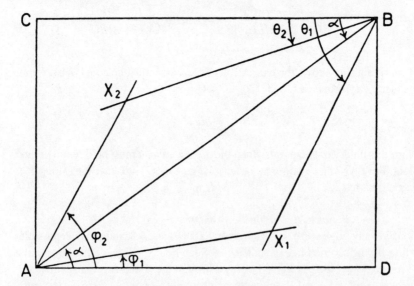

*Figure 6.8   Edgeworth box diagram for the symmetrical case*

the ray which represents the endowed ratio in Figure 6.7 sweeps around from coincidence with the axis 2 to coincidence with the axis 1, this ray being represented by *OQ*.

When *OQ* lies below *OA'* on the diagram, neither *A'*, *B'* nor any pair of points to the north-west of *A'*, *B'* will define points on the contract line, and only those portions of the isoquants in the south-east corner will be relevant to the economy.

As *OQ* moves around, *A'* and *B'* will come to define a point on the contract line so long as *OQ* lies between *OA'* and *OB'*, then will be off the contract line when *OQ* lies between *OB'* and *OT*. When *OQ* coincides with *OT*, the contract line degenerates into the diagonal and then shifts to lie to the north-east of the diagonal when *OQ* moves past *OT*, instead of south-east as when *OQ* was below *OT*. *A* and *B* will come on to the contract line when *OQ* lies above *OB* and will go off it again when *OQ* moves to above *OA*.

The factor endowment ratio corresponding to *OT* may be termed the critical ratio, since it is the ratio at which the relative factor intensities of the two commodities change places. If two countries be considered, with different factor endowment ratios, neither of which is the critical ratio, then there are two possible situations:

1. The countries have factor endowment ratios which are both less than, or both greater than, the critical ratio. In the first case *A* is the capital-intensive good in both countries, in the second case *B* is the capital-intensive good in both countries, in terms of Figure 6.7. In either case the analysis of all the preceding sections holds in full, the parts of the isoquants corresponding to

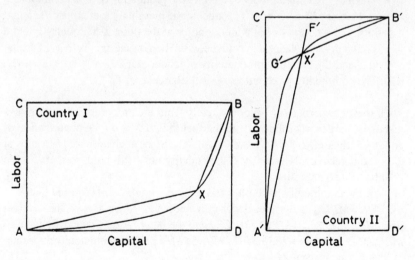

*Figure 6.9　Box diagrams for the theorem of inverse points*

endowment ratios on the opposite side of the critical ratio from the actual endowments of the countries being irrelevant.

2. The countries have factor endowment ratios which lie on opposite sides of the critical ratio. Then the good which is labour-intensive in one country is capital-intensive in the other, the contract lines lie on opposite sides of the diagonal, and the countries have no corresponding points. The analysis of the preceding sections does not hold at all, and a new type of analysis is necessary. This analysis can be made in terms of a class of points, analogous in many ways to the corresponding points of the preceding sections, which may be termed inverse points.

*The theorem of inverse points*

Consider two countries with perfectly symmetrical production functions of the type already discussed, whose factor endowment ratios lie on either side of the critical ratio. Suppose that the two countries are represented by the box diagrams $ACBD$ and $A'C'B'D'$ in Figure 6.9. Let $X$ be a point in the contract line of country I. Draw, in the box representing country II, a ray $A'F'$ through $A'$ which is inverse to the ray $AX$ in I, that is, such that $\angle C'A'F' = \angle DAX$. Similarly, draw a ray $B'G'$ through $B'$ which is inverse to the ray $BX$ in country I (i.e. $\angle C'B'G' = \angle DBX$). Then the point $X'$, which lies at the intersection of the rays $A'F'$ and $B'G'$ is the *inverse point* to the point $X$ in country I, with the following properties:

(i) If $X$ is on the contract line of country I, then $X'$ is on the contract line of country II.
(ii) The marginal productivity of labor in the production of both commodities at the point $X'$ in country II is equal to the marginal productivity of capital in the production of both commodities at the point $X$ in country I, and a similar inverse relationship holds between the marginal productivity of capital at $X$ and the marginal productivity of labour at $X'$.
(iii) The commodity price ratio at $X'$ is the same as at $X$.

Of these properties (ii) follows directly from the properties of inverse rays discussed earlier; (i) follows from the fact that, if $X$ is on the contract line of country I, then $MPL_A/MPC_A = MPL_B/MPC_B$. Since each of these two ratios at $X'$ is the inverse of its value at $X$, the equality must still hold, so that $X'$ is on country II's contract line.

Now the commodity price ratio at $X$ is given by $MPL_A/MPL_B$, and that at $X'$ by $MPL'_A/MPL'_B$, the primes denoting values at $X'$. Since $X'$ is on the contract line, $MPL'_A/MPL'_B = MPC'_A/MPC'_B$, and the latter ratio is, from (ii), equal to $MPL_A/MPL_B$. Hence $MPL'_A/MPL'_B = MPL_A/MPL_B$ and the commodity price ratio at $X'$ is the same as at $X$.

*Inverse points and the pattern of trade*

The patterns of trade which will result when two countries have factor endowment ratios which are such that they have inverse points and not corresponding points can be seen most clearly through the interposition of an intermediate step. Consider an economy whose endowments of labor and capital are in inverse ratio to those in country I: such an economy may be called the inverse economy to country I.

If the rectangle $A'C'B'D'$ in Figure 6.9 were in this relationship to the rectangle $ACBD$, so that country II were the inverse of country I, then the diagonals of the two rectangles would be in inverse relationship so that $\angle DAB = \angle C'A'B'$. It follows directly from the symmetry of the system that every point on the contract line of country II would be the inverse of a point on the contract line of country I, and that every point on the contract line of country I would be the inverse of a point on the contract line of country II. Furthermore, for all pairs of inverse points $X$, $X'$, the proportionality relationship $AX/BX = A'X'/B'X'$ would be true. The contract lines of the two economies would, therefore, present the same range of commodity price ratios, and, at every price ratio, the same in both countries, the proportions in which the two commodities were produced would be identical. In fact, if the rectangle $A'C'B'D'$ were relabelled by the interchange of $C'$ and $D'$, the new diagram $A'C'B'D'$ would be geometrically similar in all respects to the diagram $ACBD$.

*When the factor endowment ratios are thus inverse to each other, the exceptional case occurs that, with the same tastes and widely differing factor endowment ratios, there will be no incentive to trade, since the production patterns will be identical in the two countries at all prices.*

This apparently paradoxical situation can occur (and not only in the symmetrical case) because, in the particular circumstances of the case, each country is as well suited by its own factor endowment as the other. Indeed, such is the structural similarity between the two economies in this case that a description of one country, in economic terms alone, would exactly fit the other. Two travellers from the two countries, comparing notes in a third, would only discover that their countries differed when they described the factors in physical terms: it would then be discovered that the factor physically described as labor in country I was exactly equivalent in all *economic* aspects to the factor physically described as capital in country II. So long as factors were immobile between countries, labor in country I and capital in country II might just as well be regarded as the same factor, since the only relationship between them is through their economic aspects.

The method of analysis of the trade relationships between two countries with factor endowment ratios which lead to inverse points is now straightforward. The trade relationships between country I and country II are exactly the same as the trade relationships between country II and the *inverse* of country I. Since country II and the inverse of country I have the same relative factor intensities in the production of the two goods, they can be analyzed by the methods of the earlier sections, using corresponding points to determine which country will export which good. In fact, inverse points in country II relative to country I are corresponding points to points in the inverse of country I.

The general rule for determining the pattern of trade under these circumstances can be expressed in the following way. Country II will export that good which is intensive in the factor relatively abundant in comparison with the *inverse* of country I.

Suppose, for example, that $A$ is the labor-intensive good in country II, that the labor/capital ratio in country I is 0.5, and that the labor/capital ratio in country II is 1.5. Then the factor ratio in the inverse of country I will be 2.0, and country II will be relatively abundant in *capital* by comparison. Country II will export $B$, the capital-intensive good, in exchange for $A$, which is the capital-intensive good to country I, but the labor-intensive good to country II. Here is another paradoxical situation: country II, with only one-third as much capital per unit of labor as country I, will export her capital-intensive good.

If, however, all other things were the same, but the ratio of labor to capital in country II were 2.5, then country II would have abundant labor relative to the inverse of country I, and would export $A$. Country I would export $B$, her labor-intensive good.

Both countries, then, will export labor-intensive goods (in terms of their respective modes of production), or both will export capital-intensive goods. It is clear that factor prices will never be equalized, nor can one say with certainty whether they will move closer or further apart as the result of trade. Trade will cause the price of labor relative to capital to rise in both countries together, or to fall in both countries together. The ratio of the commodity price of labor in country I to that in country II may rise, fall, or remain constant as a result of trade.

### Notes

1. Originally published as 'The Heckscher–Ohlin Trade Model: A Geometric Treatment' in *Economica*, **24** (1957), 19–39.
2. Heckscher 1919.
3. Ohlin 1933.
4. See Samuelson 1953.
5. James and Pearce 1951.
6. Although the exact formulation of the relationship between relative factor endowments and the complete specialization of production seems to be new, the analysis of reversals contains new elements.
7. Rybczynski 1955.
8. This assumption is dropped later.
9. Not necessary, but introduced to give minimum difference between the countries.
10. With more than two countries, a country is relatively abundant in a factor if its endowment ratio is above the ratio of the world supplies of the factors.
11. Lerner 1952.

# 7   Protection and real wages[1]

In a paper which is now one of the classics in the literature of international trade, Stolper and Samuelson 1941 asserted that, in a two-factor economy, the absolute real wage of the scarce factor would be raised by protection. The effects of protection on real wages had been previously thought to have been confined, in general, to raising the relative share of the scarce factor, with the absolute real wage being increased only in the case of a minor and immobile factor.

The Stolper–Samuelson proof ingeniously avoided the index-number problem – formerly believed to have stood in the way of reaching definite conclusions – by choosing a two-factor, two-commodity model, and showing that the marginal physical productivity of the scarce factor would be raised, under protection, in the production of *both* commodities. Thus, the demonstration went, the real wage would increase in terms of either commodity or any fixed basket of the two commodities.

It is the purpose of the present paper to show that, in some respects, Stolper and Samuelson merely succeeded in avoiding the frying-pan for the fire. For, while they showed that, if the production pattern shifted in a particular direction as the result of protection, the direction of change of the real wage of any factor was independent of demand conditions, they ignored the fact that the demand conditions are important in determining the direction in which the production pattern moves in the first place. In other words, if the real wage goes up, or goes down, it does so in terms of either good as the wage-good, but whether the movement is up or down to start with may depend on which good is the wage-good.

This is not a criticism of Stolper and Samuelson's real contribution, which was to show that protection could raise the absolute real wage (not only the relative share) of one factor, but of the actual formulation of their theorem. This paper does not deny that protection will raise the real wage of one of the factors, but shows that no general statement about which of the factors this will be can be deduced from the relative 'scarcity' of the factors in the Stolper–Samuelson sense.

Although the Stolper–Samuelson theorem 'Protection raises the real wage of the scare factor' is shown to be an incorrect generalization, a restatement in the form 'Protection raises the real wage of the factor in which the imported good is relatively more intensive' has general validity. This correct restatement of the protection and real wages theorem is shown to throw a different light on the United States and Australian cases from that given by Stolper and Samuelson.

**Assumptions**

The general assumptions of the present analysis are exactly those used by Stolper and Samuelson. The economy is assumed to produce only two commodities, using only two factors, and both commodities are produced by the use of both factors. The production functions are assumed to be homogeneous of the first degree, so that a doubling of both factor inputs will exactly double the product. There is full employment of both factors, perfect competition internally and the country faces fixed terms of trade which are unaffected by its own actions.

Although the two commodities (henceforth, beer and clothing) use both factors, they use them in different proportions for any given relative factor prices. Beer, the more capital-intensive good, will use a higher ratio of capital to labor at any given ratio of interest to wages than will clothing, the more labor-intensive good. As the ratio of interest to wages rises, the capital/labor ratio will decline in both industries, but the ratio will always continue to be greater in the manufacture of beer than of clothing.

Since there is perfect competition, the values of the marginal products (in terms of either good) of labour and capital in the beer industry must be equal to the respective values (in terms of the same good) of the marginal products of the same two factors in the clothing industry. Given the total quantities of labor and capital in the economy, these conditions are sufficient to determine, except for one remaining degree of freedom, all the variables in the economy. If the remaining degree of freedom is used up by allocating a price ratio between the two commodities (i.e. the terms of trade), then, for this price ratio, the allocations of both factors between the two industries, the marginal productivities of the factors in the two industries and the production of the two commodities are all determined.

The economy under discussion can be analyzed geometrically in a form of the well-known Edgeworth–Bowley box diagram. This is shown in Figure 7.1, where the horizontal sides of the box represent the total quantity of capital in the economy and the vertical sides the total quantity of labor. Labor and capital used in beer production are measured from $B$ along $BD$, $BA$ respectively, and the quantities used in clothing production from $C$ along $CA$ and $CD$. Thus any point in the box represents some allocation of the two factors between the two industries.

At the point $P$, for example, the labor and capital used in beer production are given by $PN$, $PR$, and the labor and capital used in clothing production by $PM$, $PS$, $P$ will lie on isoquant contours (equal-product curves) $bb$ and $cc$, from whose labels can be read the respective amounts of beer and clothing produced with the particular factor allocations given by $P$. These contours are shown cutting each other in the diagram, so that $P$ is not an optimum allocation, since, by moving along $bb$ until it is tangential to the clothing isoquant $c'c'$ at $Q$, there is an increase

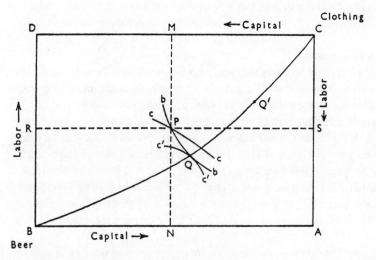

*Figure 7.1   The Edgeworth–Bowley box diagram*

in the production of clothing and no decrease in the production of beer. The series of points like $Q$ represent the allocations which will be reached under perfect competition, and $BQC$ is the 'contract line'. The term has been inherited from the original use of the box diagram in bargaining and allocation problems: it is somewhat inappropriate here, and 'equilibrium curve', might be a better choice if it did not lack conformity with the previous literature on the subject.[2]

The contract line in Figure 7.1 lies wholly to the south-east of the diagonal $BC$. This is because beer production is more capital-intensive than clothing production, so that at the same relative marginal productivities for the factors in both industries, as is the case along the contract line, the ratio of capital to labor is greater in the beer industry than in the clothing industry. That is, the angle $QBA$ is less than the angle $QCD$, so that $Q$ lies below $BC$.

Now the original Stolper–Samuelson demonstration was this. If, as has been drawn in Figure 7.1, the economy as a whole has a high ratio of capital to labor (labour is the 'scarce' factor) then, under free trade, it will produce more beer (the commodity intensive in the abundant factor, capital) and less clothing than in isolation. Hence, if $Q$ in Figure 7.1 represented the pattern of production in isolation, then the pattern of production under free trade would be some point like $Q'$, lying along the contract line, but closer to $C$.

Protection will cause a movement in the general direction $Q'Q$, away from the free trade point towards the self-sufficiency point. Since the angles $QBA$, $QCD$ are less than the corresponding angles $Q'BA$, $Q'CD$, protection will raise the ratio of capital to labour in *both* industries. The marginal physical productivity of labor will rise in both industries, so that the real wage of labor, the scarce factor, will rise in terms of beer or clothing or any combinations of the two.

**Demand conditions**

Although this proof removes the index-number problem in the sense of showing that any rise in real wages will be a rise in terms of both goods, this very approach introduces new complications in the form of demand conditions.

Suppose, initially, that the wage-good is consumed only by wage-earners, and that this is the only good that they consume. Wages must either be paid in the wage-good or else, if paid in the other good, traded for the wage-good. If beer is the wage-good, then the total demand for beer is equal to the product of the total labor force and the marginal physical product of labor in the beer industry: this is the wage-bill of the economy expressed in terms of beer. Since the internal supply is equal to the production, the net demand for imported beer is:

Net beer imports = (Labor force) × (Marginal product of labor in beer)
  − (Production of beer)

or

$$I_B = L . MPL_B - Q_B \tag{1}$$

where $I_B$ is the net import of beer *when beer is the wage-good*, $Q_B$ the production of beer, $L$ the labour force and $MPL_B$ the marginal product of labor in beer manufacture.

Referring back to Figure 7.1, any movement along the contract line in a south-westerly direction (from $C$ towards $B$) decreases both the labor ($L_B$) and capital ($K_B$) employed in the beer industry. Hence $Q_B$ declines, $L$ is constant and $MPL_B$, which depends on the ratio $L_B/K_B$, shows changes of only the second order, so that $I_B$ will increase for a movement in this direction. In other words, at a point on the contract line near $C$ beer will be exported ($I_B < 0$), while at a point near $B$ beer will imported ($I_B > 0$).

At some point in between, the net import of beer will be zero. At this point $L . MPL_B = Q_B$ and this point, a vital one for the succeeding analysis, will be referred to as 'the break-even point when beer is the wage-good'.

Suppose now that clothing were the wage-good instead of beer. Considering still the demand for beer, this now comes only from the capitalists, and the net import of beer is given as follows:

$$I'_B = K . MPK_B - Q_B \tag{2}$$

where $\Gamma_B$ is the net import of beer *when clothing is the wage-good*, $K$ the total capital in the economy and $MPK_B$ the marginal productivity of capital in the beer industry.

Just as $I_B$ in (1) increases for movements along the contract line in a south-westerly direction, so does $\Gamma_B$ in (2). $\Gamma_B$ changes to a lesser extent than $I_B$ (since the second-order changes in $MPK_B$ work in the opposite direction to $Q_B$, while those in $MPL_B$ work in the same direction), but the direction of change is the same.

As was the case when beer was the wage-good, the net import of beer when clothing is the wage-good will be large and positive near $B$ and large and negative near $C$. In between, there will be a point at which $\Gamma_B = 0$, the break-even point when clothing is the wage-good.

It will be shown that the two break-even points, when beer is the wage-good and when clothing is the wage-good, do not generally coincide, and this lack of coincidence renders uncertain the effect of protection on the real wage of any factor, given only its relative scarcity.

**Break-even points**
In order to investigate the relationship between the two break-even points (at which the economy is just self-sufficient in beer and, of course, in clothing as well), when beer is the wage-good and when clothing is the wage-good, it is necessary to indulge in some simple algebraic manipulation.

Since the production functions have been assumed (as an essential part of the original Stolper–Samuelson argument) to be homogeneous of the first degree, they satisfy, as is well known, the Euler identity. In the case of beer, this can be expressed in the form

$$L_B \cdot MPL_B + K_B \cdot MPK_B = Q_B \tag{3}$$

where the symbols have the same meaning as in II.

From (3), by rearranging terms,

$$K_B \cdot MPK_B = Q_B - L_B \cdot MPL_B$$

Hence

$$\frac{L}{L_B} \cdot K_B \cdot MPK_B = \frac{L}{L_B} \cdot Q_B - L \cdot MPL_B \tag{4}$$

At the break-even point when beer is the wage-good, $I_B = 0$ and, from (1), $L.MPL_B = Q_B$. Substituting in (4),

$$\frac{L}{L_B} \cdot K_B \cdot MPK_B = \frac{L}{L_B} \cdot Q_B - Q_B$$

$$= \left(\frac{L}{L_B} - 1\right) \cdot Q_B$$

$$= \frac{L_C}{L_B} \cdot Q_B,$$

where $L_C$ is the labor employed in the clothing industry, since $L_B + L_C = L$. Hence

$$MPK_B = \frac{L_C}{LK_B} \cdot Q_B$$

From (2),

$$\Gamma_B = K \cdot MPK_B - Q_B$$

$$= \frac{K}{L} \cdot \frac{L_C}{K_B} \cdot Q_B - Q_B$$

$$= \left(\frac{K}{L} \cdot \frac{L_C}{K_B} - 1\right) \cdot Q_B \qquad (5)$$

Taking stock of the situation, what equation (5) gives is the net import of beer which would occur if clothing were the wage-good, at terms of trade which would make the economy just self-sufficient in beer if beer were the wage-good. If, in (5) $\Gamma'_B \neq 0$, then the economy would be trading when clothing was the wage-good at those terms of trade which would make it self-sufficient if beer were the wage-good. That is, although these terms of trade correspond to the break-even point when beer is the wage-good, they do not correspond to the break-even point when clothing is the wage-good. Hence, if $\Gamma_B \neq 0$, the two break-even points do not correspond. If, on the other hand, $\Gamma_B = 0$ in (5), then the two break-even points are the same.

A glance at (5) shows that whether $\Gamma_B \gtreqless 0$ depends on whether $K/L \cdot L_c/K_B \gtreqless 1$, that is, on whether $L_c/K_B \gtreqless L/K$.

This condition is most clearly appreciated geometrically. In Figure 7.2 (which is a reproduction of the relevant elements of Figure 7.1), $X$, $Y$, $Z$ are three possible positions for the break-even point when beer is the wage-good. Consider the value of $\Gamma_B$ in (5) at each of these points.

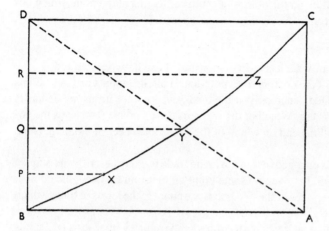

*Figure 7.2 Break-even points according to wage-good*

Suppose that $X$ represented the break-even point when beer was the wage-good. Then $I_C = DP$, $K_B = PX$. Clearly, in this case, $L_c/K_B (= DP/PX) > L/K (= DB/BA)$, so that $\Gamma_B > 0$ and the country would import beer if clothing were the wage-good. Since $\Gamma_B$ diminishes for a movement along the contract line away from $B$, the break-even point when clothing is the wage-good must lie between $X$ and $C$.

Similarly, if $Z$ represented the production pattern at terms of trade corresponding to the break-even point with beer as wage-good, then $L_c/K_B (= DR/RZ) < L/K (= DB/BA)$ and the country would export beer at these terms of trade if clothing were the wage-good. By the same argument as used previously, it can be shown that the break-even points with clothing as the wage-good must lie between $B$ and $Z$.

In both the above cases, where the break-even point for beer lies at a point on the contract line above or below its intersection with the diagonal $AD$, the two break-even points (for beer as wage-good, and for clothing as wage-good) fail to coincide. Only if the break-even point for beer as wage-good lies at $Y$, on the diagonal $AD$, is it true that $L_c/K_B (= DQ/QY) = L/K (= DB/BA)$, so that $\Gamma_B = 0$ when $I_B = 0$, and the two break-even points correspond.

The particular case that leads to identity of the break-even points requires special coincidences among the structural parameters of the economy. Contrary to what may intuitively be expected, the occurrence of this case seems to depend primarily on the factor intensities of the production functions and to have little to do with the relative endowment of the factors.

By reversing the argument, and considering the sign of $I_B$ at points where $\Gamma_B = 0$, it can be shown that, if one break-even point lies on one side of the diagonal

*AD*, the other will lie on the other side, both coinciding at the point which lies on the diagonal itself.

### Significance

The significance of what has been demonstrated can now be analyzed.

It is clear that, if the country does not trade at all, its outputs and allocations are fully determined, since only at the break-even points are its net demands for the two goods zero. Which of the two break-even points represents the no-trade position will depend on which of the two goods, beer or clothing, is the wage-good.

If the country is engaged in trade, with no trade barriers or tariffs, its outputs and allocations will be given by some point on the contract line – the point at which the relative prices of the two goods are equal to the terms of trade, which are assumed to be given.

Suppose now that, at given terms of trade, the country imposes a tariff. It is clear that the point which represents the equilibrium of the economy will move in a direction away from the free trade point towards the no-trade point, the extent of the movement depending on the size of the tariff.

The exact effect of the tariff on the real wages of the factors can now be analyzed in terms of the preceding discussion. Suppose, for concreteness, that *X* is the break-even point when beer is the wage-good. Then, since (as was shown in the previous section) the break-even point with clothing as wage-good must lie on the other side of the diagonal *AD*, it may be supposed to be *Z*. The analysis is essentially of the same type if the positions of the two break-even points are reversed. There are three possible cases:

1. If the terms of trade are such (i.e., favorable to beer) that the free trade position of the economy is represented by a point on the sector *CZ* of the contract line, then the Stolper–Samuelson conclusions hold unreservedly. For, if beer were the wage-good, then protection would result in a movement towards *X*, the break-even point for beer as wage-good. Similarly, if clothing were the wage-good, protection would result in a movement towards *Z*, the break-even point with clothing as wage-good. In either case, since the free trade point lies in the section *CZ*, the movement is in a south-westerly direction. Such a movement will increase the ratio of capital to labor in both industries, raise the marginal productivity of labor in both industries and increase the real wage of labor in terms of either beer or clothing.
2. If the terms of trade were such that the free trade position were represented by a point on the sector *BX* of the contract line, then the situation would be the exact reverse of the preceding case, and the real wage of labor would fall (in terms of both goods) as a result of protection. This case, can, in general, be ruled out, since the economy has been assumed to be relatively abundant

in capital, which means (if it means anything) that the occurrence of terms of trade distinctly unfavorable to the capital-intensive good should be unlikely.

3. If the terms of trade are such that the free trade position falls within the sector $XZ$ of the contract line (i.e., the sector lying between the two break-even points), then the Stolper–Samuelson conclusions no longer hold, and no unambiguous statement can be made about the effect of protection on real wages in terms of factor endowments only. For, if beer were the wage-good, protection would result in a movement towards $X$, the break-even point with beer as wage-good. This movement would be in a south-westerly direction, and would result in an increase in the real wage of labour, as in 1. But, if clothing were the wage-good, protection would cause a north-easterly movement (towards $Z$, the break-even point with clothing as wage-good). This would lower the capital–labor ratio in both industries and cause a decline in the real wage of labour as in 2.

## Capitalists as consumers

Before summarizing the position and examining the general relationship between protection and real wages, it is necessary to determine the effect on the analysis of the capitalists also consuming the wage-good.

Suppose that beer is the wage-good. Then, if the capitalists also consume beer, the demand for beer will be greater, at all points, than if it were consumed only by the workers. Hence the break-even point with beer as wage-good will be further away from the point $B$ in Figure 7.2 than it was previously, since the economy will now be self-sufficient only if it produces more beer than it did before.

If clothing were the wage-good, then its consumption by capitalists would diminish the demand for beer, and the break-even point with clothing as the wage-good would be closer to $B$ (i.e., lower beer production) than previously.

The effect of the capitalists' consumption of the wage-good towards $C$, and the break-even point with clothing as the wage-good would be, therefore, to shift the break-even point with beer as the wage-good towards $B$. The net effect on the distance between the break-even points depends on their initial situation. If the break-even point with beer as wage-good was originally below the diagonal $AD$ (i.e., a point like $X$), so that the break-even point with clothing as wage-good was above the diagonal (a point like $Z$), then the capitalists' consumption of the wage-good would bring the break-even points more closely together.

If, on the other hand, the break-even points were disposed in the opposite manner, with that for beer as wage-good above the diagonal (in position $Z$) and that for clothing as the wage-good below the diagonal (position X), then consumption of the wage-good by the capitalists would increase the divergence between the break-even points.

If the break-even points were coincident when the capitalists did not consume the wage-good, then they would not coincide if the capitalists did consume the wage-good.

It is clear, then, that a removal of the original assumption that the wage-good was not consumed by the capitalists merely makes the already indefinite situation more indefinite. Given the production functions, the factor endowments and the terms of trade, therefore, but not the consumption patterns of the wage-earners and capitalists, it is quite impossible to determine whether the imposition of a tariff will raise or lower the real wage of any factor, since the positions of the break-even points remain unknown.

**Conclusion**

It has been shown that the Stolper–Samuelson theorem, when expressed in the form given it by its authors, 'international trade necessarily lowers the real wage of the scarce factor expressed in terms of any good', cannot be regarded as a true universal proposition, even in the two-factor, two-commodity case.

The non-universality of the theorem is due to incorrect formulation: if the scarce factor is defined as that which is used more intensively in the good of which more is produced in isolation than in trade (the only acceptable definition), then the previous analysis has shown that different wage-goods may make for different factor scarcities. In this sense, the Stolper–Samuelson formulation is meaningless, since the phrases 'real wages … in terms of any good' and 'scarce factor' represent incompatible concepts.

Now the generality of the Stolper–Samuelson formulation breaks down only in the cases when the free trade point lies between the two break-even points, so that, in order to reach a true universal formulation of the protection and real wages theorem, it is necessary to concentrate on this case. The clearest way to see the situation is in tabular form. Table 7.1 summarizes the possibilities (as analyzed fully above) for an economy in which the demand conditions are unknown, considering only the ambiguous cases where the free trade position lies between the break-even points.

*Table 7.1   Break-even points and effect of protection*

| Break-even point which is closest to *B* (Figure 2) | Wage good | Good imported | Effect of protection on real wage of labor |
| --- | --- | --- | --- |
| That with beer as wage good | 1. Beer | Clothing | Rise |
| | 2. Clothing | Beer | Fall |
| That with clothing as wage-good | 3. Beer | Beer | Fall |
| | 4. Clothing | Clothing | Rise |

The Stolper–Samuelson proof of the irrelevance of the index-number problem as such holds, it should be noted. If the real wage rises, it rises in terms of *both* goods; the problem is to define the situations in which the rise will occur.

Given only the production functions, the factor endowments and the terms of trade, but not the conditions of demand, there is no reason, *a priori*, to assume that the free trade position does not lie between the break-even points and, if it does, any one of the four cases tabulated above might represent the position. If the situation were represented by cases 1 or 4, real wages would be increased by protection, but, if it were represented by cases 2 or 3 the real-wage level would be lowered by a tariff.

In terms of factor scarcities, the only statements that can be made about the effects of protection on real wages are in terms of probabilities. It is, in the first place, always more probable that protection will raise real wages (of labor) the higher the ratio of capital to labor in the economy, since a higher capital/labor ratio will give a free trade point closer (for given terms of trade) to $C$, and is thus more likely to lie outside the two break-even points.

Given this overriding condition, it is the more probable that real wages will be increased by protection (using the results of the above sections):

(a) If the wage-good is the capital-intensive good (beer) –
    (i) the *less* the capitalists consume of the wage good;
    (ii) the *more* capital-intensive is the wage-good.
(b) If the wage-good is the labor-intensive good (clothing) –
    (i) the *more* the capitalists consume of the wage-good;
    (ii) the *less* capital-intensive is the wage-good.

To obtain a universally valid general statement about the effect of protection on real wages it is better to scrap the 'scarce factor' approach altogether. Table 7.1 shows that, in the cases (1 and 4) in which the real wage of labor is raised by protection, the common factor is that clothing – the labor-intensive good – is imported. In other words, what is necessary in order to determine the effect of protection on real wages is not the relative endowment of the factors, but the factor intensity of the imported good. For it is universally true, in a two-factor, two-commodity economy, that protection will always raise the real return to the factor which is used most intensively in the imported good.

The true general theorem of protection and real wages is, therefore, that: *Protection will raise the real wage of labor if, and only if, the country imports the labor-intensive good.*

This is true regardless of which good is the wage-good, and which factor is 'scarce' in whatever sense is given to the word. It is important to note that, since the analysis has been carried out entirely in terms of the home country, the factor intensity of the imported good is to be reckoned in terms of the productive process in the *importing* country, not in the country of origin.

The reformulation of the theorem makes important differences to any attempts to assess real situations. It throws more light on, for example, and makes a more definite case for, the wages arguments in favour of the Australian tariff. For Australia exports, in the main, wool, which is distinctly land-intensive. Therefore her imports are, relative to her own production functions, relatively labor-intensive. Protection would increase real wages in Australia (assuming it can be simplified to a two-factor economy), and would continue to do so as long as wool remained the chief export, whatever the ratio of land to labor. This removes the tentativeness of Stolper and Samuelson's 'in Australia, where land may perhaps be said to be abundant relative to labour'. The fact is that one is more likely to know whether imports are labor-intensive or not, than to be able to assess the relative scarcity of factors.

A particularly interesting case is that of the United States. When he simplified it to a two-factor model, Leontief[3] found that its imports were capital-intensive (in terms of United States production functions). If Leontief's findings are accepted, then protection will tend to *lower* real wages and raise profits – exactly the opposite of the conclusion reached by Stolper and Samuelson on the assumption that labour was 'scarce'.

Without necessarily siding with Leontief on a contentious issue, it is worth pointing out that the analysis in this paper indicates the possibility of the real wage of 'scarce' labor being lowered by protection. In terms of the model used here, this would occur if the free trade point lay between the two break-even points. In particular, it would occur if the Unites States exports were wage-goods (in terms of her own consumption patterns, Chevrolet cars are a wage-good) *and* if the relatively more labor-intensive good were, itself, still quite strongly capital-using. Since the United States (considering the trade in finished goods) does tend to export mass-produced items (wage-goods) and import luxury goods, and since her labor-intensive industries are highly capitalized by the standards of other countries, there is some resemblance to the model.

These attempts to push economies into two-factor, two-commodity strait jackets should not be taken too seriously, of course, but they provide material for interesting armchair speculation.

Finally, it should be noted that, although the present model (as was the Stolper–Samuelson model) is cast only in the two-country, two-commodity mould, it is clear enough that the thesis is true that differences in demand functions between different sections of the community will, as a result of changing aggregate demand following shifts in relative factor prices, render more uncertain the effects of protections on real wages than would otherwise seem to be the case.

**Notes**
1. Originally published as 'Protection and real wages: a restatement' in *Economic Journal*, **67** (1957), 199–210.
2. Stolper and Samuelson 1941, p. 346.
3. Leontief 1953. See also Valavanis–Vail 1954.

# PART II

# MARKETS

# 8 Innovative entry: profit hidden beneath the zero[1]

The traditional models of free entry, zero-profit monopolistic competition equilibrium do not, of course, exclude the possibility that positive profits might still be made by intra-marginal firms if the market is non-uniform, or that collusive actions plus barriers to further entry can almost always be used to convert a zero-profit non-cooperative equilibrium into a structure which is profitable for all existing firms.

This paper is concerned with situations giving rise to a local Nash equilibrium (no firm can improve by a marginal move), which are zero-profit across all firms, but yet in which it is possible for a new firm to enter and make profits (at least in the short run) without collusive action. Entry in such situations will be referred to as *innovative entry*, since it involves potential entrants looking behind the zero-profit situation actually existing to a possible different structure in which profits are possible, or in which a larger number of firms can be accommodated without losses. This can be contrasted with *passive entry*, in which firms simply enter industries where actual profits are positive and do not enter those in which actual profits are non-positive. We shall restrict ourselves to discussion of uniform cases in which all firms make identical profits at equilibrium so as to avoid any difficulty associated with the term 'zero profit'.

The general context will be that of monopolistic competition in which product differentiation takes place by variation in the specifications (combinations of characteristics) of the goods produced. The potential variations are considered as points in a space of characteristics, with dimensionality determined by the number of characteristics actually relevant to consumer choice among the products. The market structure arising within this context when there is free entry, no collusive behavior, frictionless change and complete information, has been termed 'perfect monopolistic competition' by the author, and discussed fully (at least for the case of two characteristics) in Lancaster 1979.

Within this structure, it will be shown that innovative entry is possible, even when there is passive entry equilibrium (because actual profits of all firms are zero), in at least two cases:

1. The 'ignored characteristics' case, in which there is a zero-profit equilibrium when firms take note of $k$ characteristics, but where there is a relevant $(k + 1)$th characteristic which has been ignored. By differentiating the

product in an additional dimension, a greater number of firms can be sustained at a non-negative profit level.

2. The multiple equilibrium case (possible only if there are more than three characteristics) in which there is more than one configuration of firms over the goods spectrum, each giving a zero-profit Nash equilibrium but with more firms covering the spectrum in one configuration than in others.

### Outline of the basic model

For a product group defined over $n + 1$ characteristics, it is assumed that suitable normalization for equivalent quality permits all potential products to be represented by points in a linear subspace of dimension $n$. It is further assumed that the set of all products that could actually be produced is a convex subset of $L^n$, so that continuous product differentiation is possible. The convex subset is the product spectrum, and any point within it is a potential product specification.

Consumers are assumed to have separable utility functions, so that there is a two-stage decision process in which intra-group choices are independent of the events occurring in the market for outside goods. The consumption technology for the group is taken to be of the non-combinable kind so that the consumer must choose one product from the group – a Volkswagen or a Toyota, not half a Volkswagen plus half a Toyota. Non-combinability is not essential to the analysis, but makes it somewhat simpler and seems the most relevant for typical differentiated product markets.[2] Each consumer has a point in the product spectrum which is his most preferred specification, and is the product he would choose if all were available to him on the same terms. The utility of any other product, relative to the same quantity of his most preferred product, is taken to be a concave decreasing function of some measure of the difference between the specifications of the available and most preferred goods.

The choice of which product to buy within the group will depend on both price and specification. If the prices of all available products are the same, the consumer will obviously choose the one which is closest to his most preferred specification, otherwise he will make the choice which gives the most utility per dollar – perhaps choosing one further from his most preferred specification, but cheaper. The quantity he will purchase, which is separable from his choice of the product, depends on its price relative to the price of the outside good, the elasticity of substitution between group and outside goods, and also on the specification of the good relative to his most preferred specification.

It can be shown that the quantity, $q(u)$, that will be purchased by a consumer whose most preferred specification is at a distance $u$ (in the characteristics space) from the good actually available to him, has properties which depend on the elasticity of substitution between outside goods and goods within the group. If this elasticity be denoted by $\sigma$, then, in particular,

$$\frac{\partial q}{\partial u} \lessgtr 0 \text{ according as } \sigma \gtrless 1 \tag{1}$$

The function $q(u)$ is decreasing in $u$ if and only if $\sigma > 1$. Since $q'(u) < 0$ is necessary for satisfaction of the second-order conditions for equilibrium, as well as a sufficient condition to guarantee that no two firms will produce the identical product, it will be assumed that $\sigma > 1$ throughout.

Now consider the market for a particular product. The market consists of two elements, the market area or set of consumers (identified by the specifications of their most preferred goods) who choose to buy that product, and the market density at each point or the quantity that will be purchased by consumers at that point in the market area. The quantity per consumer is determined by an individual demand function $q^i(p, u)$, the number of persons being given by the assumed distribution of consumer preferences over the spectrum. The following two simplifying assumptions are made:

1. *Uniformity of preferences.* That is, every consumer has a utility function of the same form, with the same parameters, so that the only variation over consumers is in the specification of each one's most preferred good.
2. *Uniform density.* There is a continuous distribution of consumers (that is, of most preferred specifications) over the spectrum, with a uniform density and equal incomes. The density will be taken to be unity.

Due to these two simplifying assumptions, the quantity demanded from consumers in some element, $dv$, of the market 'area' (actually a set in $R^n$) which is at a distance $u$ from the point representing the specification of the good, is given by $q(u) \, dv$.

$$Q = \int_v q(u) dv \tag{2}$$

where the integral is taken over the whole market area $V$.

Since we shall be confining our attention to equilibrium configurations involving firms with identical cost functions under conditions of demand uniformity, equilibrium prices will be the same for all goods. Thus each consumer will buy the good which is closest to his preferred specification and the boundaries between market areas of firms adjacent on the spectrum will consist of points equidistant from those representing the specifications of the two goods. These boundaries will thus be subsets of hyperplanes (dimension $R^{n-1}$) which are orthogonal to, and bisect, the line joining the two specification points. The market areas will necessarily be convex polytopes.

Although we shall be concerned with shapes in $R^n$, it is often convenient to use traditional terminology associated with $R^3$, such as polyhedra for the total shapes, facets for their bounding hypersurfaces in $R^{n-1}$. Furthermore we shall also use the conventional term 'market areas' for what are actually the hyper-volumes of shapes in $R^n$. In all cases, the terms really refer to the equivalents in $R^n$, and it is believed that no confusion will occur.

If the price of a good is raised slightly above the prices of the adjacent goods (which are all equal and constant), a consumer who was formerly on the boundary will now shift his purchasing from the good in question to the relevant adjacent good, so that the market area will shrink. Under the conditions specified, this shrinking can be taken to be uniform in all directions for a sufficiently small change in price. Similarly, a sufficiently small price reduction will lead to a uniform expansion of the market area.

We are thus interested in how the quantity changes for a small uniform expansion or contraction of the market area. Let $r$ be any suitable linear measure of the market size, such as the radius of the smallest hypersphere enclosing the market. Then we can write $Q(r)$ as

$$Q(r) = \int_0^r f(\rho)d\rho \tag{3}$$

where $f(\rho)$ is the demand originating from the boundary layer of a market area of size $\rho$ when the shape of the market area remains unchanged. It is the integral of $q(u)$ over the outer shell of the market area. If $\rho$ increases, then the distance $u$ of every point in the shell from the point representing the specification must increase, so that $q(u)$ increases everywhere if $\sigma < 1$, and decreases everywhere if $\sigma > 1$. Thus $Q'(r) = f(r) \gtrless 0$ according as $\sigma \lessgtr 1$, and $Q$ is a concave (convex) function of $r$ if $\sigma$ is greater than (less than) unity.

The effect of a small change in price on the demand for a given product is made up of three components:

1. The market area expands or contracts slightly (according as the price falls or rises), the extent of this change being determined by the substitutability between price and specification at the market boundary.
2. Expansion or contraction of the market area will, of itself, change the quantity demanded because of the change in the number of consumers covered.
3. The value of $q(u)$ for every $u$ will change as a result of the price change, less being purchased by every consumer if the price rises.

The elasticity of demand is the product of effects 1 and 2, which form the intra-group substitution effect, plus effect 3 which accounts for the substitution of outside goods and the income effect.[3] The resulting demand elasticity is not constant in this model, but varies with the distance between adjacent goods because the factors determining it depend on the size of the market ($r$). It can be shown that the elasticity increases as goods move closer to each other on the spectrum, implying that adjacent goods are better substitutes if they are closer in specification. (Substitution becomes perfect as the specifications coincide, with $E = \infty$.) Note also that the elasticity relations change if the *shape* of the market changes.

The uniformity and uniform density assumptions give an isotropic demand spectrum, so that the demand for any good (given all prices) depends only on the specifications of other goods relative to its specifications, and not on the absolute specifications. Thus the demand for a good is unchanged if the whole constellation of goods is translated or rotated in the spectrum, provided the relative positions remain fixed.

Given the demand structure outlined above, each firm's sales, and thus its profits, are a function of its specification and its price. The firm will be in equilibrium, given the behavior of other firms, when its profit is stationary for first-order changes in either specification or price and declining for second-order changes in either separately or both together. We are interested here only in the free entry Nash equilibrium, in which every firm takes the specification and price of other firms as given and in which the number of firms is such as to give zero profits for all firms. All firms have identical cost functions.

It will be assumed that the reader is willing to accept the following properties of any equilibrium configuration as either obvious or following directly from the two-characteristics analysis set out in Lancaster 1979:[4]

1. The market areas of all firms will be convex sets of the same size and shape.
2. These market areas will form a proper partitioning of the spectrum.
3. The prices of all goods will be the same, as will be the marginal revenues, marginal and average costs, and elasticities associated with them.
4. For every firm, marginal revenue will equal marginal cost, and price will equal average cost.

These properties follow from the isotropic nature of demand, identity of the cost functions, and dependence of the quantity functions $Q$ on both the shape and size of the market areas. If the goods produced by the various firms are each represented by their appropriate specification points in characteristics space, what configurations are possible for zero-profit equilibria which satisfy the conditions given in the last section (convex and space-filling) and which can

be shown to be profit maximizing for each firm, given the prices and specifications of the other firms?

The dimensionality of the spectrum (number of characteristics) is clearly of
very great importance. If there are only two characteristics, so that the spectrum
is one-dimensional, there will be a unique configuration with the goods spread
evenly along the linear spectrum at a spacing which depends on the parameters
of demand and of cost, but is unique. Since much of the study of product differentiation when product characteristics are variable has been based on the linear
model, itself derived from the Hotelling linear spatial competition model, the
problem of non-uniqueness of equilibrium has received less attention than it
deserves.

Just as the two-characteristic line spectrum analysis can be related to
Hotelling's linear location model, it would seem that a first step towards
analyzing the multi-characteristic model would be to examine the work on location
in a plane, corresponding to the specification space for three characteristics. For
a uniform distribution of consumers over an infinite plane (so that there are no
boundary problems), the classic argument of Lösch 1954 was that free entry
by firms having identical cost functions and in which existing firms can relocate
costlessly as new firms enter, would lead to market configurations in which firms
equally spaced in such a manner as to give identical market areas, each of which
was a regular hexagon. More recently, other authors, especially Eaton and
Lipsey 1976 have shown that the market solution is not confined to hexagonal
markets but may include a great variety of shapes, so that the market equilibrium is not unique. The optimum (planning solution) is a unique hexagonal
arrangement, but this not necessarily the only market equilibrium.

Since the demand and cost functions in the characteristics analysis are more
general and more complex than the simplified functions typical of location theory,
the relationship between the two analyses is not exact. Nevertheless, the non-
uniqueness result that will be proved is similar to, and directly inspired by, the
work of Eaton and Lipsey.

Locational theory is confined to two dimensions at most and thus is directly
analogous only to the two- or three-characteristics case. For an $n$-dimensional
spectrum ($n + 1$ characteristics) there is no analog in physical location, and the
geometry of potential market shapes is complex. For example, contrary to what
might perhaps be expected, there is no simple progression in the number of space-
filling regular polyhedra as the dimensionality of the space increases. In $R^2$, for
example, there are three such figures: equilateral triangles, squares, and hexagons.
In $R^3$, there is only one figure, the cube, but in $R^4$ there are again three – the
hypercube, a 16-facet figure, and a 24-facet figure.

The requirements that all market areas should be convex sets of the same size
and shape and form a partition (that is, exactly fill the space) clearly reduces
the field, but still leaves many potential candidates for equilibrium configura-

tions. In $R^2$, for example, the requirement is satisfied by equilateral triangles, squares and hexagons, but it is also satisfied by right-angled triangles, rectangles, parallelograms, and hexagons elongated or shrunk along the principal axis. In $R^3$, it is satisfied by cubes, but also by hexagonal prisms, certain pyramids, and arbitrary rectangular boxes, but not by tetrahedra (which are not space-filling).

We shall show that equilibrium conditions for zero-profit monopolistic competition, namely the convexity and space-filling properties already given, plus first- and second-order conditions for profit maximization with respect to specification, together with conditions guaranteeing that no two firms will produce the same product and that profits of all firms converge uniformly to zero as the number of firms increases, are satisfied by all convex space-filling market shapes possessing the following symmetry property.

*Basic symmetry property*
A market area in $R^n$ (that is, with $n + 1$ characteristics) possesses the basic symmetry property if there exists an orthogonal set of $n$ hyperplanes (dimension $n - 1$) such that the market area is symmetric across every hyperplane, perhaps after rotation of one half-area about the normal to the hyperplane.

The basic symmetry property does *not* confine the equilibrium market areas to regular polyhedra. In fact, a wide variety of shapes satisfy it – in $R^2$, for example, these include arbitrary rectangles, parallelograms and stretched and skewed hexagons. Equilateral triangles, however, do not satisfy it, even though they are regular polyhedra, nor do any figures with an odd number of faces.

Consider a market area which satisfied the basic symmetry condition, and consider an arbitrary small change in specification. Such a change can be measured with respect to the normals to the hyperplanes of symmetry, since these normals form an acceptable set of coordinate axes, so we shall consider a small movement along one of these normals. Since we are concerned only with equilibrium configurations, prices of all goods will be the same, so that all market boundaries will be equidistant from the two goods between which it forms the boundary.

To set the basis for the argument, consider the simple case of a hypercube, illustrated as a square in $R^2$ in Figure 8.1, and choose the normal to any face as our primary reference axis. In the figure, this axis is $OA_1$, with $S$ as the hyperplane of symmetry. Since the facet must be normal to the line joining the specification points for the good and the relevant adjacent good, the point representing the specification of the latter lies on the primary axis, at the point $A_1$. Since the line $OA^1$ must be bisected by the facet (since prices are equal), $OF_1 = \frac{1}{2}OA^1$.

Now consider a small change in the specification of the good, represented by a movement of $2\delta$ along the primary axis so that the new specification is represented by point $O'$. The boundary between $O$ and $A_1$ will now shift so that it is normal to, and bisecting, the segment $O'A_1$. That is, the boundary will remain vertical and intersect $OA_1$ at $F'_1$ where $F_1F'_1 = \delta$. Since $OO' = 2d$, the distance $O'F'_1$ is less than the distance $OF_1$ by an amount $\delta$. The total demand for the product from consumers whose relevant choice is between goods $O$ and $A_1$ has thus shrunk by an amount equal to the integral of $q(u)$ over the facet $F_1$, and multiplied by $\delta$.

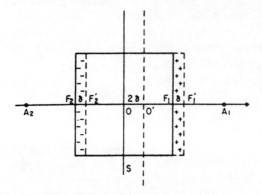

*Figure 8.1   Market area – hypercube*

On the other side of the origin, $OA_2$ must equal $OA_1$ because of the assumed symmetry, and the shift from $O$ to $O'$ will shift the facet $F_2$ rightward to $F'_2$ by an amount $\delta$, so that the distance $O'F'_2$ is larger than $OF_2$ by $\delta$. Demand from consumers choosing between $O$ and $A_2$ has increased by $\delta$ times the integral of $q(u)$ over the facet $F_2$.

For the first-order condition, we ignore the slight change in the average distances of the two facets from the center which results from the small change in specification. Since the facets $F_1$ and $F_2$ are the same size and shape, from the symmetry condition, the integral of $q(u)$ is the same over both facets so that the gain of new consumers in direction $A_1$ is balanced by an equal loss of consumers in direction $A_2$ and thus demand is stationary for a first-order change.

For the second-order condition, we do not ignore changes in distances for the consumers. In the original situation, the market area extended from the symmetry plane $S$ to $F'_1$ (a distance $r - \delta$ from $O'$) in one direction, and to $F'_2$ (a distance $r + \delta$ from $O'$) in the other. The difference resulting from the spec-ification shift is a loss of consumers situated between two hyperplanes at distances $r$ and $r - \delta$ from the origin, and a gain of consumers between two hyper-planes at distances $r$ and $r + \delta$. The average distance from the origin of the consumers lost is less than that of the consumers gained. If the elasticity of sub-stitution is greater than unity, $q(u)$ is a decreasing function of $u$, so that the demand associated with the lost consumers is greater than that associated with the consumers gained, and total demand falls. Since price is constant and average cost does not increase with output, the second-order specification change results in lower profits. Thus the first and second-order conditions are satisfied in this case if the symmetry and elasticity of substitution conditions are satisfied.

For market areas having shapes such that there are facets which are neither perpendicular nor parallel to the primary reference axis, the argument follows similar lines. Slight changes in the angles of the facets can be ignored and the effect of small changes along the primary axis treated as pure translations in that direction. The loss on a facet in one direction will be the integral of $q(u)$ over the facet times the amount of translation, and this will be balanced by a gain from a facet of the same size, shape, and relative position in the other direction, if the symmetry condition is satisfied. The second-order condition will be satisfied if $q(u)$ is a decreasing function of $u$, and thus if the elasticity of substitution is greater than unity.

Note that the first-order condition will not, in general, be satisfied by a market area which does not satisfy the symmetry condition, such as the triangle in Figure 8.2. For a movement in the direction of the arrow, the net gain or loss in demand involves comparing the integral of $q(u)$ over facets $F_1$ and $F_2$ with the integral over facet $F_3$. Since the values of $u$, and thus of $q(u)$, follow quite a different pattern in traversing the facet $F_3$ from what they do over facets $F_1$ and $F_2$, the balance necessary to give stationarity in demand for a small change in specification could occur, if at all, only for some very special form of the function $q(u)$ and thus would be destroyed by a small arbitrary variation in $q(u)$.

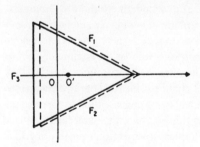

*Figure 8.2  Market area – triangle*

It is now necessary to show that no two firms will produce the same product under the conditions already given. To prove this, we shall show that, if a given product were being produced by more than one firm, at least one firm would always gain by changing the specification of its good to differ from that of the other. In particular, if there is more than one firm producing a product there is always a firm with sales no greater than half the total sales of the good. This firm can always gain by producing a product of its own.

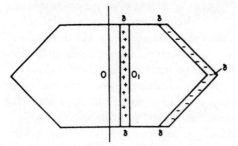

*Figure 8.3    Market area – effect of a new product*

Consider a change by this firm to the production of a new product with specification differing from that of the original good by an amount of $2\delta$ in a direction normal to any of the hyperplanes of symmetry in the original market area, as shown in Figure 8.3 for $R^2$ space, where the new product is sold at the same price as the old. The new product's market area will have boundaries in the direction of movement but they are translated in the direction of movement by an amount of $\delta$, since the new good is closer to the adjacent goods in that direction by $2\delta$. Thus this boundary is closer to the specification point of the new good than the original boundary was to that of the original good by an amount $\delta$. In the other direction, the original and new goods will divide the part of the market between their two specifications exactly in half, so that the boundary between them will be parallel to the hyperplane of symmetry and at distance $\delta$ from the new specification. Thus the market area for the new good is equivalent to the part of the original market area on one side of the symmetry plane (exactly half the original area because of symmetry) *less* a volume equal to that lost when the boundary in the direction of change is moved laterally inward by $\delta$ (marked – in the figure), *plus* a volume equal to the cross-section of the original area at the center times $\delta$ (marked + in the figure). Since the outer face consists of parallelepipeds having aggregate 'heights' (projections on the vertical hyperplane) equal to the central cross-section and bases of width $\delta$, so the volume of the market area lost is equal to the volume gained. But every small element of volume in the lost portion can be paired with an element in the gained portion which is closer to the product specification and is thus associated with a smaller value of $u$ and thus a larger value of $q(u)$, since the elasticity of substitution is greater than unity. The total demand for the new good is therefore greater than half the total demand for the original good, and thus greater than the firm's sales in the original position. Since price is unchanged and average cost non-increasing, the firm's profits are increased by moving out of the original cluster to produce a product unique to itself.

Finally, we need to show that the maximum profit $\pi^*(r)$ associated with a market area of given shape (satisfying the conditions) and size $r$ is a continuous increasing function of $r$, so that profits decline uniformly to zero as the number of firms increase (ignoring the integer problem) for all shapes having basic symmetry. This follows from the property that the elasticity of demand increases as $r$ shrinks, so that the ratio of price to marginal cost falls as the market area gets smaller. The quantity sold obviously declines with $r$, and the ratio of average to marginal cost will not fall as quantity falls. Thus a decline in $r$ implies a lower ratio of price to average cost and a smaller quantity, hence necessarily a smaller profit.

### The scope for innovative entry

A passive entry equilibrium is a configuration such that no firm can increase its profit by price changes or small variations in specification, and all firms make zero profits. Innovative entry is still potentially profitable if there is another arrangement of the *same number* of firms which is also a Nash equilibrium but in which all firms make positive profits. Whether innovative entry would be actually profitable depends on whether new entry in an appropriate position on the spectrum would, of itself, induce such a rearrangement. The analysis here will be confined to the question of potential profitability, leaving the dynamics of rearrangement and actual profitability open except for one or two pointers from location theory.

The basic proposition to be established is the following: *There is scope for innovative entry in any passive-entry equilibrium in which the market areas are not regular polyhedra.*

A sketch of a proof proceeds as follows. Any market area which is space-filling and satisfies the symmetry conditions of the previous section can be related to some regular polygon by a process of uniform stretching or shrinking along one or more principal axes and/or skewing the principal axes so that they are no longer at the angles appropriate for regularity. In $R^2$, the four-facet market areas which give a passive-entry equilibrium but are not regular are the rectangle (stretching of the square along one axis) and the parallelogram (skewing of the rectangle, thus skewing plus stretching of the square). We shall show that since $q(u)$ is a decreasing function of $u$ because the passive-entry equilibrium conditions are satisfied, the square market area gives higher total demand for a given coverage of the spectrum than does a rectangle or parallelogram.

Figure 8.4 shows a rectangle (in (a)) and a rhombus (in (b)), superimposed on a square with the same center and of the same area. The portions marked with plus signs (+) represent consumers gained in moving from the original figure to the square, while the portions marked with minus signs (−) represent consumers lost. Since the area remains the same, the number of consumers lost is equal to the number gained, but the consumers gained are all closer to the center (the specification of the good) than those lost. Since $q(u)$ is a decreasing function of $u$, total demand is greater for the square than for the non-regular figure.

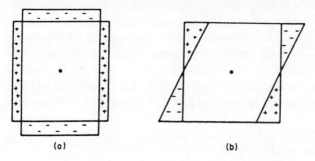

*Figure 8.4    Market area – superimposed rectangle (a) and rhombus (b)*

A similar argument can be given for stretched and skewed hexagons in $R^2$ and for equivalent deformations of regular figures in $R^n$. The regular figure gives greater total demand for a given coverage of the spectrum than the equivalent non-regular figure. Thus any configuration in which the market areas are deformations of some specified regular figure can be rearranged so that the spectrum is covered by the same number of firms, but each firm has larger sales at the original prices. Since average cost is non-increasing, firms will make positive profits at the new configuration if they made zero profits at the old, which will be the case if the old configuration was a passive entry equilibrium. Note that the rearrangement will, in general, change the elasticity of demand and thus the old prices will no longer be optimal, but the subsequent adjustment of prices can only increase profits further.

The above result relates demand in a specific regular polyhedron to demand in deformations of that polyhedron which have the same area. It does not compare configurations which consist of different regular polyhedra – a configuration of squares with a configuration of hexagons in $R^2$, for example, since these cannot be deformed into each other in any simple fashion. Can it be shown that a hexagonal market area of the same coverage (area) as a square will generate a larger demand, given only that the quantity function $q(u)$ is a declining function of $u$? The answer seems to be, no, although it is easy to generate acceptable functions $q(u)$ that do give this result, and the author has not yet been able to generate a counter-example. It does not seem impossible that each of some subset of the space-filling regular polyhedra associated with $R^n$ may be found to give the greatest demand per unit coverage of the spectrum, for a specific choice of $q(u)$. Given $q(u)$ and the system parameters, however, there can be presumed to be a unique member of the set of space-filling regular polyhedra which gives a full innovative-entry equilibrium, at least in general.

We have shown the potential for innovative entry, but actual attainment of a full innovative-entry equilibrium is another matter. Location theorists[5] have studied the problems of entry and the dynamics of rearrangement for patterns in $R^2$ under simpler demand conditions than those of the present model, and the results are complex and somewhat uncertain. A general study is that of Eaton and Lipsey 1976, using numerical methods, the overall tenor of which is that entry into a rectangular system is likely to generate other rectangles, perhaps squares, but not hexagons, while entry into a hexagonal configuration is likely to break up the hexagons. Nothing is known of the entry dynamics of systems in $R^n$ with $n > 2$, but it can be presumed to be more complex, if anything, than that for $R^2$. There seems to be some evidence that passive-entry equilibria in which the market shapes are far from regular could result in innovative entry which moves the system closer to regularity, but that a smooth transition to the full innovative-entry equilibrium would be a rare event. The difficulties associated with innovative entry are, of course, much greater in an abstract space of characteristics than in location theory – maps of the market areas can at least be drawn in the latter case on the basis of fairly simple information. It is obvious that the point at which entry stops, even if that is not the full innovative-entry equilibrium, is likely to depend on the configuration which develops (perhaps due mainly to random factors) at early stages of the industry growth.

**The 'ignored characteristics' case**

Although this case could be analyzed separately, it is convenient to treat it as a special case of the multiple equilibrium phenomenon in passive-entry equilibrium. Consider a market in which a passive-entry equilibrium has been achieved on the misperception by all present firms that there are only two relevant characteristics, whereas there are really three. The existing industry can be considered to be organized along a line spectrum like $AB$ in Figure 8.5. Each firm, such as that producing the good of specification $X_i$, perceives its potential customers' most preferred specifications as distributed along the line $AB$ and its actual customers as distributed along the market segment $y_{i-1}y_i$. If this were the true situation, the passive-entry equilibrium would be a partitioning of the spectrum into line segments of equal length, the length being determined by the parameters of the system and thus the equilibrium being unique. Since the true spectrum is in $R^2$, however, the firm's potential customers are not confined to the line $AB$ but may have preferred specifications all over the plane. The true market area for the $i$th firm is not the line segment $y_{i-1}y_i$, but the *rectangle* (shaded in Figure 8.5) having sides perpendicular to $AB$ and which pass through $y_{i-1}$, $y_i$, respectively. The distance of the ends of the rectangles from the line $AB$ depends on how fast $q(u)$ declines as $u$ increases – if $q(u)$ approaches zero

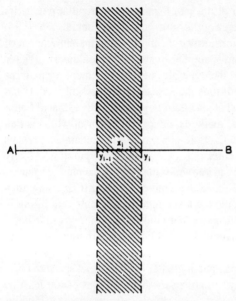

*Figure 8.5   Market area – rectangle*

asymptotically, the rectangles are infinite in length. In any case, it is necessarily true that the heights of the rectangles are always greater (much greater in general) than the widths $y_{-1}y_i$. Thus the true market areas generated by the false supposition that there are only two characteristics will be elongated rectangles, and the previous proof has shown that innovative entry is possible because the passive-entry equilibrium configurations are not regular figures.

Note that the 'ignored characteristics' case brings out the difference between perceptions in location theory and those in the theory of product differentiation in characteristics space perhaps more sharply than the question of multiple equilibria itself. To assume population was distributed along a line when it was actually distributed over a plane would be gross ignorance of reality in location theory. In characteristics space, however, it is not at all obvious which properties of goods are relevant characteristics for choice, nor are the goods clearly displayed with respect to their characteristics. From an operational point of view, all that could be observed for multiple equilibria under passive entry would be two zero-profit equilibria for identical industries in identical markets, or the same industry at two different periods, but with different numbers of firms and a different array of goods actually produced.

**Conclusion**
The main result that has been shown here is that it is quite possible for a product-differentiated industry to be in a stable local Nash equilibrium, with

zero profits for all firms, and yet in which it is possible for the same number of firms to form a different configuration, also a stable local Nash equilibrium, in which all firms make positive profits. Looked at from another point of view, an industry may be in a passive-entry equilibrium in which there may seem no room for any new firms, yet in which the restructuring induced by new entry may result in greater profits for all even though the number of firms has increased. The analysis has been confined to examining the potential for innovative entry of this kind (essentially a multiple equilibrium phenomenon) rather than mechanisms by which new entry may set up movements appropriate to attaining the alternative equilibrium configuration.

The possibility that an industry may settle down to a passive-entry equilibrium, in which profits per firm are less than they might otherwise be, is very real in an industry in which products are differentiated by variations in their characteristics rather than by observable physical location. Multiple equilibria are then different configurations in an abstract space of characteristics, and the possibility of being in a less profitable configuration, but no firm in the industry being aware of it, is considerable.

The importance of innovative entry may be less in a closed economy than in an open one, where the impact of import competition may bring about major restructuring. The author has shown in Lancaster 1980, 1982 that intra-industry trade implies considerable such restructuring in monopolistic competition industries, and innovative entry effects would increase these structural strains – but perhaps profitably.

**Notes**
1. Originally published in *Journal of Industrial Economics*, **31** (1982), 41–56.
2. Note that the emphasis on non-combinability makes the analysis of demand somewhat different from that in the author's original statement of the characteristics approach, Lancaster 1966, but non-combinability was discussed in the more extended analysis of Lancaster 1971.
3. The elasticity of demand can be shown to be given by the expression

$$E = Se_Q + (1 - m)\sigma + m$$

where $S$ is the elasticity of market size with respect to price, $e_Q$ the elasticity of quantity with respect to market size, $m$ the expenditure on the group as a proportion of total consumer expenditure, and $\sigma$ as already defined.
4. It is assumed that boundary conditions on the spectrum can be ignored, by treating the spectrum as infinite in length or otherwise. It is common to do this for the one-dimensional location model by assuming everything is distributed on the circumference of a circle, but it is difficult to make sense of this in characteristics space.
5. See, for example, Mills and Lav 1964, Beckmann 1968, Eaton and Lipsey 1976.

# 9　Product differentiation in two-tiered industries[1]

## Introduction

The purpose of this paper is to analyze potential industry structures in which both large-scale and small-scale firms are present and competing. The motivation is simple: most industries, from automobiles to clothing to software contain both very large and very small firms, but typical theoretical models tend to be based on firms of approximately the same size. The disparity in size between the large and small firms is typically very great, so much so that their production can be taken to be based on different technologies with different cost structures.

The term *two-tiered* will be used to describe industries in which firms are either very large or quite small, but in which both sizes of firms coexist. We are interested in such industries only when the large and small firms are actually competing. Many of the small firms in some industries are auxiliaries of the large firms, supplying parts and services, rather than competitors.

In a homogeneous product industry, it is obvious that there will be limited scope, if any, for the long-run coexistence of firms having quite different marginal and fixed costs. Thus the analysis of two-tiered industries is primarily concerned with industries in which products are differentiated.

The modeling involved in carrying out this analysis covers several interesting topics:

- Nash equilibria with two quite different classes of players.
- An important role for contestability.
- A major difference between the properties of markets for products differentiated in only two characteristics and those differentiated in more than two.[2]
- The resemblance between the problem of a two-tiered industry structure and that of the *two-price* equilibrium associated with work on imperfect information.[3]
- The conclusion that, under some circumstances, increased competition leads to higher prices.

## The basic model

The analysis will be based on the simplest model, an industry in which the two technologies are in their most basic form:

1. *LS technology.*   This large-scale technology is characterized by a plant set-up which incurs a fixed per-period cost of $F$ plus a relatively low marginal cost (taken to be constant at level $m$). A firm cannot enter at any output level or even change its product without incurring the fixed set-up cost. It is assumed that capacity is not limiting over the range relevant to the analysis.[4] Most of the analysis is concerned with differentiated products, in which every firm's market is limited on the demand side, so it is easy to ignore capacity. It is also ignored in the brief discussion of homogeneous product industries, since this is simply a brief preliminary to the rest of the paper. All LS firms are identical except, in a product-differentiated industry, as to product specification.

2. *SS technology.*   The small-scale technology has a relatively high marginal cost, taken to be constant at $c$, but has no fixed set-ups, commitments, or costs. Thus SS firms can freely enter, exit, or change their product, unlike the LS firms. It is assumed that $c > m$, otherwise the LS process would never be used.

Firms are simple profit maximizers operating with full information and perfect mobility, except as limited by fixed set-up costs. In particular, LS firms are taken to be aware of SS costs even if no SS firms are active in the industry.

### Homogeneous products

Consider an industry with both large- and small-scale technologies available, producing a homogeneous product for which the aggregate demand function is $Q(p)$.

Initially consider the market structure when only the LS technology is available. If there are $n \geq 1$ LS firms, there will be some equilibrium, which we shall take to be symmetrical, at price $p^*(n)$ with profit per firm $\pi^*(n)$. The details of the equilibrium need not concern us, but we assume that both $p^*(n)$ and $\pi^*(n)$ vary inversely with $n$.

Now consider the effect of making an SS technology available. Since this requires no set-up, SS firms can freely enter and if they choose later, freely exit: the industry is potentially contestable.[5] If $p^* > c$, SS firms will enter and bring the price down to $c$. Thus $c$ places an upper limit on the equilibrium price, which is now given by

$$p^{**}(n) = \min \{p^*(n), c\} \tag{1}$$

For a given number of LS firms, there are two possible structures: it is clear that the industry is contestable for $n$ LS firms if $p^*(n) > c$ for an $n$. No LS firms will operate in the industry unless $\pi(p^M)$ is non-negative. Thus there are two possible structures, determined jointly by the cost and demand functions:

*Type 1: Contestable.* $p^{**}(n) = c$. The pricing strategies of the LS firms are constrained by potential entry of SS firms rather than competition from other LS firms.

*Type 2: Non-contestable.* $p^{**}(n) = p^*(n)$. The equilibrium price due to competition among the LS firms is less than $c$, so SS firms cannot compete and the SS technology has no influence on the outcome.

In long-run (zero-profit) free-entry equilibrium, there are three possibilities:

1. $\pi^{**}(1) < 0$. Note even a single LS firm can break even under the market conditions given.[6] The industry will consist entirely of SS firms.
2. $\pi^{**}(n) = 0$ at $n = n^{**}$ and $p^{**}(n^{**}) = c$. There is a contestable long-run equilibrium. The industry will consist of LS firms only, but the influence of the SS technology is felt in the constraints on price.
3. $\pi^{**}(n) = 0$ at $n = n^{**}$ and $p^{**}(n^{**}) = p^*$. The industry consists entirely of LS firms, with no contestability or influence from the SS technology.

Thus we can assert:

**Proposition I**   *In the long-run equilibrium of a homogeneous product industry in which both SS and LS technologies are available, only one technology will be in active use and the industry will be made up of either LS firms or of SS firms. For some range of parameters, however, the industry will be contestable, with the threat of potential entry by SS firms determining the pricing strategies of the LS firms which are actually present.*

In the short run (which includes uncertainty and imperfect information), a homogeneous product industry might be two-tiered. Since LS set-ups can be presumed to take time to put in place, there is scope for SS firms to take advantage of temporary supply shortages. If potential demand is initially uncertain, or is unstable, LS firms may deliberately choose minimum capacity with slack to be taken up by SS firms. If there is imperfect information among consumers, SS firms may still find customers even at higher prices than LS firms. These are a few of the many possibilities. But in the long run, only one of the technologies will be in active use.

### Differentiated products

The analysis follows the general lines set out in Lancaster 1978 and elsewhere, and used by the author in various papers. It will be assumed that it is possible in principle to make a product to any specification (characteristics proportions) over a continuous range, but that any fixed set-up commits a producer to a single specification. Thus the economies of the LS process in the differentiated-product case apply only to production of a single specification (model).[7] On the other hand, the SS process requires no special set-up and thus can reproduce goods to the existing specification or produce goods to new specifications, all at the same cost. Goods of different specifications are assumed to be of the same 'quality', always having less of some characteristic(s) if possessing more of another. It is assumed that the firm cannot identify a particular consumer's 'location' and thus cannot discriminate as in a pure spatial model.[8]

On the demand side, each individual is assumed to have some *ideal specification* of the characteristics mix he would prefer in the good, other things (particularly price) being equal. The desirability of a particular good to a particular individual diminishes with the distance in characteristics space[9] between his ideal specification and that of the good.

For simplicity, the factors determining demand and supply are taken to be isotropic with respect to a space of characteristics. That is, on the demand side, consumers are assumed to react only to *relative* distances between actual and ideal specifications, all consumers are assumed to have identical demand functions except for their choice of ideal specifications, and the distribution of incomes and of consumers' ideal specifications is of uniform density over the space. On the supply side, the set-up and variable costs are the same for goods of all specifications (standardized for quality).

Since consumers are assumed to have identical preferences except as to ideal specifications, we shall associate with all consumers the same *compensating function* $h(x)$ which expresses how an individual's view of a good is affected by its distance from his ideal.[10] One unit of an ideal good is perceived as equivalent to $h(x)$ units of a good at distance $x$, with $h(0) = 1$, $h'(x) > 0$ and $h''(x) \geq 0$.[11]

The consumer purchases only one good in the group, choosing that which has the best combination of price and distance from his ideal, lower price being substitutable for closer distance. The aggregate demand for a particular good depends on which consumers choose it rather than a rival good, and how much of it each purchases.

Choices between different goods are made by comparing the prices in terms of ideal good equivalents, $p_i h(x_i)$, so that the market boundary between LS firms with goods specifications at $2\overline{w}$ spacing is determined by the location of the *boundary consumer*, for whom:

$$p_1 h(w) = p_2 h(w_2) = p_2 h(2\overline{w} - w_1) \tag{2}$$

Under isotropic conditions, the market area of each good (the set of ideal specifications of consumers who purchase that good) will be non-overlapping areas in characteristics space. The market width is the distance between the ideal specification of the boundary consumer and the specification of the good actually produced, which may be different in different directions if competition is asymmetric. An important part of the effect of price on market demand is through changing the market width and thus the number of customers.[12] Since we do not wish to become involved with end-of-spectrum effects, it will be assumed that the characteristics space can be treated as if it extends indefinitely in all directions.

## Unidimensional product space

With only two characteristics, the space of goods adjusted for quality is unidimensional and representable by a line. Distances between specifications become simple differences, and markets extend in just two directions, up and down the line. Each firm has at most two neighbors and its boundary consists of at most two separated points. Since we are interested in equilibria within an isotropic market, we shall confine discussion to symmetric cases in which there are either two neighbors or none, and if two, both are at the same distance (in opposite directions) and sell at the same price. A neighbor may be either an SS firm or another LS firm.

As a preliminary to examining market equilibrium with free entry of both LS and SS firms, consider two special cases.

### Competition between LS firms only

Consider initially the case of a fixed number of LS firms, distributed uniformly at distance $2\overline{w}$ and selling at price $\overline{p}$. Any firm which contemplates varying its price to $p$ faces the market demand function

$$Q(p; \overline{p}, \overline{w}) = 2\beta \int_0^{w(p)} q(p, x)dx \tag{3}$$

where $w(p)$ satisfies the dividing condition (2), $q(p, x)$ is the individual demand at price $p$ from a consumer whose ideal is at distance $x$ from the market center, and $\beta$ is the density of consumers over the space, taken to be uniform.

The profit function for the firm has the form

$$\pi(p; \overline{p}, \overline{w}) = (p - m)Q(p; \overline{p}, \overline{w}) - F \tag{4}$$

Providing $q(p, x)$ is non-increasing in both $p$ and $x$, a simple extension of well-known results indicates that there is a symmetric profit-maximizing Nash equilibrium price

$$p^*(\overline{w}) = \text{arg max } \pi(p; p^*(\overline{w}), \overline{w}) \qquad (5)$$

for all values of $\overline{w}$.

The Nash equilibria for different values of $w$ will be such that $\pi^*(\overline{w})$ is increasing in $\overline{w}$.

### A single LS firm facing SS firms

The essential difference from the previous case lies in the dividing condition. Since SS firms have no set-up costs they can enter at (or change specification to) any point in the spectrum. The LS firm has a fixed specification but a variable price, while any SS competitor has a variable specification but a fixed price, since it cannot charge more than $c$ because of SS competitors and cannot break even at less than $c$.

The dividing condition (2) is now modified, since $h(w_2) \to 1$ and $p_2 \to c$, to give

$$h\big(w(p)\big) = \frac{c}{p} \qquad (6)$$

The demand function has the same basic form as before

$$Q(p;c) = 2\beta \int_0^{w(p)} q(p,x)dx \qquad (7)$$

In this case, the situation facing the LS firm is like that of a monopolist in a market where consumers all have a reservation price of $c$. There is a 'monopoly' solution $p^M$ for the single LS firm facing SS competitors only, given by

$$p^M = \text{arg max } (\pi(p) = (p - m)Q(p; c) - F) \qquad (8)$$

Denote the market width at this equilibrium by $w^M$ so that $w^M = c/p^M$. We shall refer to the situation as that of 'competitive monopoly' since the firm has a local monopoly relative to other LS firms, but is competitive with SS firms. Unlike the homogeneous good case, SS competition here does not place a simple upper limit of $c$ on the price. The dividing condition implies an effective upper limit strictly smaller than $c$.

**Lemma 1** $p^*(w^M) > p^M$ and $\pi^*(w^M) > \pi^M$. *That is, an LS firm has a higher equilibrium price and higher profit in competition only with other LS firms at spacing $2w^M$ than in competition only with SS firms.*

Any equilibrium price satisfies the relationship.

$$p = \left(1 - \frac{1}{E(w)}\right)^{-1} m \tag{9}$$

where the $E$ is the elasticity appropriate to the case. The proposition is proved by showing that $E$ is higher for SS competition alone than for LS competition alone.

Taking the demand function for the SS case, equation (7), we obtain:

$$E = -2\beta \frac{p}{Q} \int_0^w \frac{\partial q(p,x)}{\partial p} dx - 2\beta \frac{pq(p,w)}{Q} \frac{dw}{dp} \tag{10}$$

Using the dividing condition (6), the second term in the above expression becomes

$$2\beta \frac{wq}{Q} \frac{h(w)}{wh'(w)} \tag{11}$$

For the firm with LS competition only, the elasticity expression will have the same structure as (10) but the different dividing condition will result in the second term becoming

$$2\beta \frac{wq}{Q} \frac{h(w)}{2wh'(w)} \tag{12}$$

For the same values of $p$ and $w$, (12) is smaller than (11) and the elasticity associated with LS competition is smaller than that for competition with SS firms.

Thus at $w = w^M$ and $p = p^M$, $E^* < E^M$ so that $p^* > p = p^M$. Since the same market width has been taken in both cases, $\pi^* > \pi^M$, and the latter is the highest profit attainable with competition from SS firms.

*Firms facing both LS and SS competition*
There is a special property of the LS–SS game in unidimensional space which simplifies the analysis, namely that the interface with other firms is limited to two discrete points. Since we are concerned primarily with symmetric situations, the typical interface is the single point which is the common boundary between

one half-market of an LS firm and the corresponding half-market of the rival, whether it is an LS or an SS firm.

The above property implies that the firm is not in competition simultaneously with different kinds of rivals. The point interface can be thought of as a narrow pass, through which can come only one enemy at a time.

The firm's strategy consists in identifying the type of rival posing the maximum threat in the given situation, then taking appropriate action. The situation is defined by the spacing between adjacent LS firms (which are taken to be distributed uniformly), the action is the choice of $p$, the firm's only strategy variable.

Let the spacing between adjacent LS firms be $\bar{w}$ and consider one of the these firms situated symmetrically between LS neighbors both selling their products at price $\bar{p}$. In the absence of SS firms, the optimal price would be $p = \arg \max \pi(p; \bar{p}, \bar{w})$ with the market width $w(p)$ satisfying the appropriate dividing condition (2). But if $p > c/h(w(p))$, SS firms will enter on the edge of the market and the desired market width $w(p)$ cannot be attained. Thus the choice of $p$ must be made subject to the constrain $p \leq c/h(w(p))$. Note that this involves both dividing conditions: (2), which determines $w(p)$, and (6), which directly constrains $p$.

From Lemma 1 it is clear that the constraint on $p$ due to potential SS competition is binding at $\bar{w} = w^M$ if $\bar{p} = p^*$. Note that it is never optimal to charge less than $p^M$ even if the constraint permits.

The above constraint due to potential SS competition is not always binding, however:

**Lemma 2**  *For sufficiently small values of $\bar{w}$, $p^*(\bar{w}) < c/h(\bar{w})$, provided $m < c$. The latter relationship is assumed throughout this analysis.*

Inspection of (10) and (12) shows that $E^*(w) \to \infty$, and thus $p^* \to m$, as $w \to 0$. But $c/h(w) \to c > m$ as $w \to 0$.

The optimal strategy for an LS firm facing competition both from other LS firms and from SS firms can be summarized as follows:

$$p^{**} = \min \{\arg \max \pi(p; \bar{p}, \bar{w}), \max (c/h(w(p)), p^M)\} \qquad (13)$$

**Equilibrium**

**Proposition II**  *In an isotropic unidimensional market with a uniform density of consumers and a uniform distribution of LS firms at spacing $2w$, there is a joint Nash equilibrium for SS firms together with the LS firms. The equilibrium prices are $c$ for products of SS firms and*

$$p^{**}(w) = \min \{p^*(w), \max (c/h(w), p^M)\}$$

*for products of LS firms, where p\*(w) is the Nash equilibrium price that would exist for the LS firms in the absence of SS firms.*

To show that this is a Nash equilibrium, we first note that the SS firms are always in equilibrium at a price $c$, whatever the prices charged by the LS firms. As to the LS firms, we need to consider the different possibilities.

1. $p^*(w) < \max (c/h(w), p^M)$. At the LS-only Nash price, the closest distance at which SS firms could become competitive is further than the distance at which the nearest LS firm competes for boundary customers. Thus the LS-only equilibrium is the relevant one and $p^*(w)$ the equilibrium price.
2. $p^*(w) > c/h(w) > p^M$. The equilibrium price is $c/h(w)$. Since $dw/dp = h(w)/ph'(w)$ for the boundary with SS firms and $dw/dp = 2h(w)/ph'(w)$ for the boundary with LS neighbors (see (11) and (12)), a reduction in price would increase the distance to the nearest SS competition by more than the distance to LS competition, making the LS competition the effective one. But $c/h(w) < p^*(w)$, so a reduction in price can only reduce profit. By the symmetric argument, increasing the price would make the SS competition effective, but $c/h(w) > p^M$ so this again would reduce profit.
3. $p^*(w) > p^M > c/h(w)$. The equilibrium price is $p^M$. Note that this case implies $w > w^M$, so that the LS competition is further than the boundary of the local pseudo-monopoly area. The effective competition is from SS firms, and any change in price will reduce profit, by definition of $p^M$.

Thus the proposition is established.

**Two-technology market structures**
If both LS and SS technologies are available, three different symmetric market structures are possible, depending on the system functions and parameters relative to the spacing of LS firms.

*Type 1: Competitive monopoly.* $p^{**} = p^M$. For $w > w^M$. Each LS firm interacts solely with SS firms and sets price $p^M$ like a monopolist whose customers have a reservation price of $c$. Between each pair of LS firms will be a band of width $2(w - w^M)$ supplied entirely with custom goods by SS firms, isolating the LS firms from each other. Both LS and SS firms are active in this configuration.
*Type 2: Contestable oligopoly.* $p^{**} = c/h(w)$. For $w$ such that $p^*(w) \geq c/h(w)$. The constraint is effective because any higher price will attract SS firms. The market is truly contestable in the sense that the existence of potential SS firms

keeps the ideal good equivalent price at the market edge ($ph(w)$) down to the competitive level of the SS firms even though none of the latter actually enter. Only LS firms are active in this structure, although behavior is dominated by the potential SS firms. The existence of a Type 2 range for $w$ is guaranteed by Lemmas 1 and 2.

*Type 3: Pure oligopoly.* $p^{**} = p^*(w)$. For $w$ such that $p^*(w) < c/h(w)$, a range with existence guaranteed by Lemma 2. This is a regular oligopoly structure involving LS firms only. The Nash equilibrium prices are too low, and the market widths too small, to attract entry by SS firms even at the outer fringes of the market. The SS technology is simply irrelevant.

Note an interesting and special property of Type 2 structures. Since $p^{**} = c/h(w)$, price *increases* (but profit per firm does not) as the number of firms (and thus, in one sense, the degree of competition) increases. What is happening is that ologipolistic competition is increasing, but contestability is decreasing.

**Long-run equilibrium**
Now consider the effect of free entry (and exit) combined with costless relocation.[13] The market width becomes an equilibrium variable instead of an independent parameter.

Denote by $\pi^{**}(w)$ the maximum profit per LS firm under both SS and LS competition when the LS firms are distributed uniformly at a spacing of $2w$. This is the profit at optimal price $p^{**}$ when the latter is determined as in the preceding discussion.

Since $\pi^{**}(w) \leq \pi^M$, the first possibility is that $\pi^M < 0$. In this case LS firms will not enter the industry at all (or will exit if they entered under different conditions) and in the long run the equilibrium structure will consist entirely of SS firms producing custom goods to ideal specifications at price $c$.

Note that $\pi^{**}(w) = \pi^M$ for all $w \geq w^M$ and is independent of the spacing between firms so long as it is no less than $w^M$. Thus if $\pi^M \geq 0$, LS firms will be attracted into the industry[14] until the inter-firm spacing is $w^M$ or less. As soon as the spacing falls to this level, $\pi^{**}(w)$ commences to decline with $w$. There are then two possibilities:

1. If $\pi^{**}(w) = 0$ for some $w$ such that $p^{**}(w) = c/h(w)$, the equilibrium structure is of Type 2 and is contestable. The industry will consist entirely of LS firms, but the influence of the SS technology will be apparent in the price behavior of the firms.
2. If $\pi^{**}(w) > 0$ for all $w$ such that $p^{**}(w) = c/h(w)$, the spacing will fall until the structure is of Type 3 and no longer contestable. The competitive structure is that of conventional oligopoly or monopolistic competition in LS firms only. The SS technology exerts no influence of any kind.

Note that the long-run equilibrium structures in the model analyzed consist of either SS firms only or LS firms only. Hence:

**Proposition III**   *With an isotropic unidimensional market and uniform market density, the active firms in an industry will all be LS firms or all be SS firms in the long run, even though LS and SS technologies are always both available. For some range of parameters, however, contestability will result in the behavior of the LS firms being determined by the cost properties of the SS technology, even though no SS firms are actually present. There will be a single price.*

### Non-uniform consumer density

The market demand depends on the consumer density over the market area. If the density is uniform, demand is directly proportional to its value for given price and market area. Inspection of equations (3) and (4) shows that the density $\beta$ does not affect the demand elasticity and thus the Nash equilibrium price, given the spacing between firms. Nor does it affect the monopoly price $p^M$ or the contestable price $c/h(w)$.

But the density directly affects the equilibrium profit per LS firm, given the spacing, including the 'monopoly' profit $\pi^M$. Since $d\pi/d\beta > 0$, lowering the density while keeping other parameters constant can switch $\pi^M$ from positive to negative and thus change the long-run equilibrium from one in LS firms only to one in SS firms only.

Consider a system represented by a goods space in which the density of consumers is high in some areas and low in others, but in which the variations are negligible over the market area of any one firm. Then the long-run equilibrium can be approximated by considering firms in the high- and low-density areas as achieving equilibria in high-density and low-density systems, respectively. If $\pi^M > 0$ in the high-density area but $< 0$ in the low-density part, then the long-run equilibrium will consist only of LS firms in high-density areas and only of SS firms in low-density areas. The industry as a whole will then appear as a mixture of the two types of firm.

It is thus possible to have a two-tiered structure in a unidimensional market with non-uniform density, the dense part of the market being supplied by LS firms, the thin part by SS firms.

### Multidimensional product spaces

In some respects the analysis of competition in multidimensional product spaces (more than two characteristics) is a direct extension of the unidimensional analysis. There is, however, one fundamental structural difference between unidimensional and multidimensional market arrays. In the former case market areas are line segments and boundaries are points, so that in a uniform partition of the whole market every boundary customer is at the same distance from his relevant market center as every other boundary customer. In two-dimensional space (three characteristics), any uniform partition, whether in squares, triangles, or hexagons (the only possibilities) is such that some boundary customers are further from their market center than others. Those at the apices of the areas are furthest from the center, those at the centers of the sides are closest. The same is true for three-dimensional space, in which cubes are the only symmetric space-filling figures, and analogous properties hold for all multidimensional spaces.

For multidimensional spaces and a two-tiered technology, an LS firm could have a market in which some boundary customers were on the margin of buying from adjacent LS producers, while others were on the margin of buying custom goods from SS producers. The possibility arises that there can be a true long-run Nash equilibrium in which both LS and SS firms are active and in which LS firms interact simultaneously with SS firms and with other LS firms. The following analysis explores that possibility.

*Multidimensional demand*
The market demand function for the multidimensional case in which all neighbors are at distance $2w$ and sell at price $\bar{p}$ has the form

$$Q(p; \bar{p}, w) = \beta \int q(p, \rho) \, dV \tag{14}$$

where the integral is taken over the appropriate figure. In this analysis $\rho$ is the Euclidean distance from the market centre, discussion being confined to Euclidean spaces.

For any symmetric figure in Euclidean $n$-space, the space enclosed (area, volume, hypervolume, depending on $n$) can be expressed as $A(w) = Kw^n$ where $w$ is the distance of a facet from the center and $K$ is a constant which depends on the figure being considered. For inelastic individual demand with $q(p, \rho) = 1$, $Q = K'w^n$ where $K' = \beta K$. Then

$$\frac{dQ}{dp} = nK'w^{n-1}\frac{dw}{dp} \tag{15}$$

so that

$$E(w) = -n\frac{p}{w}\frac{dw}{dp} = n\frac{h(w)}{2wh'(w)} \tag{16}$$

using the dividing condition (2), which remains the same for any number of dimensions. The effect of varying $w$ is given by

$$\frac{dE}{dw} = -\frac{n}{w}\left((E-1)+\frac{hh''}{h'^2}\right) < 0 \tag{17}$$

since $E > 1$ and $h'' \geq 0$ are good behavior conditions, assumed to hold.

### Nash equilibrium in LS firms

Consider the Nash equilibrium configuration of LS firms in the absence of the SS technology. If the inter-firm spacing is $2w$ and the environment strictly isotropic, the equilibrium structure must be such that all market areas are equal regular figures making up a uniform partition of the market space.

For a three-characteristic two-dimensional space, which will be our primary context, these market areas must be equilateral triangles (each firm with three neighbors), squares (four neighbors), or hexagons (six).

While it is well known that the hexagonal configuration is optimal for pure location models with uniform inelastic demands because it gives lowest average transport costs for a given area, as compared with other symmetric space-filling figures, the same argument cannot be used for the structure of a Nash equilibrium.

An outline of the appropriate reasoning is as follows:

1. For figures of equal area (and thus equal numbers of firms covering the same overall market), the spacing between the firms is greater for hexagons than squares (by a factor of $\sqrt{(2/(\sqrt{3}))}$) or triangles (by a larger factor).
2. The greater the spacing between adjacent firms, the lower the elasticity of demand (see (17) above) and so the higher the equilibrium price. From this it follows that firms will have the highest Nash equilibrium prices and highest profits with hexagonal market areas, given the number of firms (market area per firm).[15]
3. The above argument is based on the case of inelastic individual demands. In the more general case in which individual demand for a product falls with distance from ideal (elasticity of substitution greater than unity), the argument holds *a fortiori*. Because the hexagon gives the lowest average distance of consumers from the center, for a given area, it gives the highest sales per unit area for a given price, strengthening the previous argument.

For hexagonal market areas in which all six adjacent firms are at the same distance $2w$ and sell at price $\bar{p}$, the market demand function is:

$$Q(p; \bar{p}, \bar{w}) = 12\beta \int_0^{\frac{\pi}{6}} \int_0^{w \sec \theta} q(p, \rho) \rho d\rho d\theta \qquad (18)$$

The Nash equilibrium price with LS competition only will satisfy

$$p^*(w) = \arg \max (\pi(p; p^*, w) = (p - m) Q(p; p^*, w) - F \qquad (19)$$

With the hexagonal market structure, note that the distance $w$, which is half the inter-firm spacing, is the distance from the center to the closest point on the boundary (the center of a side). The distance to the furthest point on the boundary (an apex) is $2w/\sqrt{3}$.

## Competition with SS firms

The multidimensional analysis of competition between a single LS firm and actual or potential SS firms follows the same general lines as that for unidimensional space. The market area of the firm is limited by the dividing condition $h(w(p)) = c/p$, and is now a circle (or sphere or hypersphere) of radius $w(p)$. As before, there is a local pseudo-monopoly situation and an optimal profit-maximizing price $p^M$ giving a market width $w^M$ and profit $\pi^M$. Lemma 1 can be shown to hold, so that $p^*(w^M) > p^M$ and $E^*(w^M) < E^M$.

## Two-way competition

If an LS firm faces both SS firms and other LS firms, every potential customer has a three-way choice, between the firm's product, that of the nearest LS neighbor, and a custom product from an SS firm. The major difference between this two-way competition in the multidimensional case and that in a single dimension is that it is possible for some boundary customers to be on the margin of buying from an SS firm while others are on the margin of buying from an LS firm. This is because the hexagonal partitioning results in different portions of the boundary being at different distances from the center.

Consider a target LS firm surrounded by six LS neighbors spaced at distance $2w$ from the target firm and each other, in a context of free entry by SS firms. A consumer at distance $\rho$ from the market center will buy the target good at price $p$ only so long as both

- $ph(\rho) \le c$. (otherwise he will choose the SS good.)
- $ph(\rho) \le \bar{p}h(2w - \rho)$. (Otherwise he will choose the neighboring LS good at price $\bar{p}$.)

Thus the demand function now becomes

$$Q(p;\bar{p},w,c)=12\beta\int_0^{\frac{\pi}{6}}\int_0^{\min(r(p),z(p)w\sec\theta)}q(p,\rho)\rho d\rho d\theta \tag{20}$$

where $r$ satisfies $ph(r) = c$ and $z$ satisfies $ph(z) \le \bar{p}h(2w-z)$.

There are three possible market shapes for the firm:

*Type A*: If $r \ge z \sec \pi/6 = (2/\sqrt{3})z$, the market area is a hexagon with closest boundary point at distance $z$.

*Type B*: If $r \le z$, the market area is a circle of radius $r$.

*Type C*: if $(2/\sqrt{3})z > r > z$, the market is a complex figure, being a combination of a circle of radius $r$ and a hexagon of size $z$. The actual market area consists of those portions of the hexagon lying inside the circles plus those portions of the circle lying inside the hexagon, as shown in Figure 9.1.

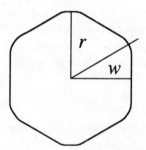

*Figure 9.1    Market area for Type C competition*

Since Type C configurations, which have no analog in one dimension, have elements of both circular market areas like firms in SS competition only and hexagonal market areas like LS oligopolists, the market properties are weighted combinations of the two, as shown by splitting the demand function:

$$Q=12\beta\int_\phi^{\frac{\pi}{6}}\int_0^r q(p,\rho)\rho d\rho d\theta+12\beta\int_0^\phi\int_0^{z\sec\theta}q(p,\rho)\rho d\rho d\theta \tag{21}$$

where $\phi = \arccos z/r$.

Total quantity and elasticity of demand are both weighted averages of the properties for the separate market types. The weights are continuous functions of the ratio $r/z$, are equal to 0 or 1 (as appropriate) for ratios 1, $2/\sqrt{3}$. As $z/r \rightarrow$ 1, the properties of the figure (including the demand elasticity) converge to that of the circle and the firm in SS competition only. As $z/r \rightarrow \sqrt{3}/2$, they converge to those of the hexagon and the firm in LS competition only. Note, however, that the weights are not linear and do not add to unity.

The following lemma, given without formal proof, summarizes the above reasoning:

**Lemma 3**    *If $E_{SS}$ is the elasticity of demand for a firm facing SS competition only, and $E_{LS}$ that for a firm facing LS competition only, the elasticity of demand $E^C$ for a firm in a Type C situation can be expressed as*

$$E^C(p, w) = \lambda(z/r)E_{SS}(p) + \mu(z/r)E_{LS}(p, w)$$

*where*

$$r \mid ph(r) = c$$
$$z \mid ph(z) = \bar{p}h(2W - z)$$

*and $\lambda$, $\mu$ have the properties*

$$\lambda(1) = \mu(\sqrt{3}/2) = 1$$
$$\lambda(\sqrt{3}/2) = \mu(1) = 0$$
$$\lambda \in [0,1], \mu \in [0, 1]$$

In the Type C case here, unlike the unidimensional case in which the constraint $c/h(w)$ fully determined the price over the equivalent range, the firm can reach an interior optimum, maximizing profit over the special market area implied by the demand function (20). The solution can be written in the form

$$p^C = \left(1 - \frac{1}{E^C}\right)^{-1} m \qquad (22)$$

From Lemma 3, $E^C(p^M, w^M) = E_{SS}(p^M, w^M) = E^M$. This implies $p^C(w^M) = p^M$ $< p^*(w^M)$ (Lemma 1). As $w$ declines, the weight of $E_{LS}$ in $E^C$ increases, reaching 1 when $h(2w/\sqrt{3}) = c/p^C(w)$. At that stage, $p^C(w) = p^*(w)$.

Thus the range of values for Type C is from $w = w^M$ at the top down to $w^0 = w \mid p^*(w) = c/h(2w/\sqrt{3})$. The existence of such a value $w^0$ is guaranteed by Lemma 2.

## Nash equilibria

**Proposition IV**  *In an isotropic multidimensional market with a uniform density of consumers and a uniform distribution of LS firms at spacing 2w, there is a joint Nash equilibrium for SS firms together with LS firms. The equilibrium price is always c for SS firms, while for LS firms it is*

$$p^{**}(w) = p^M \text{ for } w \geq w^M$$
$$= p^C(w) \text{ for } w^M \geq w \geq w^0$$
$$= p^* \text{ for } w \leq w^0$$

*where $p^*(w)$ is the Nash equilibrium price that would exist for the LS firms in the absence of SS firms, $p^C(w)$ is the equilibrium price for a Type C market, and $w^0$ satisfies $p^*(w^0) = c/h(2w^0/\sqrt{3})$.*

That the above constitutes a Nash equilibrium follows from the definitions of $p^M$, $p^C$, and $p^*$.

## Market structures in two dimensions
As in the unidimensional case, there are three different types of market structure possible, depending on the relationship of $w$ to the relevant parameters.

*Type 1: Competitive monopoly. $p^{**} = p^M$. For $w \geq w^M$.* As in the unidimensional case, each LS firm is like a monopolist whose customers have a reservation price of $c$ and thus will set an appropriate pseudo-monopoly price $p^M$. Both price and profit per firm are constant at $p^M$, $\pi^M$ for all $w$ which stays in the range. A major difference in the two-dimensional case is that the market areas are circles, which are not space-filling. Thus even when $w = w^M$ so that the market areas touch, there are interstitial spaces between each triplet of circles and SS firms will operate in these.

*Type 2: Mixed competition. $p^{**} = p^C(w)$. For $w \in [w^0, w^M]$.* In this range, firms in Type C competition, directly competing with other LS firms on part of their boundaries, and with SS firms on other parts. The complex market areas, compounded of hexagons and circles, are not space-filling, so both LS and SS firms coexist. The range is referred to here as 'mixed competition', rather than 'contestable' as in the single dimension, because SS firms are active and do not simply affect events by being *potential* entrants. The existence of a Type 2 range for $w$ is guaranteed by Lemmas 1 and 2.

*Type 3: Pure oligopoly. $p^{**} = p^*(w)$. For $w < w^0$.* This is a regular oligopoly structure involving LS firms only, prices being too low to attract even potential SS firms on the margin. Market areas are space-filling hexagons.

Figure 9.2 shows the progression of the market structure through the three types, as $w$ declines from left to right.

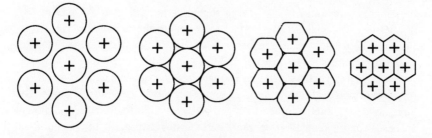

*Figure 9.2 The progression of market structure*

In long-run equilibrium the industry will consist only of SS firms if $\pi^M < 0$. If LS firms can at least break even, such firms will continue to enter until $w = w^M$ since $\pi^M$ remains constant for $w \geq w^M$. For $\pi^M = 0$, long-run equilibrium will be at $w^M$, but if $\pi^M > 0$ entry will continue into the Type C range. Over this range each LS firm is competing directly and simultaneously with both SS firms and other LS firms. The industry will contain both LS and SS firms if zero-profit values for $w$ are larger than $w^0$. Only if the zero-profit level of $w$ falls below $w^0$ will there be an equilibrium structure in LS firms only.

Thus we have

**Proposition V** *With an isotropic multidimensional market and uniform market density, an industry with both SS and LS technologies will contain active firms of both types in the long run unless:*

(a) *The LS cost structure is so high relative to SS costs that even a single LS firm cannot break even competing only with SS firms, in which case the industry will consist only of SS firms, or*

(b) *the LS cost structure is so low relative to SS costs that a Nash equilibrium with non-negative profits exists for LS firms at a price and spacing combination at which SS firms producing custom products cannot compete even for consumers at the furthest points of the LS market boundaries, in which case the industry will consist only of LS firms.*

Note that a *two-price* equilibrium with prices $c$ and $p^{**} < c$ will exist when both kinds of firms are active, which is easily possible in the multidimensional case.

### Notes on higher dimensions

For a three-dimensional product space (four characteristics), the *only* space-filling symmetric figures are cubes, so these must be the Nash equilibrium market structures in an isotropic environment. The local monopoly market areas will be spheres with radii $r^M$ satisfying the same condition as for one or two dimensions. The analysis is analogous to that given above, with the critical relationships between $r$ and $w$ now being 1, $\sqrt{3}$. In this case, the maximum market share for SS firms is $(1 - \pi/6))$ or 47.6%.

The large jump in the maximum SS share from two to three dimensions should not be extrapolated into similar large jumps at every dimensional increase. The analysis of symmetric space-filling figures in multidimensional Euclidean spaces is complex, but there are more possibilities in spaces with even numbers of dimensions than with odd. Whereas the maximum number of facets is two for one dimension and jumps to six for two dimensions, it remains at six for three dimensions and then jumps to 24 for four dimensions. The greater the number of facets, the less the difference between the hypervolume of the figure and that of an inscribed hypersphere, and the lower the share of available interstitial space for SS firms.

**Conclusion**

The analysis has shown that it is possible to have an industry in long-run two-tiered equilibrium, with both large-scale low marginal cost and small-scale high marginal cost firms present and active, provided the industry is product-differentiated in more than two characteristics. Such an equilibrium is characterized by two-way competition in which large-scale firms compete simultaneously with each other and with small-scale firms, and by the existence of different prices for the outputs of the large- and small-scale firms, prices of the latter being always higher. If costs of large-scale firms fall enough relative to small-scale firms, the two-tiered structure is replaced by a conventional oligopoly structure in large-scale firms. If the reverse is true, the industry becomes a competitive industry in small-scale firms only.

For an industry with product differentiated in only two characteristics, so that goods can be represented on a line spectrum, there is no two-tiered equilibrium in the long run unless consumer density varies greatly over the market space. However, there is a range of cost relationships between large-scale and small-scale technologies in which, although only large-scale firms are actually present, the potential entry of small-scale firms (contestability) keeps prices below what they would be if a small-scale technology did not exist. A feature of this range is that the price rises as the number of firms increases (although profit per firm falls).

The difference between the properties of unidimensional product spaces (two characteristics) and multidimensional (more than two characteristics) provides a warning against generalizing too readily from spatial analogs in one dimension.

## Notes

1. Originally presented in 1988. Published as 'Two-tiered Industries: Large and Small Firms in Simultaneous Competition' in the conference volume Gee, J. Alec and Norman, George (eds), *Market Structure and Strategy*, London, Wheatsheaf, 1992.
2. As previously noted in Lancaster 1980, 1982.
3. See Salop and Stiglitz 1976, for example. A two-tiered structure in a differentiated product industry can be misperceived as a two-price equilibrium of a homogeneous product industry.
4. It is not uncommon in the oligopoly literature to assume a fixed capacity and a zero marginal cost. See Kreps and Scheinkman 1983, Benoit and Krishna 1987.
5. The term as used in this paper is in the spirit of, if not always technically identical with, that in the seminal work by Baumol et al. 1982.
6. Traditional single-price monopoly is assumed. See Wilson 1988 for an argument that a firm may gain by using two prices.
7. It is assumed that there are no inter-product economies, so that even large-scale firms produce a single product.
8. See Greenhut and Ohta 1975.
9. Treated here as Euclidean. Other metrics are possible, but require a different analysis. See Eaton and Lipsey 1980.
10. See Lancaster 1978 for detailed discussion of this concept.
11. It is assumed that the firms relocate to preserve the uniform equilibrium spacing at each change in the number of firms. See Capozza and Van Order 1980 for discussion of relocation effects in pure spatial models.
12. Concave compensating functions lead to various kinds of ill behavior and are ruled out here.
13. Many spatial oligopoly models assume fixed demand per customer, as in Hotelling's original analysis, so market width change is the only way in which demand is affected.
14. It is assumed that firms enter so long as profit is nonnegative.
15. For unit market areas with fixed unit demand per customer, unit marginal cost, and $h = 1 + x^2$, profit per firm at Nash equilibrium (excluding fixed cost) is 27% higher with a hexagonal configuration than with squares.

# 10　Information and product differentiation[1]

In the uncomplicated world of the idealized competitive economy, there are really only two types of information that the consumer is presumed to need in order to make all his decisions – information as to the prices of goods and information as to the timing of receipts and payments. Less than full information on timing has long been accepted and forms one of the foundations of monetary theory. But informational deficiencies as to prices were long ignored, and the existence of uniform prices – for which there are no information problems – was a cornerstone of competitive market theory.

Perfect information on prices implies perfect information on the specification of goods: a price is a price *of* something, and it makes no sense to suppose that consumers have perfect price information but do not know to what things those prices refer. In the idealized competitive economy there was assumed to be a finite number of well-defined homogeneous goods, the quantities and prices of which were the outcomes of the market process, but the specifications of which were eternal and perfectly known so that there was no uncertainty whatever as to what the prices were prices of.

It was inevitable, therefore, that the modern development of the economics of information should commence, on the consumer side,[2] by assuming that the information problem was that of prices and proceed to investigate the theory of optimal search for the lowest price when the search costs time or money.[3] Although the search for price information is the basic case in the development of the economics of information, it is not the true paradigm case. This is because if the specification of the good is exactly known, price is a simple, totally objective parameter, misinformation concerning which is directly refutable,[4] and that signifies the same thing to all consumers. For these reasons, universally available price information has the properties of a public good.

In this paper we shall be concerned with a more complex decision environment for the consumer than that which underlies the basic competitive model, an environment in which differentiated products form an important part of the spectrum of consumer goods. In this environment, the specifications of goods are not eternal (or at least long established), but can be and are changed with a frequency that presents the consumer with a real problem in finding out what the specifications are. In this context, even if prices are known perfectly, there remains a problem of establishing of what manner of things these are prices. The first steps in this direction have been taken in the work on 'quality' information and signaling.[5]

## Pure vertical differentiation

A product can be considered to be vertically differentiated if it possesses a single characteristic, which we shall call 'quality' and is made available in versions of different quality content. For this to be an interesting case, the consumption technology is taken to be non-combinable so that it is not possible to take two differentiates of qualities, $q_1$, $q_2$ and consume them in combination to obtain some new quality $q(q_1, q_2) > \max (q_1, q_2)$. Differentiates of different qualities can be viewed as different-sized packages of the same single characteristic, with consumption restricted to a single package. The differentiation is vertical in the simple sense that if offered a free choice between differentiates of qualities $q_1$, $q_2$, every consumer will choose the differentiate with the greater value of $q$. Implicitly this assumes that quality is a universal 'good' and that there is no satiation.

In order to make a fully informed choice in a budget situation, a consumer needs to know the following:

1. The exact nature and relevance to him (her) of the single characteristic possessed by all goods in the group. (This information will be taken to be known because the emphasis is on other aspects of the situation in the present analysis.)
2. The quality content (characteristic quantity) of each good within the group that is offered in the market.
3. The price of each good within the group.

With full information, the choice situation for the individual consumer can be imagined in a space of two characteristics, one being a Hicks-type aggregate characteristic from all other goods, the other being the quality content to be derived from goods within the group. The budget constraint will be a set of discrete points if there is only a finite number of product differentiates in the group, or a budget curve if a continuous spectrum of goods is available. There are few restrictions on the pattern of points or the shape of the curve and, in particular, the latter may be convex or concave to the origin (or part convex, part concave). It will be linear only if the prices of goods are a linear function of their quality contents. Whatever the relationship between price and quality for different goods, there is a potential consumer (in the sense of a preference map with acceptable properties) for a good with every degree of quality excepting only a good of lower quality that is priced at or above the level of some good of higher quality.

The full-information market equilibrium will then depend on the supply side which, in turn, will depend on the technical production conditions and the competitive structure. The production conditions can be taken to be summarized by a cost function of the form $C(q, x)$, where $C$ is the cost of producing quantity

$x$ of a good having quality $q$. It is obvious that unless $C$ is an increasing function of $q$ for given $x$, only the highest quality good will be produced and sold, and then there will be no product differentiation. Taking $\partial C/\partial q$ to be positive everywhere, the outcome will depend crucially on the properties of $C$ as a function of $x$, given $q$, which are essentially the returns to scale properties of the technology. The results from Lancaster 1975 are applicable here even though these were designed for the horizontal product differentiation case, and we can conclude that:

1. If the production technology shows increasing returns to scale, only a finite number of quality variants will be produced.
2. If there are constant or decreasing returns to scale, an infinite spectrum of quality variants will be produced, *whatever the market structure*, provided that there is a continuous spectrum of preferences.
3. If consumers are divided among a finite number of groups, with all consumers in each group having identical preferences and incomes (or identical homothetic preferences), there will be, at most, as many quality variants as groups, and there may be less if there are increasing returns to scale.

Whatever the returns to scale properties or the market structure, the equilibrium can be represented by a schedule in the form of discrete values or a continuous function $P(q)$ showing the relation between the market price of a good and its quality. This schedule will certainly be such that $P$ increases as $q$ increases, but otherwise few restrictions can be placed upon it in general. In particular, $p = P/q$ (the price per unit of the quality characteristic) may vary in any way as $q$ varies, subject only to the restriction that if $p$ falls as $q$ rises, the elasticity of $p$ with respect to $q$ is greater than $-1$. The relationship between $p$ and $q$ will depend on the relationship between the cost of production and the quality, the competitive structure of the market, and the distribution of preferences over consumers.

There are of course special cases worth noting. If there are constant returns to scale (with respect to the number of 'packages' of given quality produced), constant costs per quality unit for packages of different size, and a competitive market structure, then $p$ will be constant. It is possible to have constant $p$ under other circumstances, such as constant costs per quality unit, increasing returns to scale, and a distribution of consumer preferences that is 'uniform' in a particular sense, giving a monopolistic competition solution with this property.[6]

## Incomplete quality information

We now consider the market for a vertically differentiated group of goods in which the quality content of the goods is not known completely and in advance of purchase. Initially we shall suppose that all prices are known in advance, that is, that the consumer knows the price of the $i$th differentiate to be $P_i$, but does not know its quality content.

It is convenient to divide goods according to the circumstances under which the consumer is able fully to determine their quality content. We can commence with the useful classification by Nelson 1970 into 'search goods', the quality of which can be determined by direct inspection of the actual goods before purchase, and 'experience goods', the quality of which can only be determined after actual purchase and consumption. We may add another category of 'hidden property goods' for which the quality cannot be clearly determined even after consumption. The latter category, which is more realistic in a multicharacteristic context, covers goods that have long-term or subtle properties (such as carcinogenesis for cigarets) that would count in the utility function if they were known.[7]

If the goods under consideration are search goods, the consumer's problem of determining quality is confined to that of inspecting the goods before purchase. If the whole spectrum of goods can be inspected at one location, the search is trivial. If each outlet sells only one of the goods, the search is non-trivial but *provided the consumer can be certain that the price (of the whole package) is a monotonically increasing function of quality*, a simple convergent search procedure can easily be devised because after each inspection the consumer will know whether he should next inspect a good of higher price (therefore, quality) or lower price. If the number of goods is very large, the consumer will stop when the potential gain from finding a good closer to his optimal specification is no longer greater than the cost of an additional inspection. If the number of goods is finite, the consumer can find his optimal choice by inspecting not more than half the number of goods (or half of one plus the number, if the number is odd) because each inspection halves the number of goods yet needing inspection.

Can the consumer be assured that the price and quality will move together? This is a very simple signaling situation and, as in all signaling, it involves some game aspects. In the case of search goods, the consumer can reason that a firm that cheats (sets a price higher than that of other goods of comparable or higher quality) will easily be found out, and thus that the price can be taken to be ordinally related to quantity. There is still room here for the 'fly-by-night' firm that cheats and catches some consumers for whom the good offered is sufficiently close to optimal for them to search no further, but the expected payoff for the firm is not potentially very great.

Even in the search goods case, the cost of the search can be greatly reduced by the presence of additional information. If, for example, the consumer knows that the price per quality unit is constant, he needs but one inspection to determine that constant. He then faces a linear budget constraint of known slope, can determine his optimum quality package, and determine his chosen good immediately from its price.

**The effect of random price**
Still keeping to the context of search goods, let us now consider the effect of having price as a random variable. Models of search in which price is a random variable but the good is homogeneous are well known and have been the subject of much study.

We shall assume that the price per unit of quality ($p$) is a random variable with a distribution that is independent of the quality $q$. This is equivalent to assuming that the expected value and the standard deviation of the distribution of the price of the good as a package ($P$) are both proportional to the quality content. Even under this highly simplifying assumption, however, the problem does not reduce to that of the standard search model, of finding the lowest price for a good of predetermined quality. This is shown in Figure 10.1, in which different prices per unit of quality for goods within the group give rise to budget lines with different slopes. At price per quality unit $p$, the consumer's optimal choice is a good of quality $q$, but if he can find a lower price per quality unit $p'$, his optimal choice is no longer a good of quality $q$, but one of quality $q'$ – greater than $q$, presumably, because we can take $q$ to be a normal characteristic rather than an inferior one.

The analog of the Stigler search here is the inspection of what is offered at $n$ outlets and at what prices, after which the consumer chooses the $(p,q)$ com-

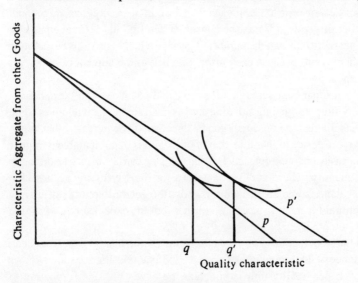

*Figure 10.1   Budget lines with different slopes*

bination that maximizes utility, with the number $n$ to be determined from the relationship of search costs and potential utilities. Inasmuch as prices are not known, the consumer has no easy way of choosing outlets selling goods within the general quality range in which he is likely to make his final choice. Thus a random choice of a store or outlet will turn up a $(p, q)$ combination that depends both on the distribution of prices and of qualities. Although it is not unreasonable to assume that the distribution of price (that is, the price per unit quality) is known on the basis of experience in market situations, the distribution of quality is another matter. If all sales outlets sell approximately the same number of units, the quality distribution over stores will be a function of the relative popularities of goods of different qualities – unlikely information for the consumer to possess.

The search problem is of course made much simpler if sales outlets sell a range of goods of different qualities rather than a single good, as implicitly assumed above, especially if (as seems reasonable enough) it can also be assumed that the store sells all goods at the same price per quality unit. In that case, the consumer can search for the store with the lowest prices and choose the quality that suits him within that store (provided it carries sufficient range), constituting something very close to the conventional search model.

In the context under discussion, there is no potential signaling function for price (that is, of the whole package), for the price can be found only by visiting the store, at which time the quality can be found by inspection.

## Prices as signals of quality

Under pure vertical product differentiation, prices (referring now to the price of the good as a package, not the price per unit of quality) become relevant as signals in the case of experience goods. For search goods, as we have seen, the signaling properties of price may reduce the cost of search, but they are ultimately dominated by the possibility of determining quality by inspection. Where quality cannot be determined by inspection, the price must be treated seriously as at least one of the pieces of evidence of the quality of the product.

Let us first consider a rather special case, but one with a long history in economics, in which price plays a particularly strong part not only in signaling quality but actually in determining it. This is of course the 'snob' or 'Veblen' good. In its purest form, this is a good valued for its exclusiveness or for its demonstration of the wealth of its owner, and it is a special case because it involves externalities. The higher the price of the good, the fewer the number of people who can afford it and the better it fulfills its role as a snob good, whatever its actual physical characteristics. In a sense, therefore, the price *is* the quality, and the physical properties are irrelevant to a large extent. They are not entirely irrelevant, however, because the market equilibrium for such a good requires that it cannot easily be supplied by competitors at a lower price to capture the market of aspiring but poorer snobs. Thus the good must be inherently costly to produce or have a natural or institutional limit on its supply. The signaling role of price is in generating the externalities – the high price is a signal to *other* consumers from the owner of the good, not from the seller to the potential buyer.

Our primary interest here is in the cases in which the quality is an objective characteristic of the good, in which the consumer is interested in the lowest price for a good of a particular quality, but in which he must consider using the price of the good as a signal containing quality information. In the context of experience goods, the consumer can determine quality only by purchase and consumption or attempt to estimate quality before purchase by the use of whatever information is available. Much depends on the feasibility and the cost of repeated trial consumption. If the item is consumed in small quantities at frequent intervals and costs only a small part of the budget (candy bars, for example), the situation is closely analogous to that of the search good. But if it is a major indivisible item (a house or a car), the cost of a trial-and-error search is prohibitive.

If the only information available to the potential buyer of an experience good is its price, he must attempt to assess the possibility of using that price as some index of quality. As has already been emphasized, any signaling situation is also a game situation in which the signal recipient (the buyer) must consider the potential payoff to the sender (the firm) of making different price quality offers. The special feature of the situation we are examining is of course that price is not a pure signal in the Spencian sense, nor is the consumer's reaction to price one of pure screening for quality. The primary function of the price to the seller is to generate revenue; the primary impact on the buyer is payment from the budget.

Consider a very simple situation in which goods are produced in only two qualities, high $(q_h)$ and low $(q_l)$, there are constant returns to scale in the production of both varieties, and the average and marginal costs are higher for the high-quality good. On the demand side, we suppose that the market is segmented into rich and poor consumers with incomes and preferences so different that changes in the relative prices of high- and low-quality goods cause no switching of consumers between qualities except that if the price of the high-quality good is not greater than that of the low-quality good, everyone will buy the high-quality good *if he can identify it*. There is assumed to be no information available to the buyer other than the price of the good, which is an experience good. In particular, no information passes between consumers so that the experience of other consumers with a particular good is unknown to a potential buyer. Finally, we shall make the case an extreme one by supposing that the good is a major purchase and thus that trial-and-error search will be prohibitive.

With competitive markets and full information as to price and quality there would be some equilibrium situation in which the high- and low-quality goods were sold at prices $P_h$, $P_l$, with $P_h > P_l$, and the quality of the goods could be gauged from the relative prices. Let us commence from this equilibrium and then suppose that the information has vanished from the memories of consumers. What incentives will the suppliers have to change their behavior?

1.  Producers of the high-quality good will have no incentive to change their pricing strategy in the first instance.
2.  Some producers of low-quality goods will realize that if they price their good at the high-quality price, consumers will believe it to be the high-quality good and will buy it. Because the low-quality good has lower production costs, such a move has its attractions, but it also means that the firm leaves an assured market for a situation involving some risk. However, the firm can eliminate the risk by selling the same good at both prices and thus be assured of at least the profit to be made in the low-quality market.
3.  In the extreme case, there will be a Gresham's Law tendency to have only the low-quality good actually produced and sold in the two markets at different prices.
4.  Any modification of the extreme conditions, such as allowing limited information to pass among consumers, or applying the analysis to goods when the individual will purchase the good more than once, will prevent the full Gresham's Law effect. But as long as information is less than complete there remains some probability that a good being sold at the higher price is really the lower-quality good.

Thus we see that price signaling is asymmetric. The lower price correctly identifies the lower-quality good, but the higher price identifies the higher-quality good only to some degree of probability, which could be as low as zero in an extreme case of non-information or as high as unity with complete information. From this we can conclude that *only the consumers interested in the higher-quality product will seek information additional to price.*

The conclusion obviously becomes fuzzier if there are many goods of different degrees of quality, but the general presumption is that the reliability of inferring that the higher-priced of two goods close together on the scale is the higher-quality good will diminish as we move up the scale. On the other hand, we can expect that the probability that the higher-priced good is the higher-quality good will increase with the number of goods available at prices between the two. Both presumptions depend on the possibility that cheaters may be found out either because there is some feedback between experienced buyers and potential new buyers or some repeat purchasing.

It is a necessary property of a signal that the cost of signaling, say, quality, should decrease with the actual amount of quality embodied. In the classic education examples[9] this cost relationship is independent of the market equilibrium because those of higher ability are assumed to find it easier to obtain qualifications whatever the relative wages of more and less skilled workers. In the price–quality case, any relationship that exists is imposed by the market itself – it is not *inherently* less costly for the high-quality seller to announce a high price than for the low-quality seller. Thus the signaling properties of price, which are secondary and not primary, are very closely tied to the market structure itself.

### Advertising as signaling

Nelson 1970, 1974 has discussed advertising as information in a variety of contexts and has shown that advertising is more important in industries selling experience goods than in those selling search goods, which is what we would expect from the information problems facing the consumer in the two cases. We are interested here in the rather narrow context of how advertising fits together with price to give a joint signal of quality.

In a recent paper Johnsen 1976 has attempted a formal analysis of 'informationless' advertising (that is, advertising that does not itself make any statement as to quality) in the tradition of contemporary signaling theory, using a simple two-quality market for a good of the experience kind. The Johnsen model has some features that make it rather difficult to mesh fully with the approach here, but it does lead to the conclusion that an equilibrium is possible if consumers accept the *volume* of advertising (its content, if any, is irrelevant) as a signal positively correlated with quality, but not if it is believed to be negatively correlated. This is consistent with our conclusion in the preceding section that the potential buyers of the lower-quality product need no information other than price and thus that the sellers of this product would be wasting money by bothering to advertise, although the reasoning in the two analyses is considerably different. In both cases it is assumed that advertising does not reach customers who would not otherwise buy the product at all, nor does its content influence consumers in any way.

Real-world advertising is sometimes of the contentless variety, but it is often of the kind that makes claims for the product. In the present context, advertising with content would be advertising that not only identified the product and its price but made a claim that it was of a particular quality. In the two-quality model advertising is unnecessary for the lower-quality good and so any advertisement would necessarily be for the higher-quality good, in which case explicit mention of the quality would not be necessary. With more than two qualities, however, it would be necessary for the advertiser to identify the quality level being claimed.[10]

To what extent will firms find it advantageous to cheat in their quality claims? This depends very much on the general structure of the market situation. In the most extreme case in which there is no transfer of information gained from experience between consumers and each consumer will buy only once, there is the same incentive to cheat on quality claims as on price signals – ultimately, we are likely to reach a situation in which only the low-quality good is actually produced but is marketed at both a high price with a high-quality claim and at a low price with no quality claim. The quality claim simply becomes irrelevant. If there is some cost to cheating then, as in the price case, the quality claim can be accepted with some probability that it is true.

The real issue when cheating carries a probable cost is whether an advertising claim of quality adds to the information already conveyed by price. This will obviously be so if the probability of the firm's incurring costs through false price signals is not perfectly correlated with the probability of incurring costs through quality-claim cheating. The seller of the low-quality product has four cheating options – he can claim the high quality but offer his good at the low price, he can claim the low quality but offer the good at the high price, he can claim the high quality and offer the good at the high price, or he can offer the good at the high price with no explicit claim.

Only the last two of these options are potentially viable strategies. They differ to the extent that cheating on quality can be found out more easily, or will be more costly if found out than cheating on price, or if the costs are borne by different agents. There are many realistic circumstances under which these conditions will be satisfied if the same product can be identified under different marketing conditions, as in the case of brand-name goods. One is that there are externalities in quality cheating so that, for example, all goods identified with the manufacturer become downgraded if a consumer finds cheating on one item, while overpricing has less externality effect. It is not altogether unrealistic to suppose that because prices fluctuate with market conditions while quality is built into a product, consumers will give fewer bad marks for a good that is overpriced than for one that is below the quality claimed. Finally, if the manufacturer advertises the quality but the store sets the price – a very common situation – cheating by the manufacturer will lose sales over many outlets, while overpricing will lose sales only to the single store.

The seller who plans to cheat on price under the conditions mentioned above will run a greater risk of loss if he cheats on the quality claim as well. His preferred strategy will be to avoid making a quality claim. On the other hand because consumers know the seller is taking a greater risk in cheating on the quality claim than on price, they will choose a seller who quotes the higher-quality price *and* claims the good to be of the higher quality over a seller who merely quotes the higher price. Thus once quality claims enter the picture at all, those who purport to be selling the higher-quality product will be forced by competition to make the claim explicit.

Thus there are some grounds for supposing that the advertising of quality claims (or advertising at all, in the two-quality case) does add information to that implicit in the price. The probability that a seller offering a good at the high-quality price and claiming it to be the higher-quality good will be cheating is less than the probability that the seller offering the good at the high-quality price without making an explicit claim will be doing so. It is the willingness to make a refutable claim that provides the signal rather than the form of the claim itself. If the claim is not refutable, as when there is no feedback between consumers and the good is a one-shot purchase, or if the good is of the 'hidden property' kind, then advertising claims add no information. Note that the more the consumer must rely on the unsubstantiated claims of the sellers, the less reliable those claims are.

### Other information and signals

The two information parameters discussed so far are those provided by the seller but tempered by market forces. The other potential information sources are family and friends or professional assessments by presumably objective experts, such as those by government bureaus, in certain consumer publications, or by paid assessors or valuers. As shown previously, the higher the quality of product in which the consumer is interested, the more the risk in accepting the seller's signals and the more likely the consumer will seek reliable information elsewhere. Since the quality range can be expected to be positively correlated with income, one would expect the market for consumer reports (or even for virtually free government ratings) to be among people in the middle and upper incomes, not among lower-income groups. The use of outside information will also depend on the ease with which sellers' claims can be directly verified, and thus will be greater for experience goods than search goods and greater for one-shot purchases than for those things that will be purchased more often.

The reliability of seller-orientated signals can of course be increased by influencing the market context. Laws against deceptive advertising (if it is ever legally possible to define 'deception' in relation to claims of quality) can be marginally useful, but publicity on 'cheating' is probably more valuable for the consumer than suits by the Federal Trade Commission (FTC). Anything that increases the risk of being found out or the costs incurred by cheating will increase the reliability of seller-provided signals to the consumer.

### Horizontal product differentiation

The consumer information problem is most acute in the case of horizontal product differentiation in which products differ in the proportions of characteristics and no product has more of all characteristics than another. This occurs in the traditional product differentiation context in which a consumer (having already chosen the quality range in which he is interested) must choose between goods of approximately equal 'quality' but with these differences in characteristics proportions. Such differentiation exists because individuals differ in preferences, and different individuals will prefer goods with different mixes of characteristics.

The full information analysis of this case is easy enough and is given in Lancaster 1966, 1971. The consumer is assumed to know the technology that gives the characteristics proportions of the goods and then can choose which good or combination of goods is optimal for him. Our interest here is in how the consumer can obtain information as to these characteristics proportions and what signals the seller might provide.[11]

Inasmuch as we are concerned with goods of approximately the same 'quality' (the definition of which now becomes a difficult matter in itself), they can be expected to sell at approximately the same price if there is a reasonably uniform distribution of consumers over the preference spectrum and price conveys no information in the horizontal case.

What about advertising? We might assume sellers would attempt to provide some guidance as to where their product lies in the goods spectrum, but this may not necessarily be so. Consider a two-characteristics model in which goods can be arranged horizontally in the order of the ratio of the two characteristics and in which the spectrum of preferences is uniform in the sense that the number of consumers who would choose each of $n$ goods spaced evenly over the goods spectrum is the same. Suppose that there are only two goods $A$ and $B$, with $A$ to the left of $B$ on the spectrum, and such that with full information half the consumers would choose $A$ and half $B$. Now let us suppose that there is no information as to the characteristics and consumers assign equal probability to $A$ being to the left of $B$ and $B$ being to the left of $A$. Thus, of the consumers interested in the left half of the spectrum, half will correctly choose $A$ and half mistakenly choose $B$. On the right portion, half the consumers will correctly choose $B$ and half incorrectly choose $A$. If $A$ advertises that it is really to the left of $B$ on the spectrum, it will lose as many customers from the right half as it gains in the left half. With a uniform distribution of preferences, both firms may do as well when the consumers are in total ignorance as when they are fully informed, and there is no reason for them to emphasize their true place on the spectrum.

In the case above, there is a clear *social* gain from having the consumers fully informed because those making the incorrect choice of product are in a suboptimal state. Because there is no private gain to the firms, however, in correctly identifying the place of the different products on the spectrum, there seems to be a good case for having the appropriate information provided by an outside agency. One would probably argue that if the class of goods involved was purchased by all consumers, the information should be provided by the government, but if the goods were purchased by only a small group of consumers, the information could be provided by a private consumer magazine or similar information source.

The situation is somewhat different if the distribution of preferences is not uniform. Correct identification of the place of the good could then gain more customers than it loses – but the reverse is also possible, in which case it would pay the firm to misinform deliberately as to its true position. Thus there seems to be no general presumption that firms will wish to identify their places on the spectrum nor, if they identify it, to do so truthfully.

Advertising of horizontally differentiated products, which occurs widely, tends to do what we would expect from the above considerations – avoid horizontal comparisons. Most commonly, perhaps, it does this by trying to make the horizontal into a vertical by attempting to persuade potential buyers that its mix of characteristics is more desirable (for everyone, not just one segment of consumers) than those of other differentiates, or by stressing those character-istics in which it is particularly strong compared with alternatives, while remaining silent on those characteristics that it possesses to a lesser extent (or those that are undesirable ones).

Thus although the information problem is particularly acute with horizon-tally differentiated goods, the analysis is very simple: there is little incentive for the sellers to provide the appropriate information. Insofar as they do provide information as to the place of a good in the spectrum, there is no particular bias toward cheating in general – but no bias toward the truth either. Any such infor-mation is more likely to reflect the firm's market research as to where higher densities of consumers occur on the preference spectrum than anything else.

## Notes

1. Originally presented in 1976 and published in the delayed conference volume Galatin, M. and Leiter, R.D. (eds), *Economics of Information*, Boston, Martinus Nijhof, 1991.
2. On the production side, information on the technology is probably the main problem except under imperfect competition where it is information on the demand function.
3. Stigler 1961 is the seminal paper of a considerable literature in which the work of Rothschild 1973, 1974 has been of particular note.
4. That is, exact price information. Vaguer statements, such as 'the cheapest in town' are less easily refutable.
5. With seminal work by Spence 1973, 1974 and work by other writers including Riley 1975, Stiglitz 1975, Salop 1973. The initial applications were to labor markets.
6. See Lancaster 1975.
7. An interesting pursuit of the point is given in Auld 1972.
8. See Rothschild 1974, for example.
9. As in Spence 1973.
10. With only two goods, there is little problem in making a quality claim ('high' or 'low' or, more likely 'high' and 'super high'). With many goods, there is a real problem in formulating a quality claim unless it is the highest or lowest. See Lancaster 1976.
11. We assume that the characteristics proportions are not determinable by simple inspection. Note that in the multi-characteristics case, the division into 'search' and 'experience' goods is not clear-cut because some of the characteristics may be determined by inspection, others only by consumption.

# 11 The economics of product variety[1]

## Introduction

This paper attempts to survey the problem of product variety from the economist's point of view. The term *product variety* is being used here to refer to the number of variants within a specific *product group*, corresponding broadly to the number of 'brands' as the term is used in the marketing literature or the number of 'models' in consumer durable markets. Pure conglomeration, in which firms expand the number of product groups but not the variety within a group, is not considered.

Implicit or explicit theories of product variety are to be found at various points in economics, management theory, and marketing. In each context, the view of product variety and the kind of questions being asked about it are rather different from those in others. In economic theory, for example, the emphasis placed by a general equilibrium theorist is on the socially optimal degree of product variety, given some welfare criterion, and on the relationship of the degree of variety generated by the market to this. Economists primarily interested in market structure theory will tend to emphasize competitive relationships, product differentiation and product variety as decision variables for the firm, and the types of market equilibria that result.

An attempt is made in this survey to do two main things. One is to give a broad overall picture of how analytical economists have approached the study of product variety; the other is to touch base with the large number of contributions that have been made to specific problems or to the development of particular models. The study is confined to models in which product variety is the outcome of an optimizing, strategic, or competitive process, determined by the structure of the system and its parameters. Purely descriptive studies as to the actual degree of product variety in specific markets are not considered, although some reference is made to empirical studies relevant to particular analytical models. There is a considerable amount of ongoing work (especially in relation to oligopoly models), but discussion has been confined to work already published. With the exception of certain classic papers, almost all the work discussed has been published since 1975.

## Overview

In a market economy, it is clear that variety within a product group will persist only if one or more of the following is true:

- Each individual consumer seeks variety in his own consumption.

- Different consumers want different variants because tastes vary.
- Individual firms can increase profits by producing a variety of models.
- Firms can increase profits by differentiating their products from those of their competitors.

Note that none of the above (nor any combination of them) is *sufficient* to guarantee variety in the market.

Thus there are four contexts in which to consider questions concerning the degree of product variety:

1. *The individual consumer.* How many of the available variants within a single product group will the individual choose? What determines the choice?
2. *The individual firm.* What degree of product variety is it most profitable for the firm to offer in a given competitive situation?
3. *Market equilibrium.* What degree of product variety will result from the operation of the market within a particular competitive structure?
4. *The social optimum.* What degree of product variety is optimal for society on some criterion? How is this related to the market equilibrium?

Since the analysis of product variety often involves considering several of these questions together, it seems useful to give a brief overview of each before proceeding to more detailed discussion.

*The individual consumer*

The economist's traditional model of consumer choice, based on strictly quasi-concave preferences (smooth indifference contours strictly convex to the origin) and infinitely divisible products, was really devised to describe broad choices between product groups rather than within groups. It poses some problems when used to describe intra-group choices.

Strict convexity implies an inherent preference for variety, since it asserts that, for some range of prices, there is a combination of $n$ goods that is preferred to any combination of fewer goods which costs no more. This is reasonable in describing broad choice over bundles of aggregate goods such as food and clothing. When applied literally to choice over a group of similar but differentiated goods, it predicts that the individual would consume every product in the group and every brand or variant of that product for some range of relative prices.[2]

The traditional preference structure is preserved in models using the 'representative consumer', a hypothetical single consumer whose behavior becomes that of the market when magnified sufficiently. Such a consumer necessarily consumes all varieties actually sold. Although widely used in empirical demand studies and in one class of studies in product variety,[3] such models have no well-defined place for product positioning and provide no basis for a theory of product choice and product design.

At the other extreme are the locational and locational analog models in which the individual consumer buys only a single product in the group, choosing that variant which best fits his purposes. The consumer is assumed to have a most preferred or 'ideal' location of a good in a space of product characteristics, his choice between available goods being based on a balance of prices versus distance from the ideal. In many such models, *ad hoc* assumptions, such as a fixed inelastic demand for one unit of the chosen product,[4] are made, but others use fully developed demand functions.[5] The reason why the consumer must choose only one of the goods is not always explicit,[6] but can be taken to be a property of the goods themselves (such as indivisibility) rather than of preferences.[7]

Because there are few, if any, real markets in which there are individuals who consume all available brands but there are many in which individuals do buy more than one, there have been some recent attempts to combine features of the two types of models described above, with each consumer choosing a subset of goods rather than a single good.[8]

### The individual firm

Serious analysis of product variety in multi-product firms, in the sense of attempts to explain the motives for producing a particular number of products, is quite recent in the economics literature. The approaches to the subject so far can be divided into three types:

1. Those centered on the production side, emphasizing cost advantages from joint production or economies of scope.[9]
2. Those centered on the demand side, emphasizing the balance between the increased revenue possible from a more varied product line and the loss of scale economies in the production of each variant.[10]
3. Those centered on strategic considerations, especially pre-emption in the product space as a deterrent to entry.[11]

### Market equilibrium

The potential degree of product variety in the market is limited to the smaller of (*a*) the maximum number of variants which consumers in the aggregate are willing to buy, or (*b*) the number of variants which the suppliers in the aggregate are willing and able to produce, given the technology.

While a finite number of market segments is commonly assumed in the marketing literature, economists' models of product variety have almost all assumed that the aggregate potential *demand* for variety was unlimited (or not limiting in the analysis), either because each individual was interested in unlimited variety (representative consumer models) or because there was a sufficiently wide variation of individual tastes when each preferred a single ideal good.

Thus the degree of product variety has been perceived as limited only on the supply side. Almost all analysis has been of groups made up of single-product firms, so that the degree of product variety is determined simply by the number of firms, provided no two firms produce products perceived to be identical. This is true of both of the main classes of market variety models, representative consumer (neo-Chamberlinian) and location-analog or characteristics (neo-Hotelling) models, and of almost all other kinds.

The analysis of variety in the case of a multi-product monopoly, the most fully examined case of market equilibrium with multi-product firms, has strong analytical similarities to the problem of determining the socially optimum, discussed below.

*Optimal variety*

The fundamental structure of all optimal variety problems, for the individual firm as well as society, is the interplay of two elements in the economy – the existence of a gain from variety and the existence of scale economies of some kind.[12] If there are no economies of scale associated with individual product variants (in distribution as well as in production), then it is optimal to custom-produce to everyone's chosen specification. If there is no gain from variety and there are scale economies, then it is clearly optimal to produce only a single variant if those economies are unlimited, or only such variety as uses scale economies to the limit (all products at minimum average cost output). Most cases involve a balance of some variety against some scale economies, the solution depending on the preference properties of consumers, the scale properties in production and distribution, and the way in which the social welfare criterion is derived from individual preferences.

Different criteria and assumptions can lead to quite different conclusions. Chamberlin 1933 concluded, for example, that monopolistic competition would always lead to more products than socially optimal (a view that was almost universally held until the 1970s), yet Dixit and Stiglitz 1977, using a simplified general equilibrium model that was wholly in the spirit of Chamberlin, concluded that the market would always give too few products. In other analyses, such as those of Spence 1976 and Lancaster 1979, the relationship could go either way depending on circumstances.

The optimal choice of product variety for a monopolist is based on a decision process rather similar to that in determining the social optimum, since a potential social gain from variety can usually be translated into higher monopoly revenue from a more varied product line, to be balanced against higher costs from smaller outputs of each variant.

## Monopolistic competition

The theory of product variety in economics began as an incidental byproduct of analysis primarily concerned with deviations from the competitive model in prices and numbers of firms. It has a dual lineage, with one branch descending from Chamberlin's work on monopolistic competition (Chamberlin 1933), which has been a textbook staple. The other, tracing its ancestry to Hotelling's model of spatial competition (Hotelling 1929), is somewhat less well known and is discussed in a later section.

Each Chamberlinian firm produces and sells a single product which is taken to be unique to itself, but the firm is nevertheless a member of a well-defined group or industry and not a monopolist in the classical sense. The group exists because its members share similar cost and production conditions and because there is a relatively high degree of demand substitutability among the products of its members. A key element in the Chamberlin model is that demand substitutability is evenly spread over the group, so that there are no close rivalries between particular pairs of firms or within small subgroups which would give rise to oligopolistic behavior. For a given number of firms, the equilibrium is Nash in prices with every firm assuming zero reaction by other firms to its own price changes. The number of firms, and thus the degree of product variety within the group, is determined by the result of free entry. Each entry introduces a new product into the group and, since this is assumed to be an equally good substitute for all existing products, the demand for each existing product falls a little and profits fall. Entry ceases when the demand curves for all products have fallen to the point where it is tangent to the average cost curve, with price equal to average cost and marginal revenue equal to marginal cost. Since the demand curve for the firm's specific product is downward sloping, average cost is falling at the equilibrium and so the production of each firm is less than its minimum cost output. In the strictly symmetrical case used in the traditional exposition, with firms having identical cost structures and identically structured market shares, the degree of product variety (= number of firms) is primarily determined by:

1. The extent of scale economies in output – the smaller these, the smaller the minimum average cost output, the larger the equilibrium number of firms and the greater the number of products.
2. The 'intensity' of product differentiation, in the sense of the substitutability of products within the group as seen by consumers. The more intense the differentiation (the smaller the elasticity of substitution between the goods), the steeper the slope of the firms' demand curves, the higher the margin of price over marginal cost, the smaller the equilibrium output relative to minimum average cost, and thus the greater the number of firms and products.

Since Chamberlin and his immediate followers took the optimal degree of product variety to be the number of products that would enable output per firm to achieve the minimum average cost level (thus considering only the scale economies and ignoring the gain from variety), the market equilibrium was perceived as necessarily leading to more variety than was optimal. The more intense the differentiation, the greater the deviation from optimality would be. Chamberlin's writings are much richer than suggested by the simple textbook exposition, but he was not able to give a satisfactory derivation of the demand for a newly introduced brand from a consumer choice process.

### Modern neo-Chamberlinian models

The feature that distinguishes a model as 'neo-Chamberlinian' is that of dispersed product rivalry, with any price change or product innovation viewed as impacting more or less evenly over all products in the group with no close oligopolistic rivalry between any small subset of firms.

The analysis of Dixit and Stiglitz 1977 is in the spirit of the original Chamberlin analysis but is a fully defined general equilibrium model with demand properly derived from maximization of a defined utility function. It uses the representative consumer approach and simple cost functions, but the simplicity permits derivation of demand from underlying utility and explicit determination of how particular parameters affect both the market equilibrium and the socially optimal degree of product variety.

The utility function is taken to be separable between the group and all other goods. Within the group, all goods (and potential goods) are equal substitutes for each other in the simplest version, with constant elasticity of substitution.[13] This has the property that, for given prices and income, the consumer is always better off spending $1/n$th of his group budget on each of $n$ goods, than spending $1/(n-1)$th of the budget on each of $n-1$ goods, implying an insatiable taste for variety.

Firms are assumed to be identical except as to their products (only one per firm), with the same simple cost functions determined by a constant marginal cost plus a fixed cost. An important limitation on the Dixit–Stiglitz and other neo-Chamberlinian models is that firms make no product choice – it is as though each firm, as it enters the group, is assigned a product by random choice (without replacement) from an urn containing blueprints for all possible products. In particular, no mechanism is provided for firms to contemplate and then accept or reject the possibility of producing the same product as an existing firm.

As in the original Chamberlin analysis, each firm is assumed to act as though it has zero effect on any other single firm, operating with a *perceived* demand curve rather than the true one.[14]

Entry will occur until all firms have zero profit, determining the equilibrium value of the number of firms and thus of product varieties.

This equilibrium degree of product variety will be greater:

1.  The smaller the economies of scale (due here to the existence of fixed costs).
2.  The less effective are goods in the group as substitutes for each other.
3.  The larger the market, measured by aggregate income, and the more important the group.

Note that, as the size of the market increases without limit, the number of goods does also, but the monopoly markup of price over marginal cost does not change. That is, the market does not converge to perfect competition but preserves its monopolistic competition structure.

Since consumers are identical and preferences are homothetic, the social welfare function can be treated as simply a magnified version of the individual utility. On this basis the model can be shown to imply that the socially optimal degree of product variety is greater than the variety generated by the working of the market.

A neo-Chamberlinian model with the opposite welfare result from the Chamberlinian one is less paradoxical than it may seem – the reason is that the original Chamberlin analysis assumed there was no welfare gain from variety as such, while the Dixit–Stiglitz version implies unbounded gains from variety for every individual. Thus Chamberlin understated the benefits of variety and Dixit–Stiglitz overstates them.

*Neo-Chamberlinian variations*
In Hart 1985a,b and Perloff and Salop 1985, Chamberlin-type structures are generated without representative consumers or the necessity of anyone buying everything. Neither model is fully developed from a standard consumer choice mechanism, and so both contain important *ad hoc* assumptions.[15]

Perloff and Salop assume that each individual has a vector of relative values (expressed in dollars per unit) which he places on each of the available brands, relative values that are invariant with respect to the quantities consumed. Given the prices, the consumer chooses his 'best buy' – the brand for which the net surplus of his valuation over the price is greatest – and purchases only that. The vectors of relative values are randomly distributed over a large population so that, in aggregate, the demands for all brands are the same when prices are the same. As the price of one good rises, it becomes the best buy for fewer and fewer individuals, giving the demand function. The more 'intense' the preferences (the larger the gap between the value of the most preferred good and the next), the less elastic the demand.

The structure is Chamberlinian in the sense that every good competes symmetrically with every other. Firms produce a unique single product, so the degree of variety is determined by the outcome of the free entry process. Perloff and Salop do not relate the market equilibrium degree of variety to any optimal concept, so the results cannot be compared with those of, say, Dixit and Stiglitz.

Perhaps the most interesting result in this analysis is the attempt to examine the effects of imperfect information. If each consumer is aware of only $k$ brands, for example, then the equilibrium price is that for a $k$-brand market, even if the true number of goods is $n > k$. Although the authors do not make the point, it is obvious that a free entry equilibrium will then result in a greater overall degree of variety than in the full information case.

The Hart model has similarities to the Perloff–Salop model, but is somewhat more elaborate. The basic assumptions concerning consumer preferences are that

- in the overall group of $N$ potential goods there is a subgroup of $m$ goods which are relevant to a particular individual
- all other goods in the group are useless to the individual (give zero utility)
- different individuals have different relevant subgroups, and all possible subgroups of $m$ goods are represented equally in the aggregate population.

In general, each consumer will buy up to $m$ different brands. If the number of firms is $n < N$ (as assumed always to be the case), some individuals will not have all their particular $m$ goods actually available. When an $(n + 1)$th good is introduced, it will be a desired but hitherto missing good for consumers having all possible combinations of other goods in their sets, and thus the new good will substitute uniformly for all other goods in the aggregate, including goods not yet available. Thus there is a Chamberlinian demand structure in the aggregate, although individuals consume only a few of the brands.

Hart does not derive any propositions concerning the degree of variety from this general model, being primarily concerned with the existence of equilibrium and whether the system preserves its monopolistic competitive character as the size of the economy becomes very large (yes). In a more specialized version (Hart 1985b) in which the individual regards all brands in his subgroup of $m$ as perfect substitutes for each other and thus chooses only the best buy, a comparison is made between the market equilibrium degree of variety and the optimal degree. The conclusion is that the market might generate more brands than optimal, or it might generate less, depending on values of the various parameters.

Although these models can generate uniformly distributed substitutability without multiple brand consumption by individuals, they carry a built-in presumption that a new entrant might just as well choose its product at random, provided it was not being produced by an existing firm. Such models cannot provide a basis for the analysis of problems of brand positioning and product design, or of the degree of differentiation as opposed to the number of brands. The solution of problems like these requires an analysis with some concept of location (perhaps in an abstract space) – models that can be classified as neo-Hotelling rather than neo-Chamberlinian.

**Using locational concepts**

Hotelling's classic paper (Hotelling 1929) introduced the idea of firms competing on more than one level – on both price and location. The model introduced was that of a one-dimensional space (Main Street in his basic example) in which firms could locate and sell products that were identical except as to the location of the sales outlet.

Potential buyers were assumed to be uniformly distributed in the space but identical otherwise, to be intending to buy a fixed quantity of the good, and to have a transport cost that was a linear function of the distance between their location and that of the sale. Each buyer would assess the full cost of buying from each outlet (price plus cost of transport) and choose the least cost one. For a consumer located between two outlets, the choice would depend on both the relative locations and the relative prices. Since the consumers were identical except as to location, if any consumer chose outlet A, then so would all consumers located between him and the outlet. Thus the market for each firm or outlet was a connected segment of the space with the firm's location somewhere in it. The edge of the market in the direction of another firm was defined by the location of the dividing customer, to whom the delivered cost from each firm was the same. If a firm raised its price, customers on and close to the fringes of the market would shift to the next firm in that direction. Since individual demands were inelastic, the total demand for a firm's product was directly proportional to the width of its market.[16] Firms were assumed to have identical costs, to have free entry, and to be able to choose and vary their location and price at will.

Hotelling examined the possible equilibrium for the duopoly case in the above structure. He concluded that the two firms would locate close to each other near the center (principle of minimum differentiation), but that conclusion, due essentially to boundary effects (as shown later), is much less important than the framework created for product differentiation theory using locational ideas.

In a large market *without* boundary effects (often depicted as a circular road as in Salop 1979), a symmetric equilibrium for the Hotelling model exists[17] and has the property that market equilibrium gives more than the optimal number of firms, the optimality criterion being to minimize production plus transport cost while supplying everyone with his one unit.

*The characteristics approach*

While a theory of real spatial location is a topic of importance in itself, the expansion of the locational framework to cover 'location' in non-spatial contexts has been largely responsible for the recent revival of interest in models of the Hotelling type. Although Hotelling himself suggested that the location results might be applied to products differentiated in non-spatial respects, there was no full formal structure for doing so prior to the development of the characteristics approach.[18]

In this analysis, goods are perceived as bundles of 'characteristics'. These have similarities to, but are somewhat more specific than, the 'attributes' of marketing and psychology. The characteristics are taken to be objective and measurable in the basic version. Consumers' preferences are assumed to be over collections of characteristics and not over collections of goods *per se*, the role of goods being analogous to inputs in a consumption process with the demand for goods derived from the demand for characteristics. Within this framework a large number of different situations can be modeled according to whether goods can or cannot be combined in consumption to give characteristics combinations different from those of either good separately, whether such combining is linear or not, whether the number of relevant characteristics is larger or smaller than the number of available goods containing them, and so on.

The strict neo-Hotelling models[19] of monopolistic competition are built, implicitly or explicitly, on the special case in which consumption is not combinable within the group of goods being considered and the consumer chooses only one of the available brands. In the simplest versions the goods group is defined on the basis of two relevant characteristics so that the relative quantities of the two characteristics can be mapped into a one-dimensional spectrum analogous to the Hotelling 'street'. The 'location' of the firm is then given by the specification (characteristics mix) of the good it chooses to produce. The 'location' of the consumer is a rather more complex concept, which can be expressed as his 'ideal good' or 'most preferred specification' and is the specification of the good that he would prefer if goods of all possible specifications were available on equal terms. The analog of 'transport cost' is the diminution in the consumer's valuation of a good as the 'distance' between its specification and that of the consumer's ideal good increases.

Although it is common for authors to assert that their location analysis can be directly converted into an analog in characteristics space,[20] there are some considerable methodological problems involved. These are discussed in Lancaster 1979. Note that the simple symmetric Hotelling model described earlier, when converted by direct analog into characteristics space,[21] gives the following results:

1. The market equilibrium number of products is larger, the larger the market, the less the degree of substitutability between products in the group (the analog of transport cost), and the smaller the fixed costs in production.
2. The market equilibrium generates more than the optimum number of products.

Qualitatively (although not necessarily quantitatively) these are essentially the same results as those of the basic Chamberlin model. Before proceeding to the more general neo-Hotelling models, however, it is necessary to comment on the fate of the principle of minimum differentiation since it has important implications for product differentiation theory.

### Product clustering

The basic Hotelling proposition was that the equilibrium competitive location for two firms in a linear market with distinct boundaries at each end and uniformly distributed customers would be as close together as possible without actually coinciding, and in the center of the market area. The basic argument was that, if they were close together but not at the center then the market would be larger for the firm on one side (east, for example) than on the other, since each firm's market would extend out to the boundary on its own side. Then it would pay for the west firm to jump over to the east of its rival, continuing the process until the markets were equal on both sides. If the firms were not close together, then one firm might increase its market by moving closer to the other. When extended beyond pure geographical location, the proposition is concerned with the degree of differentiation rather than the number of goods, answering the question: if there are two firms in the market, will their best strategy be to choose products which are very similar or very different?[22]

The Hotelling result is a fragile one and was the subject of debate in the 1930s and 1940s. Revival of the scrutiny in recent years[23] has given the definitive answer to applicability of the result: minimum differentiation is not the general outcome to be expected from spatial oligopoly but is a special result.

It was shown early (Lerner and Singer 1937) that arguments that may hold for two firms do not necessarily hold for three. If a third firm enters, it will be optimal for it to move close to one of the existing firms. But then there will be a firm flanked by two others with almost no market. It will move to the outside, leaving a new inside firm, and so on, with no equilibrium. Eaton and Lipsey 1975 examined the *n*-firm case in some detail and showed that there could be no equilibrium with three firms, but there could be equilibria with more than three, typically involving pairings of firms at certain locations but with separation between the pairs. Expansion of the space dimension from one to two does not remove the three-firm equilibrium problem (Shaked 1975).

In D'Aspremont et al. 1979, it was shown that a two-firm Nash equilibrium in prices might not exist if the firms were located close together, since either firm could attempt to gain the other's market by undercutting. Closeness increases market width, but at the expense of greater sensitivity to price competition.[24] Thus the attempt to find a locational equilibrium by moving close together would destabilize an existing price equilibrium. Shaked and Sutton 1982 argue that a three-stage process (entry, product quality, then price) will result in differentiation, not clustering.

Hotelling assumed inelastic individual demands, so that a firm's sales were determined only by the width of its market area and were independent of its location within that area – hence the location very close to one end of the area as implied by minimum differentiation causes no revenue loss. If the quantity purchased is sensitive to distance in real or characteristics space, the outcome can be very much changed, and there is then an incentive for the firms to separate so that each is closer to the center of its own market area. See Salop 1979, Lancaster 1979, Graitson 1982, Economides 1984, for this and also for the case in which there are no boundary effects and the centrist forces vanish.

Recent location or location-analog models have tended to embody assumptions which differ from Hotelling's, particularly in removing boundary effects (by circular or infinitely long markets) and in taking demand to be sensitive to distance between the location of the good and the consumer, in either real space or some goods spectrum. Such models generate equilibria in which firms are evenly spaced and not clustered at all. For examples see Lancaster 1979, Salop 1979.

It is still possible to have clustering effects without the highly special Hotelling assumptions. The case so obvious that it is often forgotten is that in which consumers are clustered geographically or consumer preferences are clustered in characteristics space, instead of being uniformly distributed as most of the theoretical models assume. Clustering may occur in geographical space if there is also differentiation between the goods in characteristics at some other level (de Palma et al. 1985), and there is a variety of search cost and other imperfect information arguments that can explain many types of clustering, particularly the geographical clustering of stores. Studies designed to test for clustering in characteristics space, notably Shaw 1982 and Swann 1985, have tended to find it.

### Locational analog models

These are models in which locational or geographical space is replaced by a virtual space of goods or their characteristics. They are variously known as 'locational analog models', 'neo-Hotelling models', 'characteristics models', 'Lancastrian models' or 'address models'.[25]

The most elaborate of the earlier models in this category is that in Lancaster 1979, and this is representative of the approach. In this analysis, characteristics are taken to be measurable and a good is defined by its 'specification', the bundle of characteristics contained in one unit of the good. It is assumed that all goods in the group under consideration have the same characteristics but in different proportions, and that the set of characteristics relevant for both manufacturing and consumer choices is a small subset of all the actual physical characteristics. The sharing of common characteristics is what defines the group. For the basic model it is assumed that a subset of two characteristics ('speed' and 'size', for example, or 'power' and 'fidelity') is sufficient, so that potential combinations of characteristics can be represented along a line spectrum, giving the analog to the Hotelling analysis.

Each consumer is presumed to have a 'most preferred' (or 'ideal') goods specification. If his most preferred good is not available, it requires $h(x)$ units of a good at distance $x$ from the ideal to be equivalent to a unit of ideal good, where $h(x)$ is an increasing strictly convex function with $h(0) = 1$. The function $h(x)$ is referred to as the 'compensating function', since it shows how distance from the ideal can be compensated for by increased quantity. It is assumed throughout that all individuals have the same compensating function, individual differences being confined to their choice of ideal goods.

The model is based on a two-sector economy with a differentiated sector and a single undifferentiated outside good. Within the differentiated sector, products are taken to be non-combinable.[26] Combinable products are those that can readily be mixed or consumed together to give characteristics proportions between those of the components (sugar and lemon juice). Half a Mercedes combined with half a Hyundai does not, however, give the characteristics of a mid-level automobile – automobiles are non-combinable. Due to the non-combinability, each consumer chooses only one good in the group, the choice based on the relationship between the price and the divergence from ideal specification of each good actually available.

The utility function is modeled as being of constant elasticity of substitution (CES) form in two subutilities, one from the outside good, the other from the group, with substitution elasticity $\sigma$. The individual demand function which is derived has the expected properties, demand decreasing in price and in distance from the ideal (provided $\sigma > 1$, as assumed). All consumers are considered to have the same form of utility function, but express their individuality in their choice of ideal specification.

Aggregate demand for a good is the sum of all individual demands from all consumers within the market area. Its properties depend on those of the compensating function (how the utility of a good varies with its deviation from the consumer's ideal specification), the individual demand functions, and the distribution of consumers over the space. No simple expression can be written for the aggregate demand function even when consumers are identical and uniformly distributed over the space. It can be shown that the elasticity of demand is never less than $\sigma$ and increases with increasing proximity to other goods in characteristics space, approaching infinite (perfect substitutability) as goods become very close.

If there are no boundary effects, firms have identical cost structures, and consumers are uniformly distributed, it can be shown that there will be a symmetrical monopolistic competition equilibrium in which firms will choose to produce products different from those of other firms and in which the firm's product choice is fully explained as an optimal choice. The equilibrium degree of product variety generated by the market is then, as in all monopolistic competition models, determined by the number of firms at which excess profit per firm drops to zero.

The equilibrium product variety will be greater

1. The smaller the economies of scale.
2. The lower the substitutability between group goods and outside goods.
3. The more important the group in the economy (share of total expenditure).

These are somewhat similar to the properties of the neo-Chamberlinian models except for one very important point. Whereas a larger market, measured by total consumer expenditure, unambiguously predicts more variety in Chamberlinian models, it does not necessarily do so here. This is because there is a distinction in this case between the width of the market (the degree of dispersion of preferences) and the depth of the market (density of consumer purchasing power at each location). It is possible for the market with the larger consumer expenditure to have less variety because it may have consumers with less diverse preferences but more of them.

The relationship between the market equilibrium and the optimum is more complex and more difficult to establish in this model than in simpler ones. In terms of the criterion most similar to general usage in the monopolistic competition literature, the market will generate more than the optimal degree of variety under most circumstances. It is possible, however, that the market might produce too few products if the degree of substitutability between group goods and outside goods is relatively high.

Although the market in question is that of a multi-product oligopoly, we might note Scherer's 1979 attempt to determine empirically whether the degree of product variety in the ready-to-eat breakfast cereals industry was more than socially optimal or not. His approach was to estimate the welfare gain from each new variety (capitalized into present value form) and compare it with the launching costs. Scherer's conclusion was that the number of varieties was more than socially optimal, although the problems in reaching any firm conclusion were made clear. Wildman 1984 criticized Scherer's method and showed that it understated the socially optimal number of varieties, leaving the final results more uncertain.

### Dimensionality of the product space
The structure of the market equilibrium and the optimum choice of product variety for the firm depend, in the locational analog models, on the dimensions of the product space on which the market model is based. This fact is often obscured

because almost all the best known models have assumed that there were only two relevant characteristics in the group, so that all goods could be represented along a line measuring the ratio of the two characteristics, thus following Hotelling's original location model. But the two-characteristics single-dimension model possesses special features that one cannot generalize to higher dimensions. The most important of these is the number of neighbors for any good. In the two-characteristics case this is always just two (one to the left and one to the right in the usual line diagram), and the firm's market area is always a simple line segment with two boundary points. If there are many characteristics, however, the number of potential neighbors escalates. In the three-characteristics case, a product may have many neighbors, each in a different direction. In particular, one product could have any number of equidistant neighbors if the latter were positioned around a circle with center on the former or, with three products only, all could be equidistant from each other if arranged as the vertices of an equilateral triangle. Indeed, the locational model and the Chamberlinian model can coincide when there are at least $n-1$ relevant characteristics for $n$ different products. Because two dimensions (three characteristics) correspond to real geographic space, the results of pure locational analyses, as in Eaton and Lipsey 1976, can be drawn upon with suitable modifications. The most important result from the two-dimensional location models is that there may be multiple market equilibria with different arrangements of the firms in the space, different market area shapes (rectangles versus hexagons for example), different numbers of immediate neighbors (rivals) for the firms, and different levels of profit per firm. It is possible for the same demand and cost conditions to generate different free-entry ('zero-profit') equilibria with different levels of product variety. A discussion of such cases together with other aspects of many-characteristics models is given in Lancaster 1982. As the number of relevant characteristics increases the configurations become very complex, with no locational models to draw upon.

*Variety in product quality*
The discussion up to this point has been concerned almost entirely with 'horizontal' product differentiation, that is, with products which could be considered to be broadly of equivalent quality, even though different consumers prefer different variants because of their specific characteristics proportions. If one product has more of *all* characteristics than another, or is *universally* ranked as better (like a Rolls Royce relative to a cheap subcompact), then there is 'vertical' product differentiation with products ranked in a universally accepted order of preference by product quality. The latter is generally similar to single-attribute analysis in marketing, while the former requires at least two attributes.

Since all consumers have the same preference ranking for the products in vertical differentiation, something other than different preferences is required to provide markets for different qualities. The most usual is to assume variations in income, as in Gabszewicz and Thisse 1979.

One problem to be solved is the relationship between the quality level that will be produced under competition in the single-product case, compared with the optimum or the competitive outcome, as in Mussa and Rosen 1978. The problem of interest here is the number of different qualities that will be offered by a multi-product monopolist, a problem that has been tackled by Itoh 1983 and Moorthy 1984. As might be expected, the outcome depends very heavily on the way in which the demands for products of different quality are distributed over the population and on the cost of incorporating higher quality in a product.

Shaked and Sutton 1982 and others (unpublished) have considered the case in which the production cost was the same for all qualities. A monopolist will sell either the highest quality alone, or the highest quality and a lower quality (at a lower price) if the range of consumer incomes is varied enough. If entry is possible, the first firm will sell at the high quality, the second entrant at lower, and there will be, in general, room at most for two firms (and thus two quality levels). Simple models tend to reinforce an old proposition, that intermediate quality classes vanish at market equilibrium.

## Multi-product firms

As noted earlier, there are three main potential influences on the firm's choice of product variety:

1. The existence of inter-product economies on the production side.
2. The potential for increasing demand by offering more variety.
3. Use of product variety for strategic purposes.

Recent work approaching the problem of product variety in the output of a firm from the production side has placed the emphasis more on the degree of market straddling by large firms, especially in regulated sectors, and less on product variety as such. It is notable for the considerable progress that has been made in the formal analysis of the potential economies from simultaneous production of two or more goods, as in Panzar and Willig 1981. This work has been thoroughly surveyed by Bailey and Friedlaender 1982 and is discussed extensively by Baumol, Panzar, and Willig 1982, so it is not proposed to deal further with this material here. Approaches that emphasize organizational, management or financial economies[27] rather than technical production economies throw more light on conglomerates than on product variety in the sense being used here.

On the demand side, the most fully developed work has been for a firm having an uncontested monopoly over the whole goods group. The incentive for a monopolist to provide variety, even if there are no economies of scope, occurs when revenue can be increased by additional products either because representative individual consumers gain utility from variety and thus are willing to pay more for a varied collection or because preferences are heterogeneous and increased variety taps consumers in new segments of the market. The profitability of increased variety, given the potential revenue gain, is diminished by the existence of scale economies in the production of each variant and reinforced by any economies of scope. In general, a monopolist cannot capture all the potential consumer surplus without perfect price discrimination and so the revenue gain from variety to an ordinary non-discriminating monopoly understates the social gain.[28]

Thus one might expect the monopolist to produce less than optimal variety. Some of the early papers in this area, such as Swan 1970 and Lancaster 1975, concluded that the monopolist would produce optimum variety, but these used restricted demand formulations. Using the more complete demand specification of the companion monopolistic competition model, Lancaster 1979 showed the earlier results to be false in general – rather, that a monopolist would produce less than the optimal variety under most conditions.[29] Moorthy 1984 obtains a similar result using a finite number of market segments instead of a demand continuum.

In the simplest linear Hotelling-type model with inelastic demand, a monopolist will have the whole market even if it sells at only one point – which it will do if there are unlimited scale economies associated with each point of sale.[30] In this case the monopolist will certainly produce less variety than would emerge from monopolistic competition. It is not difficult to show that the general relationship continues to hold (although the monopolist now provides more than one variety) if demand is inelastic up to a reservation price (Salop 1979). When demand is fully responsive to price and distance in product space, as in Lancaster 1979, the relationship is more difficult to prove, but still holds.

There have been few attempts at a theory of optimal product variety and positioning for multi-product oligopolists although the oligopoly case is very important in real business situations. Brander and Eaton 1984 tackle the problem by considering two possible types of outcome for the duopoly case, one in which each firm has a complete segment of the market and the rivals have close substitutes only at the boundary between the segments, and the other in which the firms' products are interlaced so that each product is flanked by rival products.[31]

Using a somewhat specialized demand structure, both outcomes are shown to be potential Nash equilibria if there is simultaneous product selection, but the market segmentation outcome (which gives rise to higher prices and profits) will be the Nash equilibrium if the product selection is sequential. If there is a threat of further entry, however, the interlaced pattern can be better for the two incumbents than the segmented pattern.

*Strategic considerations*

This last result of the Brander and Eaton model is related to the work on pre-emptive product differentiation, the third of the approaches outlined at the beginning of the section. This work commenced with pure locational models as in Hay 1976, Prescott and Visscher 1977, Eaton and Lipsey 1979. See the discussion in Dorward 1982.

The argument in the simple case of the one-dimensional locational model with inelastic demand and without boundary effects (the non-clustering case) is that if outlets are evenly spaced at distance $d$ apart and all sell at the same price, each outlet will have revenue proportional to $d$. A new entrant will have to locate between two existing ones and thus will have revenue proportional only to $d/2$. If monopoly, common ownership, or collusion permits the incumbent(s) to choose $d$, it can be made large enough so that a profit can be made on market width $d$ but not so large that a loss can be avoided on a market width of $d/2$, and thus entry is inhibited. Analysis along similar lines appears in Bonanno 1987, who shows that the incumbent will tend to produce more than the minimal entry-deterrent variety, measured by the number of stores in his particular model.

Schmalansee 1978 applies the locational reasoning to product space and makes a specific application to the ready-to-eat breakfast cereals group, in which he argues that such pre-emptive brand proliferation occurs and gives a welfare loss. Since a monopolist without threat of potential entrants will generally produce too little variety, a pre-emptive increase in variety under threat of entry may merely be a move towards the optimum. It is obvious that pre-emptive strategy will not result in fewer products than under guaranteed monopoly (and almost always more) and that there will be fewer products than under monopolistic competition (else the strategy has failed), but the relationship to the optimum is unclear and is probably sensitive to the specification of the model.

**Other aspects of product variety**

There is a growing literature on the relationship between international trade and product variety. Representative works would include Krugman 1979, Lancaster 1980, 1982, Helpman 1981, Horn 1984, Eaton and Kierzkowski 1984. This is regarded as a specialized area and not reported here in detail. The general conclusion from this work is that the opening of trade between hitherto isolated product-differentiated markets may increase or decrease world product variety. However, the variety available to consumers in each country will generally increase, even though the variety produced within each country will generally decrease. Stokey 1988 has explored the relationship between economic growth and product variety, using a learning model in conjunction with a characteristics approach.

Virtually all the work on the economic theory of product variety has been within a perfect information framework and, in location and location-analog models, for a uniform distribution of consumers. Even with these simplifications, much still remains to be done at the core of the analysis.

There have, however, been a few scattered attempts to address the problem of imperfect information in relation to product variety.[32] Stahl 1982, for example, considers a two-level product-differentiation model (firms produce different varieties and can vary location) with imperfect information as to the firm's product characteristics, leading to a geographic search. His conclusion is that there will be geographical clustering to more than the optimal degree. Wolinsky 1984 considers a location-analog model in product space, with consumers who are imperfectly informed about the specifications of the goods. The central argument of this paper is that the optimal degree of variety is less than would be the case under perfect information, and thus that the market equilibrium gives too much variety when the market is large and/or the economies of scale are small.

There is a section of Lancaster 1979 concerned with imperfect information as to specification: the conclusion is that this would result in a softening of rivalry between adjacent firms, a greater emphasis on price competition as compared with product differentiation, and a structure closer to Chamberlinian competition. Imperfect information also receives some consideration in a section of Perloff and Salop 1985, where each consumer is assumed to be aware of only a subset of all the available goods. In Ireland 1985, the uncertainty is in the other direction – firms are uncertain about the demands for their products. Such uncertainty can lead to an equilibrium with either more or less product variety than is optimal, according to the parameters of the situation.

## Conclusion
Although there is wide variety in the supply of models of product variety, there appear to be certain conclusions on which almost all models agree:

1.  The degree of scale economies (in the production of each variant) is a major determinant of the degree of product variety, and an increase in scale economies reduces product variety for both monopolistic competition and multi-product monopoly. The socially optimal degree of product variety also falls when economies of scale increase.
2.  The 'intensity' with which consumers view the differences between similar products (in those models in which there is a demand parameter capable of this interpretation) is also important. In all structures, the degree of variety will be less when similar products are viewed as satisfactory substitutes.
3.  The degree of product variety increases with the 'competitiveness' of the market, in the sense that the variety is greater under monopolistic compe-

tition than under monopoly, and greater under monopoly threatened by potential entry than under protected monopoly.

There are other aspects of product variety, however, on which different models reach different conclusions. For example, a larger market will be associated with greater variety in models based on the idea of the representative consumer, but not necessarily in locational analog models where there is a distinction between the breadth of the market (width of the spectrum of diverse tastes) and depth (density of consumers at each point). There is much disagreement on an important policy issue – whether particular market structures produce more or less variety than is optimal. The conclusion in this regard varies from model to model, and in the more complex models, from situation to situation. A fair statement, however, is that most of the models predict that the monopolistic competition equilibrium will give more than optimal variety under most circumstances, and that protected monopoly will give less variety than is optimal. There seems to be no clear-cut answer to such a question as whether an oligopolistic structure of multi-product firms, or a monopolist attempting to deter entry, will result in more or less than the optimal degree of variety.

## Notes

1. Originally published as 'The economies of product variety: a survey' in *Marketing Science,* **9** (1990), 41–56.
2. If the indifference contours are asymptotic to the origin, as often modeled, the individual will *always* consume *all* available products.
3. Spence 1976a, Dixit and Stiglitz 1977, for example.
4. Hotelling 1929, Salop 1979.
5. Lancaster 1975, 1979.
6. In a pure location model it is because one cannot be in two places at once.
7. Lancaster 1966 draws the distinction between 'combinable' and 'non-combinable' goods as properties of the consumption technology.
8. See Hart 1985a, Perloff and Salop 1985.
9. This material has been surveyed by Bailey and Friedlaender 1982.
10. The work in this area has been primarily concerned with the optimal choice of product variety for a monopolist. Examples include Swan 1970, Lancaster 1979, Itoh 1983, Moorthy 1984.
11. See Prescott and Visscher 1977, Schmalensee 1978 for the pre-emptive argument, Lancaster 1979 and Brander and Eaton 1984 for attempts at a theory of multi-product oligopoly.
12. An example of the interplay in its simplest form is given in Meade 1974.
13. If $V$ is the subutility from the group, $V^{(s-1)/s} = \sum_{i=1}^{n} q_i^{(s-1)/s}$, where $s > 1$ is the elasticity of substitution.
14. In this model, the perceived demand elasticity is $-s$, so the firm will choose price at $s/(s-1)$ times marginal cost.
15. See Archibald et al. 1986 for some specific criticisms.
16. For a firm located between two other firms at distances $d_1, d_2$ each selling at price $\bar{p}$, demand is given by: $q(p, d) = (\bar{p} - p)/t + (d_1 + d_2)/2$ where $t$ is the unit transport cost.
17. For a discussion of the problems of existence and the multiple solutions possible in the simple Hotelling-type model, see Salop 1979, Novshek 1980, Economides 1984.
18. Lancaster 1966, 1971. For a discussion and critique of the use of the characteristics model see Ratchford 1975, 1979, Bernardo and Blin 1977, Geistfeld 1977, Greeno et al. 1977, Ladd and Zober 1977. For a different and more formal approach, see Horstmann and Slivinski 1985.

Somewhat analogous developments had, of course, occurred in marketing analysis and psychology.

19. Note that not all location-analog models could be called neo-Hotelling. See Capozza and Van Order 1982, for example.
20. Salop 1979.
21. But see Lancaster 1979 or Economides 1984 on the special problems created by inelastic demand and linear transport costs in this simple analog.
22. The idea was popular with political scientists, as explaining why both political parties move towards the center in a two-party system. See Downs 1957.
23. See, for example, Eaton and Lipsey 1975, Shaked 1975, D'Aspremont et al. 1979, Lancaster 1979, Salop 1979, Novshek 1980, Graitson 1982, Economides 1984, de Palma et al. 1985, Neven 1985.
24. Hotelling assumed firms chose prices first, then locations.
25. The term 'address' is an attempt to generalize the idea of location to non-geographical contexts. See Archibald et al. 1986.
26. Not all treatments of monopolistic competition in characteristics space assume non-combinable consumption or a neo-Hotelling structure. See Archibald and Rosenbluth 1975, Leland 1977.
27. Such as Williamson 1975.
28. See White 1977.
29. The exception being rather special conditions involving comparison with what is really a second-best optimum, rather than a first-best situation, and require that the elasticity of substitution between the group and outside goods be low.
30. The same will be true for the simplest Dixit–Stiglitz model, if the elasticity of substitution between the group and outside goods is unity.
31. Similar ideas (with terms 'split' and 'interleaved') appear in analyzing rivalry between home goods and imports under conditions of product differentiation in Lancaster 1984.
32. There is, of course, a very large literature on imperfect information in relation to prices, including prices in product-differentiated markets.

# PART III

# WELFARE

# 12  The general theory of second best[1]

There is an important basic similarity underlying a number of recent works in apparently widely separated fields of economic theory. Upon examination, it would appear that the authors have been rediscovering, in some of the many guises given it by various specific problems, a single general theorem. This theorem forms the core of what may be called *the general theory of second best*. Although the main principles of the theory of second best have undoubtedly gained wide acceptance, no general statement of them seems to exist. Furthermore, the principles often seem to be forgotten in the context of specific problems and, when they are rediscovered and stated in the form pertinent to some problem, this seems to evoke expressions of surprise and doubt rather than of immediate agreement and satisfaction at the discovery of yet another application of the already accepted generalizations.

In this paper, an attempt is made to develop a *general* theory of second best. The first section gives, by way of introduction, a verbal statement of the theory's main general theorem, together with two important negative corollaries. The second section outlines the scope of the general theory of second best. Next, a brief survey is given of some of the recent literature on the subject. This survey brings together a number of cases in which the general theory has been applied to various problems in theoretical economics. The implications of the general theory of second best for piecemeal policy recommendations, especially in welfare economics, are next considered. This general discussion is followed by two sections giving examples of the application of the theory in specific models. These examples lead up to the general statement and rigorous proof of the central theorem. A brief consideration of the existence of second-best solutions is followed by a classificatory discussion of the nature of these solutions. This taxonomy serves to illustrate some of the important negative corollaries of the theorem. The paper is concluded with a brief discussion of the difficult problem of multiple-layer second-best optima.

## A general theorem in the theory of second best
It is well known that the attainment of a Paretian optimum requires the simultaneous fulfilment of all the optimum conditions. The general theorem for the second-best optimum states that if there is introduced into a general equilibrium system a constraint which prevents the attainment of one of the Paretian conditions, the other Paretian conditions, although still attainable, are, in general, no longer desirable. In other words, given that one of the Paretian optimum conditions cannot

be fulfilled, then an optimum situation can be achieved only by departing from all the other Paretian conditions. The optimum situation finally attained may be termed a second-best optimum because it is achieved subject to a constraint which, by definition, prevents the attainment of a Paretian optimum.

From this theorem there follows the important negative corollary that there is no *a priori* way to judge as between various situations in which some of the Paretian optimum conditions are fulfilled while others are not. Specifically, it is *not* true that a situation in which more, but not all, of the optimum conditions are fulfilled is necessarily, or is even likely to be, superior to a situation in which fewer are fulfilled. It follows, therefore, that in a situation in which there exist many constraints which prevent the fulfilment of the Paretian optimum conditions, the removal of any one constraint may affect welfare or efficiency either by raising it, by lowering it, or by leaving it unchanged.

The general theorem of the second best states that if one of the Paretian optimum conditions cannot be fulfilled a second-best optimum situation is achieved only by departing from all other optimum conditions. It is important to note that in general, nothing can be said about the direction or the magnitude of the secondary departures from optimum conditions made necessary by the original non-fulfilment of one condition. Consider, for example, a case in which the central authority levies a tax on the purchase of one commodity and returns the revenue to the purchasers in the form of a gift so that the sole effect of the tax is to distort relative prices. Then all that can be said in general is that given the existence and invariability of this tax, a second-best optimum can be achieved by levying some system of taxes and subsidies on all other commodities. The required tax on some commodities may exceed the given tax, on other commodities it may be less than the given tax, while on still others a subsidy, rather than a tax, may be required.

It follows from the above that there is no *a priori* way to judge as between various situations in which none of the Paretian optimum conditions are fulfilled. In particular, it is *not* true that a situation in which all departures from the optimum conditions are of the same direction and magnitude is necessarily superior to one in which the deviations vary in direction and magnitude. For example, there is no reason to believe that a situation in which there is the same degree of monopoly in all industries will necessarily be in any sense superior to a situation in which the degree of monopoly varies as between industries.

**The scope of the theory of second best**
Perhaps the best way to approach the problem of defining the scope of the theory of second best is to consider the role of constraints in economic theory. In the general economic problem of maximization a function is maximized subject to at least one constraint. For example, in the simplest welfare theory a welfare function is maximized subject to the constraint exercised by a transformation

function. The theory of the Paretian optimum is concerned with the conditions that must be fulfilled in order to maximize some function subject to a set of constraints which are generally considered to be 'in the nature of things'. There are, of course, a whole host of possible constraints beyond those assumed to operate in the Paretian optimization problem. These further constraints vary from the 'nature-dictated' ones, such as indivisibilities and boundaries to production functions, to the obviously 'policy-created' ones such as taxes and subsidies. In general, there would seem to be no logical division between those constraints which occur in the Paretian optimum theory and those which occur only in the theory of second best. All that can be said is that, in the theory of the Paretian optimum, certain constraints are assumed to be operative and the conditions necessary for the maximization of some function subject to these constraints are examined. In the theory of second best there is admitted at least one constraint additional to the ones existing in Paretian optimum theory and it is in the nature of this constraint that it prevents the satisfaction of at least one of the Paretian optimum conditions. Consideration is then given to the nature of the conditions that must be satisfied in order to maximize some function subject to this new set of constraints.

It is important to note that even in a single general equilibrium system where there is only one Paretian optimum, there will be a multiplicity of second-best optimum positions. This is so because there are many possible combinations of constraints with a second-best solution for each combination. For this reason one may speak of the existence of *the* Paretian optimum but should, strictly speaking, refer to *a* second-best optimum.

It is possible to approach problems in the theory of second best from two quite different directions. On the one hand, the approach used in this paper is to assume the existence of one constraint additional to those in the Paretian optimum problem (e.g., one tax, one tariff, one subsidy, or one monopoly) and then to investigate the nature of the conditions that must be satisfied in order to achieve a second-best optimum and, where possible, to compare these conditions with those necessary for the attainment of a Paretian optimum. On the other hand, the approach used by Professor Meade is to assume the existence of a large number of taxes, tariffs, monopolies, and so on, and then to inquire into the effect of changing any one of them. Meade, therefore, deals with a system containing many constraints and investigates the optimum (second-best) level for one of them, assuming the invariability of all the others.[2] It would be futile to argue that one of these approaches was superior to the other. Meade's is probably the appropriate one when considering problems of actual policy in a world where many imperfections exist and only a few can be removed at any one time. On the other hand, the approach used in the present paper would seem to be the more appropriate one for a systematic study of the general principles of the theory of second best.

*196   Trade, markets and welfare*

## The theory of second best in the literature of economics

The theory of second best has been, in one form or another, a constantly recurring theme in the post-war literature on the discriminatory reduction of trade barriers. There can be no doubt that the theory of customs unions provides an important case study in the application of the general theory of second best. Until customs union theory was subjected to searching analysis, the 'free trader' often seemed ready to argue that any reduction in tariffs would necessarily lead to an improvement in world productive efficiency and welfare. In his path-breaking work on the theory of customs unions[3] Professor Viner has shown that the removal of tariffs from some imports may cause a decrease in the efficiency of world production.

One important reason for the shifts in the location of production which would follow the creation of a customs union was described by Viner as follows:

> There will be commodities which one of the members of the customs union will now newly import from the other, whereas before the customs union it imported them from a third country, because that was the cheapest possible source of supply even after payment of the duty. The shift in the locus of production is now not as between the two member countries but as between a low-cost third country and the other, high-cost, member country.

Viner used the term 'trade diversion' to describe production shifts of this sort and he took it as self-evident that they would reduce the efficiency of world production. Since it is quite possible to conceive of a customs union having only trade-diverting production effects, it follows, in Viner's analysis, that the discriminatory reduction of tariffs may reduce, rather than raise, the efficiency of world production.

Viner emphasized the production effects of customs unions,[4] directing his attention to changes in the location, and hence the cost, of world production. Recently Professor Meade has shown that a customs union has exactly parallel effects on the location, and hence the 'utility' of world consumption.[5] Meade isolates the 'consumption effects' of customs unions by considering an example in which world production is fixed. In this case Viner's problem of the effects of a union on the cost of world production cannot arise. Meade argues that, under these circumstances, a customs union will tend to raise welfare by encouraging trade between the member countries but that, at the same time, it will tend to lower welfare by discouraging the already hampered trade between the union area and the rest of the world. In the final analysis a customs union will raise welfare, lower it, or leave it unchanged, depending on the relative strength of these two opposing tendencies. The Viner–Meade conclusions provide an application of the general theorem's negative corollary that nothing can be said *a priori* about the welfare and efficiency effects of a change which permits the satisfaction of some but not all of the Paretian optimum conditions.

Another application of second-best theory to the theory of tariffs has been provided by S.A. Ozga who has shown that a non-preferential reduction of tariffs by a single country may lead 'away from the free trade position'.[6] In other words, the adoption of a free-trade policy by one country, in a multi-country tariff-ridden world, may actually lower the real income of that country and of the world. Ozga demonstrates the existence of this possibility by assuming that all commodities are, in consumption, rigidly complementary, so that their production either increases or decreases simultaneously. He then shows that in a three-country world with tariffs all around, one country may adopt a policy of free trade and, as a result, the world production of all commodities may decrease. This is one way of demonstrating a result which follows directly from the general theory of second best.

In the field of public finance, the problems of second best seem to have found a particularly perplexing guise in the long controversy on the relative merits of direct *versus* indirect taxation. It would be tedious to review all the literature on the subject at this time. In his 1951 article, I.M.D. Little[7] has shown that because of the existence of the 'commodity' leisure, the price of which cannot be directly taxed, both direct and indirect taxes must prevent the satisfaction of some of the conditions necessary for the attainment of a Paretian optimum. An indirect tax on one good disturbs rates of substitution between that good and all others while an income tax disturbs rates of substitution between leisure and all other goods. Little then argues that there is no *a priori* way to judge as between these two positions where some Paretian optimum conditions are satisfied while others are not. This is undoubtedly correct. However, Little might have gone on to suggest that there is an *a priori* case in favor of raising a given amount of revenue by some system of *unequal indirect taxes* rather than by either an income tax or an indirect tax on only one commodity. This interesting conclusion was first stated by W.J. Corlett and D.C. Hague.[8] These authors have demonstrated that the optimum way to raise any given amount of revenue is by a system of unequal indirect taxes in which commodities 'most complementary' to leisure have the highest tax rates while commodities 'most competitive' with leisure have the lowest rates. The reason for this general arrangement of tax rates should be intuitively obvious. When an equal *ad valorem* rate of tax is placed on all goods the consumption of leisure will be too high while the consumption of all other goods will be too low. The consumption of untaxed leisure may be discouraged by placing especially high rates of tax on commodities which are complementary in consumption to leisure and by placing especially low rates of tax on commodities which are competitive in consumption with leisure.

Professor Meade has recently given an alternative analysis of the same problem.[9] His conclusions, however, support those of Corlett and Hague. In theory at least, the tables have been completely turned and the indirect tax is proved to be superior to the income tax, provided that the optimum system of indirect taxes is levied. This conclusion is but another example of an application of the general theorem that if one of the Paretian optimum conditions cannot be fulfilled then a second-best optimum situation can be obtained by departing from all the other optimum conditions.

What is perhaps not so obvious is that the problem of direct versus indirect taxes and that of the 'consumption effects' of customs unions are analytically identical. The Little analysis deals with a problem in which some commodities can be taxed at various rates while others must be taxed at a fixed rate. (It is not necessary that the fixed rate of tax should be zero.) In the theory of customs unions one is concerned with the welfare and efficiency effects of varying some tariff rates while leaving others unchanged. In Little's analysis there are three commodities, $X$, $Y$ and $Z$, commodity $Z$ being leisure. By renaming $Z$ home goods and $X$ and $Y$ imports from two different countries one passes immediately to the theory of customs unions. An income tax in Little's analysis becomes a system of non-discriminatory import duties while a single indirect tax becomes the discriminatory tariff introduced after the formation of a customs union with the producers of the now untaxed import. A model of this sort is considered later in the paper.

An application of the general theory of second best to yet another field of economic theory is provided by A. Smithies in his article, 'The Boundaries of the Production and Utility Function'.[10] Smithies considers the case of a multi-input firm seeking to maximize its profits. This will be done when for each factor the firm equates marginal cost with marginal revenue productivity. Smithies then suggests that there may exist boundaries to the production function. These boundaries would take the form of irreducible minimum amounts of certain inputs, it being possible to employ more but not less than these minimum amounts. It might happen, however, that profit maximization called for the employment of an amount of one factor less than the minimum technically possible amount. In this case production would take place 'on the boundary' and the minimum possible amount of the input would be used. However, in the case of this input, marginal cost would no longer be equated with marginal productivity, the boundary conditions forcing its employment beyond the optimum level. Smithies then shows that given the constraint, marginal cost does not equal marginal productivity for this input, profits will be maximized only by departing from the condition marginal cost equals marginal productivity for all other inputs. Furthermore, there is no *a priori* reason for thinking that the nature of the inequality will be the same for all factors. Profit maximization may require that some factors be employed only to a point where marginal productivity exceeds marginal cost while other factors are used up to a point where marginal productivity falls below marginal cost.

Problems of the 'mixed economy' provide an application of second-best theory frequently encountered in popular discussion. Consider, for example, a case where one section of an economy is rigidly controlled by the central authority while another section is virtually uncontrolled. It is generally agreed that the economy is not functioning efficiently but there is disagreement as to the appropriate remedy. One faction argues that more control over the uncontrolled sector is needed, while another faction pleads for a relaxation of the degree of control exercised in the public sector. The principles of the general theory of second best suggest that *both sides* in the controversy may be advocating a policy appropriate to the desired ends. Given the high degree of control in one sector and the almost complete absence of control in another, it is unlikely that anything like a second-best optimum position has been reached. If this is so, then it follows that efficiency would be increased either by increasing the degree of control exercised over the uncontrolled sector or by relaxing the control exercised over the controlled sector. Both of these policies will move the economy in the direction of some second-best optimum position.

Finally, mention may be made of the problem of 'degrees of monopoly'. It is not intended to review the voluminous literature on this controversy. It may be mentioned in passing that, in all but the simplest models, a Paretian optimum requires that marginal costs *equal* marginal revenues throughout the entire economy. If this equality is not established in one firm, then the second-best conditions require that the equality be departed from in all other firms. However, as is usual in second-best cases there is no presumption in favor of the same degree of inequality in all firms. In general, the second-best position may well be one in which marginal revenues greatly exceed marginal costs in some firms, only slightly exceed marginal costs in others, while, in still other firms, marginal revenues actually fall short of marginal costs.

A similar problem is considered by Lionel W. McKenzie in his article 'Ideal output and the interdependence of firms'.[11] He deals with the problem of increasing the money value of output in situations in which marginal costs do not equal prices in all firms. The analysis is not conducted in a general equilibrium setting and many simplifying assumptions are made such as the one that resources can be shifted between occupations as desired without affecting their supplies. McKenzie shows that even in this partial equilibrium setting if allowance is made for inter-firm sales of intermediate products, the condition that marginal costs should bear the same relation to prices in all firms does not provide a sufficient condition for an increase in the value of output. Given that the optimum conditions marginal cost equals price for each commodity cannot be achieved, a second-best optimum would require a complex set of relations in which the ratio of marginal cost to price would vary as between firms. Although the analysis is not of a full general equilibrium, the conclusions follow the now familiar pattern: (1) if a Paretian optimum cannot be achieved a second-best optimum requires a general departure from all the Paretian optimum conditions and (2) there are unlikely to be any simple sufficient conditions for an *increase* when a *maximum* cannot be obtained.

## The theory of second best and 'piecemeal' policy recommendations

It should be obvious from the discussion in the preceding sections that the principles of the general theory of second best show the futility of 'piecemeal welfare economics'. To apply to only a small part of an economy welfare rules which would lead to a Paretian optimum if they were applied everywhere, may move the economy away from, not toward, a second-best optimum position. A nationalized industry conducting its price–output policy according to the Lerner–Lange 'Rule' in an imperfectly competitive economy may well diminish both the general productive efficiency of the economy and the welfare of its members.

The problem of sufficient conditions for an increase in welfare, as compared to necessary conditions for a welfare maximum, is obviously important if policy recommendations are to be made in the real world. Piecemeal welfare economics is often based on the belief that a study of the *necessary* conditions for a Paretian welfare optimum may lead to the discovery of *sufficient* conditions for an increase in welfare. In his *Critique of Welfare Economics*,[12] I.M.D. Little discusses the optimum conditions for exchange and production '... both as necessary conditions for a maximum, and as sufficient conditions for a desirable economic change'. Later on in his discussion Little says '... necessary conditions are not very interesting. It is *sufficient* conditions for improvements that we really want ....' But the theory of second best leads to the conclusion that there are in general no such sufficient conditions for an increase in welfare. There are necessary conditions for a Paretian optimum. In a simple situation there may exist a condition that is necessary and sufficient. But in a general equilibrium situation there will be no conditions which in general are sufficient for an increase in welfare without also being sufficient for a welfare maximum.

The preceding generalizations may be illustrated by considering the following optimum conditions for exchange: 'The marginal rate of substitution between any two "goods" must be the same for every individual who consumes them both.' Little concludes that this condition gives a sufficient condition for an increase in welfare provided only that when it is put into effect, '... the distribution of welfare is not thereby made worse'. However, the whole discussion of this optimum condition occurs only after Little has postulated '... a fixed stock of "goods" to be distributed between a number of "individuals"'. The optimum condition that all consumers should be faced with the same set of prices becomes in this case a sufficient condition for an increase in welfare, because the problem at hand is merely how to distribute efficiently a fixed stock of goods. But in this case the condition is a necessary and sufficient condition for a

Paretian optimum. As soon as variations in output are admitted, the condition is no longer sufficient for a welfare maximum and it is also no longer sufficient for an increase in welfare.

The above conclusion may be illustrated by a simple example. Consider a community of two individuals having different taste patterns. The 'government' of the community desires to raise a certain sum which it will give away to a foreign country. The community has made its value judgement about the distribution of income by deciding that each individual must contribute half of the required revenue. It has also been decided that the funds are to be raised by means of indirect taxes. It follows from the Corlett and Hague analysis that the best way to raise the revenue is by a system of *unequal* indirect taxes in which commodities 'most complementary' to leisure are taxed at the highest rates while commodities 'most substitutable' for leisure are taxed at the lowest rates. But the two individuals have different tastes so that commodity $X$ is substitutable for leisure for individual I and complementary to leisure for individual II, while commodity $Y$ and leisure are complementary for individual I and substitutes for II. The optimum way to raise the revenue, therefore, is to tax commodity $X$ at a low rate when it is sold to individual I and at a high rate when it is sold to individual II, while $Y$ is taxed at a high rate when sold to I but a low rate when sold to II. A second-best optimum thus requires that the two individuals be faced with different sets of relative prices.

Assume that the optimum tax rates are charged. The government then changes the tax system to make it non-discriminatory as between persons while adjusting the rates to keep revenue unchanged. Now the Paretian optimum exchange condition is fulfilled, but welfare has been decreased, for both individuals have been moved to lower indifference curves. Therefore, in the assumed circumstances, this Paretian optimum condition is a sufficient condition for a *decrease* in welfare.

### A problem in the theory of tariffs

In this section the simple type of model used in the analysis of direct *versus* indirect taxes is applied to a problem in the theory of tariffs. In the Little–Meade–Corlett and Hague analysis it is assumed that the government raises a fixed amount of revenue which it spends in some specified manner. The optimum way of raising this revenue is then investigated. A somewhat different problem is created by changing this assumption about the disposition of the tax revenue. In the present analysis it is assumed that the government returns the tax revenue to the consumers in the form of a gift so that the only effect of the tax is to change relative prices.[13]

A simple three-commodity model is used, there being one domestic commodity and two imports. It is assumed that the domestic commodity is untaxed and that a fixed rate of tariff is levied on one of the imports. The optimum level for the tariff on the other import is then investigated. This is an obvious problem in the theory of second best. Also it is interesting to note that the conclusions reached have immediate applications to the theory of customs unions. In the second part of this section the conclusions of the first part are applied to the problem of the welfare effects of a customs union which causes neither trade creation nor trade diversion, but only the expansion and contraction of the volumes of already existing trade.

*Second-best optimum tariff systems with fixed terms of trade*
The conditions of the model are as follows: country $A$ is a small country specializing in the production of one commodity ($Z$). Some of $Z$ is consumed at home and the remainder is exported in return for two imports, $X$ from country $B$ and $Y$ from country $C$. The prices of $X$ and $Y$ in terms of $Z$ are unaffected by any taxes or tariffs levied in country $A$. It is further assumed that none of the tariffs actually levied by $A$ are high enough to protect domestic industries producing either $X$ or $Y$, that country $B$ does not produce commodity $Y$ and that country $C$ does not produce commodity $X$. The welfare of country $A$ is defined by a community welfare function which is of the same form as the welfare functions of the identical individuals who inhabit $A$.

It is assumed that $A$ levies some fixed tariff on imports of commodity $Y$ and that commodity $Z$ is not taxed. It is then asked: what tariff ($\leq 0$) on imports of commodity $X$ will maximize welfare in country $A$? This tariff will be termed the optimum $X$ tariff.

The model may be set out as follows: let there be three commodities, $X$, $Y$ and $Z$. Let $p_x$ and $p_y$ be the prices of $X$ and $Y$ in terms of $Z$. Let the rate of *ad valorem* tariff charged on $X$ and $Y$ be $t_x - 1$ and $t_y - 1$.

$$u = u(x, y, z) \tag{1}$$

$$\frac{\partial u}{\partial x} = \frac{\partial u}{\partial z} p_x t_x \tag{2a}$$

$$\frac{\partial u}{\partial y} = \frac{\partial u}{\partial z} p_y t_y \tag{2b}$$

$$X p_x + Y p_y + Z = C \tag{3}$$

Equation (1) expresses country $A$'s community welfare function. Equations (2a and b) are the demand equilibrium conditions. Equation (3) gives the condition that $A$'s international payments be in balance.

These equations will yield a solution in general for any $t_x$ and $t_y$, in $X$, $Y$ and $Z$. Hence, for given $p_x$, $p_y$, $C$ and whatever parameters enter into (1):

$$X = f(t_x, t_y) \tag{4a}$$
$$Y = g(t_x, t_y) \tag{4b}$$
$$Z = h(t_x, t_y) \tag{4c}$$

Attention is directed to the sign of the change in $U$ when $t_x$ changes with $t_y$ > 1 kept constant. From equations (1) and (4):

$$\frac{\partial u}{\partial t_x} = \frac{\partial u}{\partial x} \cdot \frac{\partial x}{\partial t_x} + \frac{\partial u}{\partial y} \cdot \frac{\partial y}{\partial t_x} + \frac{\partial u}{\partial z} \cdot \frac{\partial z}{\partial t_x} \tag{5}$$

Substitute (2a and b) into (5):

$$\frac{\partial u}{\partial t_x} = p_x t_x \frac{\partial u}{\partial z} \cdot \frac{\partial x}{\partial t_x} + p_y t_y \frac{\partial u}{\partial z} \cdot \frac{\partial y}{\partial t_x} + \frac{\partial u}{\partial z} \cdot \frac{\partial z}{\partial t_x}$$

$$= \frac{\partial u}{\partial z} \left( p_x t_x \frac{\partial x}{\partial t_x} + p_y t_y \frac{\partial y}{\partial t_x} + \frac{\partial z}{\partial t_x} \right) \tag{6}$$

Next, take the partial derivative of (3) with respect to $t_x$.

$$p_x \frac{\partial x}{\partial t_x} + p_y \frac{\partial y}{\partial t_x} + \frac{\partial z}{\partial t_x} = 0$$

or

$$p_x \frac{\partial x}{\partial t_x} + p_y \frac{\partial y}{\partial t_x} = -\frac{\partial z}{\partial t_x} \tag{7}$$

Substitute (7) into (6):

$$\frac{\partial u}{\partial t_x} = \frac{\partial u}{\partial z} \left( p_x t_x \frac{\partial x}{\partial t_x} + p_y t_y \frac{\partial y}{\partial t_x} - p_x \frac{\partial x}{\partial t_x} - p_y \frac{\partial y}{\partial t_x} \right)$$

$$= \frac{\partial u}{\partial z} \left[ p_x \frac{\partial x}{\partial t_x} (t_x - 1) + p_y \frac{\partial y}{\partial t_x} (t_y - 1) \right] \tag{8}$$

It is assumed, first, that some tariff is levied on $Y$ but that $X$ is imported duty free. Therefore, $t_x = 1$ and $t_y > 1$. Equation (8) reduces to:

$$\frac{\partial u}{\partial t_x} = \frac{\partial u}{\partial z}\left[ p_y \frac{\partial y}{\partial t_x}(t_y - 1)\right] \tag{9}$$

In (9) $\partial u/\partial t_x$ takes the same sign as $\partial y/\partial t_x$. It follows that the introduction of a marginal tariff on $X$ will raise welfare if it causes an increase in imports of commodity $Y$, will leave welfare unchanged if it causes no change in imports of $Y$ and will lower welfare if it causes a decrease in imports of $Y$. Therefore, the optimum tariff on $X$ is, in fact, a subsidy, if imports of $Y$ fall when a tariff is placed on $X$, it is zero if the $X$ tariff has no effect on imports of $Y$ and it is positive if imports of $Y$ rise when the tariff is placed on $X$.

It is now assumed that a uniform rate of tariff is charged on $X$ and $Y$. Therefore, $t_x = t_y \equiv T$ and equation (8) becomes:

$$\frac{\partial u}{\partial t_x} = \frac{\partial u}{\partial z}(T-1)\left( p_x \frac{\partial x}{\partial T} + p_y \frac{\partial y}{\partial T}\right)$$

Substituting from (7):

$$\frac{\partial u}{\partial t_x} = -\left[\frac{\partial u}{\partial z}\cdot\frac{\partial z}{\partial t_x}(T-1)\right] \tag{10}$$

In (10) the sign of $\partial u/\partial t_x$ will be opposite to the sign of $\partial z/\partial t_x$. It follows that a marginal increase in the tariff on $X$ will increase welfare if it causes a decrease in the consumption of $Z$, will leave welfare unchanged if it causes no change in the consumption of $Z$ and will lower welfare if it causes an increase in the consumption of $Z$. It may be concluded, therefore, that the optimum tariff on $X$ exceeds the given tariff on $Y$ if an increase in the $X$ tariff reduces the consumption of $Z$, that the optimum $X$ tariff equals the given $Y$ tariff if there is no relation between the $X$ tariff and the consumption of $Z$ and that the optimum $X$ tariff is less than the given $Y$ tariff if an increase in the $X$ tariff causes an increase in consumption of $Z$.

In the case where an increase in the tariff on $X$ causes an increase in the consumption of $Y$ and of $Z$ the optimum $X$ tariff is greater than zero but less than the given tariff on $Y$.

*Welfare effects of a customs union causing only trade expansion and trade contraction*

It is assumed that country $A$ initially charges a uniform *ad valorem* rate of tariff on imports of $X$ and $Y$. $A$ then forms a customs union with country $B$. Now $X$ is imported duty-free while the pre-union tariff still applies to $Y$. What is the effect on $A$'s welfare of such a customs union? Some answers follow immediately from the previous analysis:

*Case 1:* Any increase in the tariff on $X$ causes a fall in the consumption of $Y$. The optimum tariff on $X$ is, in fact, a subsidy. Therefore, the customs union must raise $A$'s welfare.

*Case 2:* Variations in the tariff on $X$ have no effect on consumption of $Y$. The optimum tariff on $X$ is now zero. The customs union raises welfare in $A$. Furthermore, it raises it to a second-best optimum level (assuming that only the $X$ tariff can be varied).

*Case 3:* Variations in the tariff on $X$ have no effect on the purchases of $Z$. The optimum tariff on $X$ is equal to the $Y$ tariff. The customs union lowers $A$'s welfare. Furthermore, the union disturbs an already achieved second-best optimum.

*Case 4:* An increase in the tariff on $X$ causes a fall in the consumption of $Z$. In this case the optimum tariff on $X$ exceeds the given $Y$ tariff. Therefore, the customs union lowers $A$'s welfare.

*Case 5:* An increase in the tariff on $X$ causes an increase in the consumption of both $Y$ and $Z$. The optimum $X$ tariff is greater than zero but less than the given $Y$ tariff. The effect of the customs union on welfare is not known. Assume, however, that the $X$ tariff is removed by a series of stages. It follows that the initial stages of tariff reduction must raise welfare and that the final stages must lower it. Although nothing can be said about the welfare effect of a complete removal of the $X$ tariff, another important conclusion is suggested. A small reduction in tariffs must raise welfare. A large reduction may raise or lower it. It follows, therefore, that a partial preferential reduction of tariffs is more likely to raise welfare than is a complete preferential elimination of tariffs. Of course, this conclusion depends upon the specific assumptions made in the present model but it does provide an interesting and suggestive hypothesis for further investigation.

**Nationalized industry in an economy with monopoly: A simple model**

An interesting, and not unlikely, situation in which a 'second-best' type of policy may have to be pursued is that of a mixed economy which includes both nationalized industries and industries which are subject to monopoly control.

The monopoly is assumed to be one of the data: for one reason or another this monopoly cannot be removed, and the task of the nationalized industry is to determine that pricing policy which is most in 'the public interest'.

When there is full employment of resources then, if the monopoly is exercising its power, it will be producing less of the monopolized product than is required to give an optimum (in the Paretian sense) allocation of resources. Since there is less than the optimum production of the monopolized good, there will be more than the optimum production of the non-monopolized goods as a group.

Suppose that one of the non-monopolized industries is now nationalized. What should be its price–output policy? If it behaves competitively then it will tend to produce more of its product, relative to the monopolized good, than the Paretian optimum would require. If, on the other hand, it behaves monopolistically itself, then it will cut down the excess of its own production relative to that of the monopoly but will increase the excess of the remaining goods relative to both its own product and that of the monopolized industry. This is a typical 'second-best' situation: any policy will make some things worse and some better.

It is clear that no policy on the part of the nationalized industry can restore the Paretian optimum, for the existence of the monopoly prevents this. The nationalized industry must aim at a second-best policy, designed to achieve the best that still remains open to the economy. In purely generally terms it is impossible to be more definite than this, as will be shown in a later section. Intuitively, however, one might expect that, in some situations at least, the best policy for the nationalized industry would be to behave something like the monopoly, but to a lesser extent. In the case of the simple model to be presented in this section, one's intuitions would be correct.

There are assumed to be, in the present model, three industries producing goods $x, y, z$. Labor is the only input, costs are constant, and the total supply of labor is fixed. These assumptions define a unique linear transformation function relating the quantities of the three goods:

$$ax + by + cz = L \tag{11}$$

The production functions from which this is derived are:

$$x = \frac{1}{a}l_x, \; y = \frac{1}{b}l_y, \; z = \frac{1}{c}l_z; \; l_x + l_y + l_z = L \tag{12}$$

The marginal costs are constant and proportional to $a, b, c$.

The 'public interest' is assumed to be defined by a community preference function, which is of the same form as the preference functions of the identical individuals who make up the society. For simplicity, this preference function is assumed to take the logarithmic form:

$$U = x^\alpha y^\beta z^\gamma, \; \alpha, \beta, \gamma > 0 \tag{13}$$

The partial derivatives of this are:

$$\frac{\partial U}{\partial x} = \alpha \frac{U}{x}, \ \frac{\partial U}{\partial y} = \beta \frac{U}{y}, \ \frac{\partial U}{\partial z} = \gamma \frac{U}{z}$$

so that the marginal utilities of $x$, $y$, $z$ are proportional, respectively to $\alpha/x$, $\beta/y$, $\gamma/z$. For a utility function of this type, all goods are substitutes in both the Edgeworth–Pareto and Hicksian senses.

If there were no constraints in the economy (other than the transformation function itself), the Paretian optimum would be that found by maximizing the expression $U - \lambda(ax + by + cz - L)$, where $\lambda$ is the Lagrangian multiplier. This would lead to the three equations:

$$\left. \begin{aligned} \frac{\partial U}{\partial x} - \lambda a &= 0 \\ \frac{\partial U}{\partial y} - \lambda b &= 0 \\ \frac{\partial U}{\partial z} - \lambda c &= 0 \end{aligned} \right\} \tag{14}$$

which can be expressed in the proportional form:

$$\frac{a}{\alpha} x = \frac{b}{\beta} y = \frac{c}{\gamma} z \tag{15}$$

These conditions are of the familiar Paretian type, namely that the marginal utilities (or prices which, assuming the ordinary consumer behavior equations, are proportional to them) are proportional to the marginal costs. There being no monetary conditions, and the supply of labor being fixed, equality between prices and marginal costs is not necessarily implied.

Suppose now that the industry producing $x$ is a monopoly. The monopoly will set the price of $x$ higher (in terms of some numeraire, which will be taken to be $z$) in relation to marginal cost than in the conditions of the Paretian optimum. A numeraire is necessary since money, and money prices, are not being considered.

For the present purposes, the exact margin between marginal cost and price in the monopolized industry (relative to the numeraire) does not matter. It is necessary only for the problem that the monopolist set the prices of $x$ higher, relative to the price of $z$, than the ratio of the marginal cost of producing $x$ to the marginal cost of producing $z$.

In other words, the monopolist's behavior can be expressed by:

$$\frac{p_x}{p_z} > \frac{mc_x}{mc_z}$$

Substituting for $\dfrac{p_x}{p_z}\left(=\dfrac{\partial U}{\partial x}\Big/\dfrac{\partial U}{\partial z}=\dfrac{\alpha z}{\gamma x}\right)$ and $\dfrac{mc_x}{mc_z}\left(=\dfrac{a}{c}\right)$, this gives:

$$\frac{\alpha z}{\gamma x} > \frac{a}{c}$$
$$c\alpha z > a\gamma x$$
$$= ka\gamma x \quad \text{where } k > 1 \tag{16}$$

The actual value of $k$ (provided it is $> 1$) does not matter for the analysis. It is not necessary for the argument that $k$ is constant as the monopolist faces the changes brought about by the policies of the nationalized industries, but it simplifies the algebra to assume this.

The behavior of the monopolist, assumed unalterable, becomes an additional constraint on the system. The best that can be done in the economy is to maximize $U$ subject to two constraints, the transformation function (11) and the monopoly behavior condition (16). The conditions for attaining the second-best optimum (the Paretian optimum being no longer attainable) are found, therefore, as the conditions for the maximum of the function $U - \mu(c\alpha z - ka\gamma x) - \lambda'(ax + by + cz - L)$, where there are now two Lagrangian multipliers $\mu$, $\lambda'$. Neither of these multipliers can be identified with the multiplier $\lambda$ in the equations (14).

The conditions for attaining the second best are, therefore:

$$\alpha \frac{U}{x} + \mu ka\gamma - \lambda'a = 0 \tag{17}$$

$$\beta \frac{U}{y} - \lambda'b = 0 \tag{18}$$

$$\gamma \frac{U}{z} - \mu c\alpha - \lambda'c = 0 \tag{19}$$

To appreciate these conditions, it is necessary to compute the ratio $p_y/p_z$, compare it with the ratio $mc_y/mc_z$, and relate the result to both the Paretian optimum conditions and the mode of behavior of the monopolist.

Although there are three equations (17), (18), (19) above, these involve the two Lagrangian multipliers, so that there is actually only one degree of freedom. Hence, the policy of the nationalized industry (that which produces $y$) is sufficient for attaining the second best. If the nationalized industry sets its price, relative to its marginal cost, so as to satisfy the above conditions, it will have done all that is within its power to further the public interest.

To complete the solution it is necessary to determine $\mu$ and $\lambda'$. From (17)

$$\mu ka\gamma x = -\alpha U + \lambda' ax \tag{20}$$

and from (19)

$$-\mu ca\alpha z = \gamma U - \lambda' cz \tag{21}$$

Hence

$$\mu(ka\gamma x - ca\alpha z) = -(\alpha + \gamma)U + \lambda'(ax + cz)$$

but, from (16),

$$ka\gamma x - ca\alpha z = 0$$

so that

$$(\alpha + \gamma)U - \lambda'(ax + cz) = 0$$

$$\lambda' = \frac{(\alpha + \gamma)U}{ax + cz} \tag{22}$$

Substituting for $\lambda'$ in (20)

$$\begin{aligned}
\mu ka\gamma x &= -\alpha U + \frac{(\alpha + \gamma)U}{ax + cz} \\
&= \frac{\gamma ax - c\alpha x}{ax + cz}U \\
&= (k-1)\frac{-\gamma ax}{ax + cz}U \quad [c\alpha z = k\gamma ax, \text{ from (16)}] \\
\mu &= \frac{k-1}{k} \cdot \frac{-U}{ax + cz}
\end{aligned} \tag{23}$$

The correct pricing policy for the nationalized industry is given from the ratio $p_y/p_z$ which is implicit in the equations (17), (18), (19).

$$
\begin{aligned}
\frac{p_y}{p_z} &= \frac{\dfrac{\partial U}{\partial y}}{\dfrac{\partial U}{\partial z}} \\[2mm]
&= \frac{\beta \dfrac{U}{y}}{\gamma \dfrac{U}{z}} \\[2mm]
&= \frac{\lambda' b}{\mu c \alpha + \lambda' c} \qquad \text{[From (18), (19)]} \\[2mm]
&= \frac{b}{c + \dfrac{\mu}{\lambda'} c \alpha}
\end{aligned}
$$

$$
= \frac{\dfrac{b}{c}}{1 - \dfrac{k-1}{k} \cdot \dfrac{\alpha}{\alpha + \gamma}} \qquad \text{(From (22), (23))} \qquad (24)
$$

Now $b/c = MC_y/MC_z$, from (12), so that:

$$
\frac{p_y}{p_z} = \frac{MC_y}{MC_z} \cdot \left( \frac{1}{1 - \dfrac{k-1}{k} \cdot \dfrac{\alpha}{\alpha + \gamma}} \right) \qquad (25)
$$

Consider the expression $((k-1)/k \cdot \alpha/(\alpha + \gamma))$. Since $k > 1$, $0 < (k-1)/k < 1$, and $\alpha/(\alpha + \gamma) < 1$ since $\gamma > 0$. Thus the bracketed expression on the right hand side of (25) is greater than unity.

In other words, $p_y/p_z > MC_y/MC_z$, so that, relative to the numeraire, the nationalized industry should set its price higher than its marginal cost and, to that extent, behave like the monopoly.

But now consider the relationship between the nationalized industry and the monopoly:

$$\frac{p_y}{px} = \frac{\beta \dfrac{U}{y}}{\alpha \dfrac{U}{x}}$$

$$= \frac{\dfrac{b}{a}}{\dfrac{\mu}{\lambda} k\gamma + 1}$$

$$= \frac{\dfrac{b}{a}}{-\dfrac{k-1}{\alpha+\gamma} \cdot \gamma + 1}$$

$$= \frac{b}{a} \cdot \frac{\alpha+\gamma}{\alpha+k\gamma} \tag{26}$$

In this case, since $k > 1$, $\alpha$, $\gamma > 0$, $(\alpha + \gamma)/(\alpha + k\gamma) < 1$. Since $b/a = MC_y/MC_x$, the nationalized industry should set its price less high, in relation to marginal cost, than the monopoly.

In short, in the particular model analyzed, the correct policy for the nationalized industry, with monopoly entrenched in one of the other industries, would be to take an intermediate path. On the one hand, it should set its price higher than marginal cost (relative to the numeraire) but, on the other hand, it should not set its price so far above marginal cost as is the case in the monopolized industry.

These conclusions refer, it should be emphasized, to the particular model which has been analyzed above. This model has many simplifying (and therefore special) features, including the existence of only one input, constant marginal costs and a special type of utility function. As is demonstrated later there can be no *a priori* expectations about the nature of a second-best solution in circumstances where a generalized utility function is all that can be specified.

### A general theorem of the second best

Let there be some function $F(x_1 \dots x_n)$ of the $n$ variables $x_1 \dots x_n$ which is to be maximized (minimized) subject to a constraint on the variables $\Phi(x_1 \dots x_n)$ $= 0$. This is a formalization of the typical choice situation in economic analysis.

Let the solution of this problem – the Paretian optimum – be the $n - 1$ conditions $\Omega^i(x_1 \dots x_n) = 0$, $i = 1 \dots n-1$. Then the following theorem, the theorem of the second best, can be given.

If there is an additional constraint imposed of the type $\Omega^i \neq 0$ for $i = j$, then the maximum (minimum) of $F$ subject to both the constraint $\Phi$ and the constraint $\Omega^i \neq 0$ will, in general, be such that none of the still attainable Paretian conditions $\Omega^i = 0$, $i \neq j$, will be satisfied.

*Proof*
In the absence of the second constraint, the solution of the original maximum (minimum) problem is both simple and familiar. Using the Lagrange method, the Paretian conditions are given by the $n$ equations:

$$F_i - \lambda \Phi_i = 0 \qquad i = 1 \dots n \tag{27}$$

Eliminating the multiplier, these reduce to the $n - 1$ proportionality conditions:

$$\frac{F_i}{F_n} = \frac{\Phi_i}{\Phi_n} \qquad i = 1 \dots n - 1 \tag{28}$$

where the $n$th commodity is chosen as numeraire.

The equations (28) are the first-order conditions for the attainment of the Paretian optimum. Now let there be a constraint imposed which prevents the attainment of one of the conditions (28). Such a constraint will be of the form (the numbering of the commodities is, of course, arbitrary):

$$\frac{F_1}{F_n} = k \frac{\Phi_1}{\Phi_n} \qquad k \neq 1 \tag{29}$$

It is not necessary that $k$ be constant, but it is assumed to be so in the present analysis. There is now an additional constraint in the system so that, using the Lagrangean method, the function to be maximized (minimized) will be:

$$F - \lambda' \Phi - \mu \left( \frac{F_1}{F_n} - k \frac{\Phi_1}{\Phi_n} \right) \tag{30}$$

The multipliers $\lambda'$, $\mu$ will both be different, in general, from the multiplier $\lambda$ in (27).

The conditions that the expression (30) shall be at a maximum (minimum) are as follows:

$$F_i - \lambda'\Phi_i - \mu\left\{\frac{F_nF_{1i} - F_1F_{ni}}{F_n^2} - k\frac{\Phi_n\Phi_{1i} - \Phi_1\Phi_{ni}}{\Phi_n^2}\right\} = 0 \quad i = 1...n \quad (31)$$

If the expression $(F_nF_{1i} - F_1F_{ni})/F_n^2$ is denoted by $Q_i$ and the equivalent expression for the $\Phi$s by $R_t$, then the conditions (31) can be rewritten in the following form:

$$\frac{F_i}{F_n} = \frac{\Phi_i + \frac{\mu}{\lambda'}(Q_i - kR_t)}{\Phi_n + \frac{\mu}{\lambda'}(Q_n - kR_n)} \quad (32)$$

These are the conditions for the attainment of the second-best position, given the constraint (29), expressed in a form comparable with the Paretian conditions as set out in (28).

Clearly, any one of the conditions for the second best will be the same as the equivalent Paretian condition only if:

(i)  $\mu = 0$
(ii) $\mu \neq 0$, but $Q_i - kR_i = Q_n - kR_n = 0$

The first of these cannot be true for, if it were, then, when $i = 1$, $F_1/F_n$ would be equal to $\Phi_1/\Phi_n$, in contradiction with the constraint condition (29).

It is clear from the nature of the expressions $Q_i$, $Q_n$, $R_i$, $R_n$ that nothing is known, in general, about their signs, let alone their magnitudes, and even the signs would not be sufficient to determine whether (ii) was satisfied or not.

Consider $Q_n = (F_nF_{1n} - F_1F_{nn})/F_n^2$. If $F$ were a utility function then it would be known that $F_1$, $F_n$ were positive and $F_{nn}$ negative, but the sign of $F_{1n}$ may be either positive or negative. Even if the sign of $F_{1n}$ were known to be negative, the sign of $Q_n$ would still be indeterminate, since it would depend on whether the negative or the positive term in the expression was numerically the greater. In the case of $Q_i$, where $i \neq n$, the indeterminacy is even greater, since there are two expressions $F_{i1}$ and $F_{ni}$ for which the signs may be either positive or negative.

The same considerations as apply for the $Q$s also apply for the $R$s of course. In general, therefore, the conditions for the second-best optimum, given the constraint (29), will all differ from the corresponding conditions for the attainment of the Paretian optimum. Conversely, given the constraint (29), the application of these rules of behavior of the Paretian type which are still attainable will not lead, in general, to the best position in the circumstances.

The general conditions for the achievement of the second-best optimum in the type of case with which this analysis is concerned will be of the type $F_i/F_n = k_i(\Phi_i/\Phi_n)$, where $k_i \neq k_j \neq 1$, so that $F_i/F_j = \Phi_i/\Phi_j$, $F_i/F_j \neq F_k/F_j$, $\Phi_i/\Phi_j \neq \Phi_k/\Phi_j$, and the usual Paretian rules will be broken all round.

## The existence of a second-best solution

The essential condition that a true second-best solution to a given constrained situation should exist is that, if there is a Paretian optimum in which $F$ has a maximum (minimum) when the constraint is removed, then the expression (30) must also have a true maximum (minimum). There is no reason why this should, in general, be the case.

For one thing, whereas well-behaved functions $F$ and $\Phi$ will always have a solution which satisfies the comparatively simple first-order conditions for a Paretian optimum, it is by no means certain that the much more complex first-order conditions (31) for a second-best solution will be satisfied, since these conditions involve second-order derivatives whose behavior (subject only to convexity–concavity conditions of the functions) is unknown.

If the first-order conditions for the existence of second-best solutions present difficulties, the difficulties are quite insurmountable in the case of the second-order conditions. Let it be supposed, for concreteness, that the nature of the case is such that $F$ is to be maximized. Then the existence of a second-best solution requires that the first-order conditions (31) shall give a maximum, not a minimum or a turning point. This requires that the second differential of the expression (30) shall be negative. But the second differential of (30) involves the *third*-order derivatives of $F$ and $\Phi$. Absolutely nothing is known about these in the general case, and their properties cannot be derived from the second-order condition that the Paretian optimum represents a true maximum for $F$.

## The nature of second-best solutions

The extraordinary difficulty of making *a priori* judgements about the types of policy likely to be required in situations where the Paretian optimum is unattainable, and the second best must be aimed at, is well illustrated by examining the conditions (32) in the light of possible knowledge about the signs of some of the expressions involved.

In order to simplify the problem, and to render it less abstract, the function $F$ will be supposed to be a utility function and $\Phi$, which will be supposed to be a transformation function, will be assumed to be linear. The second derivatives of $\Phi$ disappear, so that $R_i = 0$ for all $i$, and attention can be concentrated on the expressions $Q$.

With the problem in this form, the derivatives $F_i$ are proportional to the prices $p_i$, and the derivatives $\Phi_i$ are proportional to the marginal costs $MC_i$. As an additional simplification which assists verbal discussion but which does not affect the essentials of the model, it will be supposed that price equals marginal cost for the $n$th commodity, which will be referred to as the numeraire.

From (32), with these additional assumptions, therefore:

$$\frac{F_i}{F_n} = p_i = \frac{MC_i + \theta Q_i}{1 + \theta Q_n}$$

where $\theta = \mu/\lambda'$ so that

$$p_i - MC_i = \theta(Q_i - p_i Q_n) \tag{33}$$

Thus, for the $i$th commodity, price is above, equal to, or below, marginal cost according as $Q_i/p_i$ is greater than, equal to, or less than, $Q_n$.

Since $Q_i = (F_n F_{1i} - F_1 F_{ni})/F_n^2$, the most we can expect to know is the sign of $Q_i$, unless a specific social utility function is given. From signs only, we can deduce only the following:

(i)   if $\theta > 0$,   $P > 1$ if $Q_i > 0, Q_n < 0$
$P < 1$ if $Q_i < 0, Q_n > 0$      (34)
(ii)  if $\theta < 0$,   $P > 1$ if $Q_i < 0, Q_n > 0$
$P < 1$ if $Q_i > 0, Q_n < 0$

Nothing can be said about $P$ if $Q_i$, $Q_n$ are of the same signs.

Now consider $Q_i$. The denominator is always positive, and $F_1$, $F_n$ are both positive, so that the determining factors are the signs of the mixed partial derivatives $F_{1i}$ and $F_{in}$. It is assumed that goods are known to be substitutes ($F_{ij} < 0$) or complements ($F_{ij} > 0$) in the Edgeworth–Pareto sense. There are four possible cases:

(a)  If $F_{1i} > 0, F_{ni} > 0$, then $Q_i \gtrless 0$
(b)  If $F_{1i} < 0, F_{ni} < 0$, then $Q_i \gtrless 0$
(c)  If $F_{1i} > 0, F_{ni} < 0$, then $Q_i > 0$
(d)  If $F_{1i} < 0, F_{ni} > 0$, then $Q_i < 0$

In cases (c) and (d), but not in cases (a) and (b), therefore, the sign of $Q_i$ is determinate.

To complete the picture the sign of $\theta$ is also needed. Where the sign of this can be found at all, it is found by putting $i = 1$ and substituting in the constraint condition (29). For concreteness, let $k$ be $> 1$ (the first good will be referred to as the monopolized good). Then, since $(1 + \theta Q_1)/(1 + \theta Q_n) = k > 1$, it can be deduced that, if $Q_1 < 0$, $Q_n > 0$, then $\theta < 0$, and if $Q_1 > 0$, $Q_n < 0$, then $\theta < 0$. In all other cases the sign of $\theta$ is indeterminate.

For $Q_1 > Q_n$, it is known that $F_{11}$, $F_{nn} < 0$, and $F_{n1} = F_{1n}$ so that there are only two cases, $F_{n1} > 0$ and $F_{n1} < 0$. The information conveyed in each of the two cases is as follows:

I   $F_{n1} > 0 : Q_1 < 0, Q_n > 0$, so that $\theta < 0$

II   $F_{n1} < 0 : Q_1 \gtrless 0, Q_n \gtrless 0$, so that $\theta \gtrless 0$

The combination of cases I and II with the independently determined cases $(a), (b), (c), (d)$ gives a total of eight cases. These are given in Table 12.1, showing the information which can be derived about the signs of $Q_i$, $Q_n$ and $\theta$, and the consequent information about $P$ using the conditions (34).

Table 12.1   *Determining relationship between price and marginal cost*

| Case | | Sign of $Q_i$ | Sign of $Q_n$ | $\theta$ | Relationship of price to marginal cost for $x_i$ |
|---|---|---|---|---|---|
| I $F_{ni} > 0$ | (a) $F_{ij}, F_{ni} > 0$ | ? | + | − | ? |
| | (b) $F_{ij}, F_{ni} < 0$ | ? | + | − | ? |
| | (c) $F_{1i} > 0, F_{ni} < 0$ | + | + | − | ? |
| | (d) $F_{1i} < 0, F_{ni} > 0$ | − | + | − | Price exceeds marginal cost |
| II $F_{ni} < 0$ | (a) $F_{1i}, F_{ni} > 0$ | ? | ? | ? | ? |
| | (b) $F_{1i}, F_{ni} < 0$ | ? | ? | ? | ? |
| | (c) $F_{1i} > 0, F_{ni} < 0$ | + | ? | ? | ? |
| | (d) $F_{1i} < 0, F_{ni} > 0$ | − | ? | ? | ? |

Of the eight cases tabulated, the signs of $Q_i$, $Q_n$ and $\theta$ are simultaneously determinate in only two, I(c) and I(d), and in only one of these two, I(d), does this lead to a determinate relationship between price and marginal cost. This sole case leads to the only *a priori* statement that can be made about the nature of second-best solutions on the basis of the signs of the mixed second-order partial derivatives of the utility function.

If the monopolized commodity is complementary (in Edgeworth–Pareto sense) to the numeraire, and the $i$th commodity is also complementary to the numeraire, but a substitute for the monopolized good, then, in order to attain a second-best solution, the price of the $i$th commodity must be set higher than its marginal cost.

Since knowledge of the sign alone of the derivatives $F_{ij}$ reveals only one determinate case, it would seem worthwhile to examine the situation if more heroic assumptions can be made about the knowledge of the utility function. The additional information which is assumed is that two commodities may be known to be 'weakly related', that is, that the derivative $F_{ij}$ is either zero or of the second-order relative to other quantities.

In the expression $Q_i = (F_n F_{1i} - F_1 F_{ni})/F_n^2$, for example, if the $i$th commodity and the numeraire are weakly related in this sense, then the term $F_1 F_{ni}$ can be neglected relative to the term $F_n F_{1i}$, and the sign of $Q_i$ is wholly determined by the sign of $F_{1i}$.

If the monopolized good and the numeraire are weakly related, then $Q_1 < 0$ and $Q_n > 0$. This is similar to the case I, in which the two goods were complements, leading to the same conclusions. There are now, however, four additional cases to add to $(a)$, $(b)$, $(c)$, $(d)$, for various combinations of weak relatedness with substitution and complementarity as between the $i$th commodity and the monopolized good and the numeraire. All the cases which can be given in terms of the three relationships (weakly related, complements, substitutes) are shown in Table 12.2. There are now three determinate cases, which can be summarized as follows.

*Table 12.2   Relationship between $i$th commodity, monopolized good and numeraire*

| Relationship between monopolized good and numeraire | Relationship of $i$th good to: Monopolized good | Numeraire | Signs of $Q_i$ | $Q_n$ | $\theta$ | Price of $i$th good relative to marginal cost |
|---|---|---|---|---|---|---|
| Complements, or weak | Complements | Complements | ? | + | – | ? |
| | Substitutes | Substitutes | ? | + | – | ? |
| | Complements | Substitutes | + | + | – | ? |
| | Substitutes | Complements | – | + | – | Higher |
| | Complements | Weak | + | + | – | ? |
| | Substitutes | Weak | – | + | – | Higher |
| | Weak | Complements | – | + | – | Higher |
| | Weak | Substitutes | + | + | – | ? |
| Substitutes | Any | Any | $\left.\begin{array}{c}+\\-\\?\end{array}\right\}$ ? | ? | | ? |

If the monopolized good and the numeraire are either complements or only weakly related, then the second-best solution will certainly require the price of the $i$th good to be set above its marginal cost either if the good is a substitute for the monopolized good and either complementary or only weakly related to the numeraire, or if the good is weakly related to the monopolized good but complementary to the numeraire.

With any other combinations of relatedness among the goods, it cannot be determined, *a priori*, whether the second-best solution will require the price of any particular good to be above or below its marginal cost. In particular, if there is no complementarity between any pairs of goods, and the relationship between the monopolized commodity and the numeraire is not weak, then there are no determinate cases.

As a matter of interest it is possible to work out conditions that may be likely to bring about any particular result. For example, a possible case in which the price of a good might be set below its marginal cost would be that in which the monopolized good, the numeraire, and the other good were all substitutes, but the rate at which marginal utility diminished was small in the case of the monopolized good (so that $Q_1$, $Q_n$ would both be positive, with $Q_1$ large compared with $Q_n$, giving a positive value for θ), and the relationship of the good under discussion was much stronger with the monopolized good than with the numeraire (so that $Q_i$ might be negative). There can be few real cases, however, where such guesses about the magnitudes of the quantities involved could be made.

**The problem of multiple-layer optima**
In all the preceding analysis, the problems have been conceived in terms of a single-layer optimum. It has been assumed that the constraint which defined the Paretian optimum (the transformation function, for example) was a technically fixed datum, and was not, itself, the result of an optimization process at a lower level.

The characteristic of general economic systems is, however, that they usually involve several successive processes of optimization, of increasing generality. The transformation function, for example, may have been derived as the result of competitive firms maximizing their profits. Firms are assumed to have minimized their costs before proceeding to maximize their profits, and these costs are themselves derived from processes involving optimization by the owners of the various factors of production.

It is of the nature of the economic process, therefore, that optimization takes place at successive levels, and that the maximization of a welfare function subject to a transformation function is only the topmost of these. It is also of the nature of Paretian optima (due to the simple proportionality of the conditions) that the optimization at the different levels can be considered as independent problems.

In the case of a second-best solution, however, the neat proportionality of the Paretian conditions disappears: this immediately poses the question whether a second-best solution in the circumstances of a multiple-layer economic system will require a breaking of the Paretian conditions at lower levels of the system, as well as at the level at which the problem was initiated.

The present paper does not propose to examine the problem, for it is a subject that would seem to merit full-scale treatment of its own. There seems reason to suppose, however, that there may well be cases in which a breaking of the Paretian rules at lower levels of the process (moving off the transformation function, for example) may enable a higher level of welfare to be obtained than if the scope of policy is confined to one level only.

A two-dimensional geometric illustration that is suggestive, although not conclusive, is set out in Figure 12.1. *Ox*, *Oy* represent the quantities of two goods *x*, *y*. The line *AB* represents a transformation function (to be considered as a boundary condition) and *CD* a constraint condition. In the absence of the constraint *CD* the optimum position will be some point, such as *P*, lying on the transformation line at the point of its tangency with one of the contours of the welfare function.

If the constraint condition must be satisfied, only points along *CD* can be chosen, and the optimum point *P* is no longer attainable. A point on the transformation

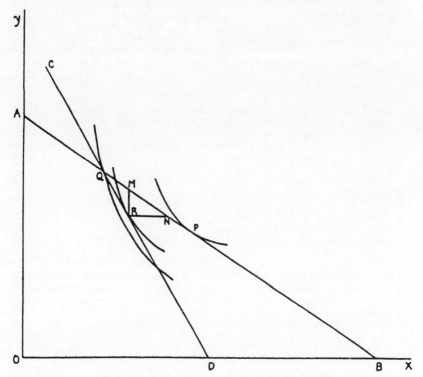

*Figure 12.1    Determining the location of the second-best solution*

line $(Q)$ is still attainable. Will the second-best solution be at the point $Q$, or should the economy move off the transformation line? If the welfare contours and the constraint line are as shown in the diagram, then the second-best point will be at the point $R$, inside the transformation line.

It is obvious, of course, that the second best will never be at a point which is technically inefficient (has less of one commodity and no more of the other) relative to any attainable point. Although there are points (the segment $MN$) on the transformation line which are technically more efficient than $R$, these are not attainable. $R$ is not technically inefficient relative to $Q$, even though $R$ lies inside the transformation line.

If the line $CD$ had a positive slope (as have the types of constraint which have been exemplified in the preceding analyses), the second best would always lie at its point of intersection with the transformation line, since all other points on $CD$ would be technically inefficient relative to it.

## Notes
1. Written with R.G. Lipsey and originally published in the *Review of Economic Studies*, **24** (1956), 11–32. At the suggestion of H.G. Johnson, then editor of the *Review*, independently written papers by the two authors, on the same topic but complementary in coverage, were combined into a single paper. The term 'second best' in this context was derived from Meade 1955b. In the original version, there was an algebraic error which affected two equations and a half page of text, but not the basic analysis, proof, or conclusions. A note was made of this when the paper was reprinted in Farrell, M.J. (ed.), *Readings in Welfare Economics*, London, Macmillan, 1973. Here the appropriate corrections have been made, affecting equations (32), (33) and some text.
2. Meade 1955b.
3. Viner 1950.
4. His neglect of the demand side allowed him to reach the erroneous conclusion that trade diversion necessarily led to a decrease in welfare. It is quite possible for an increase in welfare to follow from the formation of a customs union whose sole effect is to divert trade from lower- to higher-cost sources of supply. Furthermore this gain may be enjoyed by the country whose import trade is so diverted, by the customs union as an entity, and the world as a whole. See Lipsey 1957.
5. Meade 1955a.
6. Ozga 1955.
7. Little 1951.
8. Corlett and Hague 1953.
9. Meade 1955b, *Mathematica Appendix*.
10. Smithies 1936.
11. McKenzie 1951.
12. Little 1950.
13. If consumers have different utility functions then each consumer must receive from the government an amount equal to what he pays in taxes. However, if all consumers have identical homogeneous utility functions then all that is required is that all the tax revenue be returned to some consumer(s).
14. Obviously this is a problem in the theory of second best. The initial tariff on $Y$ causes the consumption of $Y$ to be too low relative to both $X$ and $Z$. If the consumption of $Y$ can be encouraged at the expense of $X$, welfare will be increased. However, if the consumption of $Z$ is encouraged at the expense of $X$, welfare will be lowered. A tariff on $X$ is likely to cause both sorts of consumption shift and the optimum $X$ tariff will be one where, at the margin, the harmful effect of the shift from $X$ to $Z$ just balances the beneficial effect of the shift from $X$ to $Y$.

# 13   Strategic considerations in second best[1]

## Introduction
In spite of an extensive literature on the overall topic, there are aspects of the second best that remain to be examined. The purpose of the present paper is to explore one of these, the potential for interaction between the policy maker and the private agents in the economy. Such interactions have been taken into account only in cases involving 'small' agents with no bargaining potential, as with optimal commodity taxes (Ramsey 1927) and optimal income taxes (Mirrlees 1971), where the agents react optimally, but passively, and these anticipated reactions are embodied in the design of the tax. The 'large' agent cases, such as those involving monopoly distortions, have been analyzed as though the agents simply ignored the policy maker's actions, or adjusted passively to them at most. This approach was true of the original Lipsey–Lancaster paper (Lipsey and Lancaster 1956).

The focus of this paper will be on the interactions between the policy maker and large agents, exemplified by the three-sector problem in which a regulator controls one sector and a monopolist another, while the third sector is competitive.

## The second-best problem
The problem of the second best requires three elements to be present. First, there must be a clear objective. Second, there must be a policy that can achieve this objective – the 'first-best' solution. Finally, there must be an impediment to fully implementing the first-best solution, an impediment that may arise from political, informational, administrative, or other sources. The term 'impediment' is chosen rather than 'constraint', to keep the latter term for technological, budgetary, and other basic restrictions which must be satisfied even in the first-best situation. Consider two of the classic cases:

1. Redistributive taxation. The objective is to maximize a welfare index which takes account of both the level and distribution of output. The first-best solution is an array of personalized 'lump-sum' taxes (positive and negative) which do not affect marginal choices between work and leisure or consumption and saving. For both political and informational reasons, the first-best tax system is normally unusable. If the only permissible policy instrument is an income tax on market or monetized income, what is the optimal tax schedule for a second-best solution?

221

2.  Pricing in public utility or regulated industries. If the objective is economic efficiency, the first-best solution is universal marginal cost pricing. But the existence of monopoly or other imperfectly competitive sectors beyond the scope of the regulator's power prevents implementation of the first best. What should be the pricing policy in the sectors actually regulated?

The essential feature of any second-best solution is that it must take account of the aberrant behavior that prevents first-best implementation, and attempt to partially offset it or to modify it, or both. The original Lipsey–Lancaster second-best solution to the regulation problem was pure offset. The monopoly was assumed to retain its behavior unchanged, while the regulated sector price was chosen so as to offset as far as possible the imbalance between the monopoly price and the competitive sector price. On the other hand, the optimal income tax solution to redistribution takes into account the behavior of taxpayers and attempts to modify it in a way that is optimal for the problem.

## A multiplicity of solutions

The 'second' in second best is not, of course, to be taken literally. It really means 'not as good as first' and could be considered '$n$th best' if there are $n$ impediments to attainment of the first best. Typically there will be many second-best solutions to a given problem, depending on what the impediments to the first best are, what instruments of policy are permitted, what information is available to the policy maker, and what are the expected reactions of agents to the chosen policies. The situation is made even more complicated by the existence of cases in which an appropriate mix of policy instruments may permit attainment of a first-best result in an apparently second-best situation.

Take the three-sector problem that will be the primary case considered in this paper, an economy with a competitive sector, a monopoly sector, and a regulated sector. Aggregate resource inputs are fixed, all income is consumed, and distribution is not relevant. Efficient output can be attained by marginal cost pricing in all sectors (first best). If the policy maker is permitted only to set the price in the regulated sector, we have the classic second-best problem, the solutions to which are discussed in detail later. But if the policy maker can intervene in other ways (except that the monopoly cannot be directly regulated), the first-best outcome can be achieved by matching the monopolist's price to marginal cost ratio in the regulated sector and imposing a sales tax in the competitive sector that does the same for the consumer price to marginal cost ratio in that sector, equivalent to the uniform degree of monopoly optimum.[2] Is this a first-best or a second-best solution?

It seems wisest to consider this last case to be a second-best solution that happens to lead to a first-best outcome, because it accepts the monopoly impediment as given even though it is able to offset its effects completely. Furthermore, the first-best outcome here is a special case because the same mix of policy instruments will not generally be able to achieve the first-best result if there are consumption–savings or labor–leisure decisions to be made by consumers, or if income distribution is an important consideration.

What we want to consider in this paper is the variety of second-best solutions that can exist even with a single policy instrument, and how the choice among these depends on the expected reactions of agents not directly controlled.

## Reacting to policies

In the optimal income tax problem, the policy maker is assumed to have full information as to individual's endowments and preferences, especially as to choices between market and non-market income, and to have a welfare criterion which includes distribution. The policy maker can coerce individuals to pay taxes based solely on their market income, but cannot tax non-market income or constrain individual's labor–leisure or other choices. Given a tax rate and a marginal tax rate for any specific income level, the government will know the expected reactions of the relevant households, those whose endowments will be such as to lead them to choose to generate that level of market income at those tax rates. The policy maker takes these reactions, and the utilities and tax payments resulting from them, as the basis for choosing the optimal tax schedule. Thus the relationship of the government to each taxpayer household is similar to the leader–follower relationship in the terminology of Stackelberg oligopoly analysis. In this case, the coercive nature of taxation leaves households no options but to be followers. It is also possible to think of the relationship in principal–agent terms, the households being agents with their own agendas that can nevertheless be manipulated by the incentives (or disincentives) of the tax system into contributing to an optimal outcome. The voluntary nature of the typical principal–agent contract is missing, however.

Our main interest here is in the three-sector problem when the price in the regulated sector is the only policy tool. No coercion is applied to the monopoly sector, and no taxes or other interventions occur in the competitive sector. Distribution is irrelevant or the subject of an entirely separate and non-interacting policy program. Because the monopolist is a free agent, and because the monopoly sector can well be of the same order of magnitude as the regulated sector, interactions between the monopolist and the regulator become relevant.

## The regulator and the monopolist

In the three-sector case, the relationship between the monopolist and the regulator is analogous in many respects to that between duopolists with imperfectly substitutable products, provided that the outputs of the sectors are indeed substitutes.[3] There are some important differences between the monopolist–

regulator interactions and those of a pair of duopolists, however, due to asymmetries in the first relationship that do not exist in the duopoly case:

1. The objectives of the regulator are different in kind from those of the monopolist. The latter is presumed to be interested only in the profit in his own sector, while the former is optimizing with respect to a welfare criterion which depends on outcomes in all three sectors. Note that we always assume the regulator is attempting to maximize overall welfare and not some narrowly defined sectoral objective. The term 'regulator' rather than 'government' has been chosen because limits on power are assumed, but not limits on welfare objectives.
2. The informational requirements for the regulator, who needs to know what is happening in all sectors, are much greater than those for the monopolist, who needs to know only his own cost and demand functions and market prices.
3. Since the monopolist *needs* less information, it is reasonable to suppose that he may sometimes *ignore* information. In particular, we take as one of the possible cases that in which the monopolist is simply unaware of, or ignores, the regulator's actions, and thus does not react to them – the sleepy monopolist who has been a recurring figure in industrial organization literature. This is only one case, however, and we also consider monopolists whose behavior is alert and sophisticated.
4. The regulator, in contrast with the monopolist, is assumed always to take into account the actual behavior of the latter and always to react to it. The regulator is never naive or sleepy like the monopolist, but may anticipate the behavior of the monopolist incorrectly.
5. Whereas the monopolist's objective function is known to the regulator, the monopolist may not know the regulator's exact welfare function. Thus even the sophisticated monopolist may not be able to anticipate correctly the regulator's behavior.

In spite of these differences, the regulator–monopolist relationship is much closer to symmetry than the government–taxpayer relationship in the optimal tax problem. In particular, the monopolist has the implicit bargaining power that the individual taxpayer does not.

Now consider the expectations that the two parties might hold concerning the reactions to each other's moves, embodied in $[p_m]^e$, the regulator's expectation as to the price the monopolist will set, and $[p_r]^e$, the monopolist's expectation as to the regulator's price.

Commence with the regulator's expectations about the monopolist, analysis of which will be confined to three different belief patterns which the regulator might hold concerning potential reactions by the monopolist. Where appropriate, the Stackelberg terminology is used, since this seems more to the point than either principal–agent or game theory terminology.

1. *Stationary behavior.* The monopolist is a naive or 'sleepy' one who, having determined the profit-maximizing price in the initial state, simply maintains it at this level. That is, $[p_m]^e = \bar{p}_m$, the value of $\bar{p}_m$ being determined by the initial state. The possible initial states are discussed in the next section.
2. *Follower behavior.* Complete and immediate, but non-anticipatory, adjustment to all current changes in the price of the regulated good, so that

$$[p_m^*]^e = p_m^*(p_r) = \arg \max_{p_m} \{\pi_m(p_r, p_m) \mid p_r\}$$

3. *Leader behavior.* Complete adjustment, taking into account anticipated optimal reactions by the regulator. The expected leader price is

$$[p_m^{**}]^e = \arg \max_{p_m} \pi_m(p_m, p_r^*(p_m))$$

When we come to examine the beliefs that the monopolist might hold concerning the actions of the regulator, we divide monopolists into naive and sophisticated:

1. The naive monopolist. These are not aware of, or simply choose to ignore, the effect of the regulator's actions. Thus their beliefs about the regulator, if they exist at all, are irrelevant. For analytical purposes, it can be assumed that they simply treat the regulator's price as constant at the initial level.
2. The sophisticated monopolist. The sophisticated monopolist will assume that the regulator is at least a follower, with expected price

$$[p_r^*]^e = p_r(p_m) = \arg \max_{p_r} \{W(p_r, p_m) \mid p_m\}$$

However, the monopolist might expect the regulator to take the leader role:

$$[p_r^{**}]^e = \arg \max_{p_r} W(p_r, p_m(p_r))$$

**Initial states**

Stationary behavior by the monopolist means maintaining the price that was optimal in the initial state, so we need to establish what would be relevant situations. We shall consider two scenarios, each leading to a well defined initial state:

I  Piecemeal policy. In this scenario, the regulator has already been at work in this sector, but has been adopting the so-called 'piecemeal' policy rule –

adopt marginal cost pricing because universal marginal cost pricing is a first-best policy. The regulator then becomes aware of the work on second best and changes his pricing policy accordingly. The initial state has marginal cost prices in the regulated sector, on the basis of which the monopolist has determined his price. The sleepy monopolist is assumed to maintain this price which will be given by $p_m(1)$ in the illustrative model.

This initial state would also be consistent with a scenario in which the sector which becomes regulated is initially competitive.

II  Unregulated monopoly. In the second scenario, the sector which becomes regulated was initially an unregulated monopoly. Thus there were initially two unregulated monopolies producing goods which are partial substitutes. It will be assumed in this case that the two monopolists have settled down to a Nash equilibrium in which the price of each is optimal given the price of the other. The initial prices are thus the Nash equilibrium prices for the two sectors treated as a pair of imperfect duopolists, given by

$$(\hat{p}_r, \hat{p}_m) \mid p_r(\hat{p}_m) = \hat{p}_r \text{ and } p_m(\hat{p}_r) = \hat{p}_m$$

To be consistent with the sleepy monopolist case, we can suppose that the equilibrium was reached as the result of a long period of slow adjustment.

**Potential outcomes**

The set of potential 'realistic' outcomes and their interrelationships is most easily studied by reversing the usual order of argument, giving first the results from a very specific theoretical model of the three-sector case, then analyzing those results and attempting to probe their degree of generality.

The model is that of the three-sector case in which the utility function is of the CES form, with the same elasticity of substitution between the goods in any pair of sectors, and a linear transformation relationship. The Appendix sets out the main features of this model for generalized parameters, an elasticity of substitution $\sigma$ ($> 1$), coefficients $a_1$, $a_2$, $a_3$ representing the relative importance of the regulated, monopoly, and competitive sectors, and a parameter $k$ representing the overall size. Since only limited analytical results can be obtained for general parameters, numerical solutions were generated for specific numerical values of the five essential parameters:

$\sigma = 2$
$a_1 = a_2 = 0.25, a_3 = 0.5$
$k = 100$

This is an economy with a moderate degree of substitution between outputs of the sectors, with regulated and competitive sectors of the same importance (equal quantities if prices are the same), but each only half as important as the competitive sector, and a size parameter chosen to give a first-best welfare level of 100.

Table 13.1 sets out the numerical results for this specific model in eight cases, three reference cases and five potential second-best outcomes. For each case the table gives the prices of the regulated and monopoly sectors, the welfare level, and the monopolist's profit. Cases are listed in decreasing order of welfare level.

*Table 13.1  Results for the model (eight cases)*

|  | $p_r$ | $p_m$ | $W$ | $\pi_m$ |
|---|---|---|---|---|
| First best | 1.00000 | 1.00000 | 100 | 0.00000 |
| Naive I | 1.11227 | 2.15470[a] | 93.5184 | 8.22539[b] |
| Regulator as leader | 1.09691 | 2.16328 | 93.4652 | 8.16396 |
| Nash | 1.11229 | 2.16451 | 93.4616 | 8.22562 |
| Monopolist as leader | 1.11233 | 2.18074 | 93.3863 | 8.78340 |
| Initial I (piecemeal) | 1.00000 | 2.15470 | 93.3013 | 7.73503 |
| Naive II | 1.11236 | 2.20557[c] | 93.2268 | 8.22325[d] |
| Initial II (duopoly) | 2.20557 | 2.20557 | 87.6086 | 10.2785 |

*Notes*
[a] Monopolist's optimal $p_m$ at $p_r = 1$, naively retained.
[b] Realized profit, based on true value of $p_r$.
[c] Monopolist's optimal $p_m$ at $p_r = 2.20557$, naively retained.
[d] Realized profit, based on true value of $p_r$.

The three reference cases are:

1. The first-best case, with marginal cost prices (= 1) in all three sectors.
2. The Initial I or piecemeal case, with marginal cost prices in both competitive and regulated sectors, and the monopolist setting his own best price $p_m^*(1)$.
3. The Initial II or duopoly case, with the sector that is to be regulated being initially an unregulated monopoly. Prices are Nash equilibrium duopoly prices, $\{\hat{p}_r = p_r(\hat{p}_m), \hat{p}_m = p_m(\hat{p}_r)\}$, equal here since the two sectors are of the same size.

The five potential second-best outcomes are:

1. Naive I   Commencing from Initial I, the regulator assumes the monopolist will maintain his initial price even after the regulator changes his. The monopolist is naive, and does indeed ignore the regulator's actions. In this configuration, the prices are

$$\{p_r^*(p_m^*(1)), p_m^*(1)\}$$

2. **Naive II**   Equivalent to Naive I, but commencing from Initial II, giving prices

$$\{p^*(\hat{p}_m), \hat{p}_m\}$$

3. **Nash**   A sophisticated but passive monopolist, adjusting optimally to the regulator's moves. This outcome is the Nash equilibrium of both the regulator and monopolist acting as followers, with prices given by

$$\{p_r^N = p_r^*(p_m^N), p_m^N = p_m^*(p_r^N)\}$$

4. **Regulator as leader**   The monopolist acts as a perfect follower, as in the Nash case, but the regulator foresees that this will be the case and chooses optimally, given the anticipated response. Then

$$\{p_r^{**} = \arg \max W(p_r, p_m^*(p_r)), p_m = p^*(p_r^{**})\}$$

5. **Monopolist as leader**   Here the monopolist, knowing for sure that the regulator will always adjust to his price, chooses optimally with this in mind.

$$\{p_m^{**} = \arg \max \pi_m(p_r^*(p_m), p_m), p_r = p_r^*(p_m^{**})\}$$

**The ordering of outcomes**

The descending welfare ordering of Table 13.1 is based on the results of solving a specific numerical model. At this stage, it is important to examine both the significance and the generality of this ordering, assuming that the monopoly and regulated sectors produce goods which are substitutes.

At the head of the table is the first-best outcome, with the highest welfare level. It is there by definition of 'first best', and it will hold the same place in the table for any model. It has the lowest monopoly sector profit for any outcome, although the term monopoly merely identifies the sector and not its behavior. That the profit happens to be zero is obviously not general, but due to the assumed constancy of average (total) cost.

It is perhaps surprising (and the author was certainly surprised) that the second-highest welfare level is associated with the Naive I outcome, the outcome assumed for the solution given in the original Lipsey–Lancaster paper. The significance of this ranking depends very much on whether its place in the table is general, and whether the outcome is some kind of quasi-equilibrium, or at least sustainable. Since Naive I results from policy applied to Initial I, consider first its relationship to the latter. In Initial I, the regulated sector is priced at marginal cost, while the monopolist's price is optimal for that value of $p_r$. The regulator now moves to improve welfare, assuming that the monopolist will do nothing. As shown in the Appendix,[4] $p_m > p_r^* (p_m) > 1$ for all $p_m > 1$, so that the regulator's move will increase $p_r$. Welfare is necessarily higher than in Initial I. Less obvious but more interesting, monopoly profit is also higher because $\partial x_m / \partial p_r > 0$ and the monopolist will be selling more even though his price is unchanged.

Note that Naive I dominates Initial I, since *both* the regulator and the monopolist gain by the move to Naive I. It is for this reason that Naive I can be regarded as a kind of quasi-equilibrium. The regulator obtains a welfare gain, while the naive monopolist, ignoring the regulator's policy move, obtains an unexpected increase in profit and finds no reason to change his price.

Suppose that the sleepy monopolist, having arrived at Naive I, is woken up by the appearance of unanticipated profits and decides to reconsider his pricing policy. Since he finds he is now selling more at his original price than in Initial I, he can expect to gain by raising his price a little. The regulator will then find it optimal to increase $p_r$ a little. Assuming that we reach an equilibrium in a stable manner by such incremental adjustments, the result will be the Nash outcome.

The Nash outcome will necessarily be more (in an extreme case, no less) profitable to the monopolist than Naive I, since he exercises an additional choice. The opposite side of this is that the regulator will find Nash less desirable than Naive I. Note that the differences in both welfare levels and profit between the Nash and Naive I outcomes are very small in the numerical model, although in the expected directions. The idea that Naive I could be a quasi-equilibrium is certainly suggested in the numerical values, where the monopolist would gain less than 0.01% by moving to the Nash, but there is absolutely no warrant as to generality.

Now consider the two leader cases. Since setting a price that gives the Nash outcome is always an available option to whoever takes a leader role, the leader outcome will be more favorable to the leader than will the Nash. At the same time, it will be less favorable to the non-leader than Nash, for otherwise there would be a consistent price pair that dominated Nash, which is impossible by the definition of the latter. Thus the regulator as leader outcome will give higher welfare and a lower monopoly profit than Nash, while the monopolist as leader outcome will give a lower welfare but higher profit than Nash. The ordering of the trio, regulator as leader, Nash, monopolist as leader, will be the same as in Table 13.1 even in the most general model. The leader role for the monopolist will necessarily give the highest profit among the second-best outcomes.

The lowest entry in the table is that of the Initial II or duopoly reference case. This ranks lowest in welfare since no agent's actions take any account of the level of aggregate welfare, and the price-taking constraint of competition is absent in two of three sectors of the economy, and that rank will hold in general. Lower ranking configurations, such as collusion or merger to make a two-product monopoly rather than a duopoly, are not considered here, nor are any non-cooperative solutions other than simple Nash duopoly.

Naive II is the outcome that emerges from imposing welfare-maximizing regulation on one, but not both, of a pair of initially unregulated duopolists. It necessarily ranks higher in welfare than the Initial II configuration from which it is developed, just as Naive I ranks higher in welfare than Initial I. In this case, however, monopoly profit drops because the relationship $p_m > p^*(p_m) > 1$ now means that $p_r$ falls as a consequence of optimization, instead of rising as in the Naive I case. Thus Naive II does *not* dominate Initial II, and the monopolist is most unlikely to be content with taking no action when his profit is falling. He is also much less likely to take a naive approach if he has competing as a duopolist rather than acting as an isolated monopolist.

Since $dp_m^*(p_r)/dp_r > 0$ (See the Appendix), the monopolist will cut his price below the Naive II level if he ceases to be passive and this will increase his profit. Since $\partial W^*/\partial p_m < 0$, such a move will also increase welfare. Thus the Nash outcome, the potential equilibrium if these moves continue in a convergent way, will dominate Naive II, as it does in the numerical example, reinforcing the view that Naive II would be, at most, a temporary outcome.

Putting all this together, it is clear that much of the welfare ordering as set out in Table 13.1 is not just specific to the numerical example, but is quite general. In particular, we can assert that the following order relationships hold generally:

* First best > regulator leader > Nash > monopolist leader > Initial II.
* First best > Naive I > Nash > Initial I > Initial II.
* First best > Nash > Naive II > Initial II.

The ambiguities in the order, therefore, are those for second/third place between Naive I and regulator leader, and for fifth/sixth/seventh place between monopolist leader, Initial I and Naive II. We cannot show that the ordering Naive I > regulator leader for the numerical example is general. The order might be reversed between the two, but certainly both outcomes lie between first best and Nash. Nor can we be certain in general as to the relative ordering of the trio of contenders for fifth, sixth, and seventh place, except that all three must lie between Nash and Initial II.

**The optimal second-best strategy**
Three features in the ordering of outcomes stand out with special prominence, and must play a substantial role in determining strategy even though the generality of the first is unclear:

1.  That first best is better than any second-best strategy by a clear margin, and that uncontrolled monopoly in both sectors is clearly worse than any piecemeal or second-best strategy. The welfare levels of all the potential second-best outcomes are remarkably close in the numerical example given, but it is impossible even to guess at the generality of this result.
2.  That Naive I ranks high in the order, certainly above Nash, although its ranking above regulator as leader cannot be shown to be general.
3.  That the monopolist as leader outcome is relatively unfavorable to the policy maker, but is the best available if the monopolist sets its leader price.

The choice of optimal strategy depends to some extent on the initial situation. If the sector about to be regulated by second-best principles has been setting prices at marginal cost, because of existing 'piecemeal' policy regulation or otherwise (Initial I), and the regulator is certain that the monopolist will not react, then Naive I is an available policy choice and reaches, in the example given, the highest welfare level short of first best. As has been shown above, the monopolist will find his profit increased as a result of this policy and the naive monopolist will have no incentive to react, the primary reason for treating this non-equilibrium outcome as a quasi-equilibrium and a potentially usable policy.

The danger in this policy is that any reaction to it by a monopolist who turns out not to be naive will lower overall welfare. If the monopolist is sophisticated but a follower, the regulator can move immediately to a leader role. This will commit the monopolist to a follower role and give the regulator leader outcome which is only slightly lower in welfare than Naive I, at least in the example. If the regulator does not move immediately to become leader at the first sign of action by the monopolist, the two sectors may converge to the Nash solution, which is worse than regulator leader in all cases and which leaves open to the monopolist the possibility of taking a leader role and lowering welfare still further.

If the regulator does not seize the leader role, it remains open to the monopolist. The latter has a good incentive in the example, since the profit as leader is some 7% higher than in Naive I or Nash and is the best outcome short of Initial II, a relationship that has generality. The monopolist as leader is equivalent to perfect rational expectations in this model – the regulator is locked out of an active decision role and is forced to follow, achieving at best a welfare level worse than Naive I, regulator leader, or Nash.

The Nash outcome is not likely in the second-best case. If the monopolist is truly passive, the regulator can choose Naive I and then move to regulator leader if the monopolist shows sign of reacting. If the monopolist is sophisticated and active, he may be able to pre-empt the leader role before the regulator can set up his shop, and if the regulator can move quickly enough, he may be able to pre-empt the pre-emption. If the system were at the Nash outcome, either the regulator or the monopolist could *always* gain by seizing leadership.

The only sure and safe policy for the regulator is immediately to force the regulator leader outcome, even if it happens to be worse than Naive I, and if the leadership role has not already been taken over by a sophisticated monopolist who has inevitably received ample notice of the impending regulation.

## Appendix   A three-sector CES model

*Basic structure*
There is an aggregate single price-taking consumer, three sectors, and constant unit cost in all sectors. The first sector ($r$) is the regulated sector, the second sector ($m$) is a monopoly sector, the third ($c$) a competitive sector. Goods units are chosen to equalize costs in all sectors. The competitive sector's price, equal to marginal cost in that sector and thus to the unit cost in all sectors, is the numeraire.

The model is defined by

$$U = \left( \sum_{i=1}^{n} a_i^{\frac{1}{\sigma}} x_i^{\frac{\sigma-1}{\sigma}} \right)^{\frac{\sigma}{\sigma-1}} \tag{1}$$

$$\sum_{i=r,m,c} x_i = k \tag{2}$$

*Demand functions*
These are 'true' demand functions, derived by assuming consumers make decisions as if money income were constant, then substituting for true money income by using the resource constraint:

$$x_r(p_r, p_m, 1) = \frac{a_1 p_r^{-\sigma}}{a_1 p_r^{-\sigma} + a_2 p_m^{-\sigma} + a_3} k \tag{3}$$

$$x_m(p_r, p_m, 1) = \frac{a_2 p_m^{-\sigma}}{a_1 p_r^{-\sigma} + a_2 p_m^{-\sigma} + a_3} k \tag{4}$$

$$x_c(p_r, p_m, 1) = \frac{a_3}{a_1 p_r^{-\sigma} + a_2 p_m^{-\sigma} + a_3} k \tag{5}$$

*Monopoly sector*
We can write

$$x_m = \frac{1}{1 + M p_m^{\sigma}} k$$

with

$$M = M(p_r) = \beta + \gamma p_r^{-\sigma}$$

where $\beta = a_3/a_2$ and $\gamma = a_1/a_2$. Note that $0 \leq M \leq \beta + \gamma$ for $p_r \geq 1$ and $M$ is decreasing in $p_r$. The parameter $\beta$ is a measure of the importance of the competitive sector relative to the monopoly sector, and $\gamma$ of the importance of the regulated sector relative to the monopoly sector. Note that $\beta$, $\gamma$ and hence $M$ are larger, the smaller is the monopoly sector relative to the others.

Then

$$\frac{\partial x_m}{\partial p_m} = -\frac{\sigma M p_m^{\sigma-1}}{\left(1 + M p_m^\sigma\right)^2} k \tag{6}$$

$$\varepsilon = -\frac{1}{1 + \dfrac{1}{M p_m^\sigma}\sigma} \tag{7}$$

Since $|\varepsilon| < \sigma$, must have $\sigma > 1$ for monopoly solution. The smaller the monopoly sector relative to other sectors (hence the larger is $M$), the closer is $|\varepsilon|$ to $\sigma$.

We have

$$\frac{\partial \pi}{\partial p_m} = \frac{1 - (\sigma-1)M p_m^\sigma + \sigma M p_m^{\sigma-1}}{\left(1 + M p_m^\sigma\right)^2} k$$

so that $p_m^*(p_r)$ is solution of

$$(\sigma - 1)M p_m^\sigma - \sigma M p_m^{\sigma-1} - 1 = 0$$

and

$$\pi^* = \pi_m^*(p_r) = (p_m^*(p_r) - 1)x_m(p_m^*(p_r), p_r)$$

*Example* For $\sigma = 2$, the only case in which we have a simple analytical solution:

$$p_m^* = 1 + \sqrt{\frac{(\beta+1)p_r^2 + \gamma}{\beta p_r^2 + \gamma}}$$

Note that $p_m^* > 2$ in this case, because $|\varepsilon| < 2$

*Monopolist's reaction function*    The properties of $p_m^*(p_r)$, which is the monopolist's reaction function and conveniently identified as $f_m(p_r)$, are determined by

$$f'_m = \frac{\left(p_m - \dfrac{\sigma}{\sigma-1}\right)p_m}{(p_m - 1)(a_1 + a_3 p_r^\sigma)p_r}$$

Since $|\varepsilon| < \sigma$, $p_m^* = (1 + 1/\varepsilon)^{-1} > \sigma/(\sigma-1) > 1$ so that $f'_m > 0$ over the relevant range.

Since

$$\frac{\partial x_m}{\partial p_r} = \frac{\sigma \gamma p_m^\sigma p_r^{-\sigma-1}}{\left(1 + M p_m^\sigma\right)^2} k > 0$$

and $f'_m > 0$

$$\frac{d\pi^*}{dp_r} > 0 \quad \forall p_m \geq 1$$

which is an important result.

*Regulated sector*
Taking the welfare function $W$ to be identical with the aggregate utility function $U$, and substituting for $x_r$, $x_m$ in terms of $p_r$, $p_m$ we obtain

$$W(p_r, p_m) = \frac{\left(a_1 p_r^{1-\sigma} + a_2 p_m^{1-\sigma} + a_3\right)^{\frac{\sigma}{\sigma-1}}}{a_1 p_r^{-\sigma} + a_2 p_m^{-\sigma} + a_3} k$$

From which we derive

$$\frac{\partial W}{\partial p_r} = \frac{a_2 p_m^{-\sigma}(p_m - p_r) - a_3(p_r - 1)}{\left(a_1 p_r^{1-\sigma} + a_2 p_m^{1-\sigma} + a_3\right)^{\frac{1}{1-\sigma}}} k$$

Thus maximization of $W$ with respect to $p_r$, taking $p_m$ as given, implies

$$p_m - p_r = \beta p_m^\sigma (p_r - 1)$$

and hence, since the only relevant solutions are those with $p_r, p_m \geq 1$, one of the following:

(a) $p_m = p_r = 1$ (the first-best solution)
(b) $p_m > p_r > 1$ (the classic second-best result)

In case (b), $p_r$ will normally be closer to 1 than to $p_m$, since $p_m$, $\sigma > 1$ while $\beta > 1$ if the monopoly sector is smaller than the competitive sector, which will be the usual case.

Since

$$\frac{\partial W}{\partial p_m} = \frac{a_1 p_r^{-\sigma}(p_r - p_m) - a_3(p_m - 1)}{\left(a_1 p_r^{1-\sigma} + a_2 p_m^{1-\sigma} + a_3\right)^{\frac{1}{1-\sigma}}} k$$

substitution of the optimal condition gives the result

$$\frac{\partial W^*}{\partial p_m} = -\frac{a_1 \beta p_r^{-\sigma} p_m^\sigma (p_r - 1) + a_3(p_m - 1)}{\left(a_1 p_r^{1-\sigma} + a_2 p_m^{1-\sigma} + a_3\right)^{\frac{1}{1-\sigma}}} k < 0$$

*Regulator's reaction function*　From the optimization above

$$p_r^*(p_m) = \phi_r(p_m) = \frac{\beta + p_m^{1-\sigma}}{\beta + p_m^{-\sigma}} = 1 + \frac{p_m - 1}{\beta p_m^\sigma + 1}$$

with

$$\phi_r' = \frac{1 - (\sigma - 1)\beta\left(p_m - \dfrac{\sigma}{\sigma - 1}\right)p_m^\sigma}{\left(1 + \beta p_m^\sigma\right)^2}$$

The notation $\phi_r$ has been chosen for the reaction function of the regulated sector rather than $f_r$ to emphasize the difference in criterion from the monopoly sector.

Now $\phi'_r > 0$ for $p_m \leq \sigma/(\sigma-1)$ so $\phi_r$ is certainly an increasing function of $p_m$ in the range $1 \leq p_m \leq \sigma/(\sigma-1)$. But $\phi'_r < 0$ for $p_m > \sigma/(\sigma-1)$ by a sufficient margin, so that $\phi_r$ has at least one point of inflection in the range $p_m \geq \sigma/(\sigma-1)$. But this is the range in which $p_m$ has already been shown to lie, if the monopolist is optimizing. At $p_m = \sigma/(\sigma-1)$ we have $\phi'_r = 1/(1 + \beta p_m^\sigma)^2$. This is certainly $< 1$ and, since $\beta$, $p_m$, $\sigma$ are all $> 1$, it can be taken to be small. Thus we can treat $\phi_r(p_m)$ as nearly flat over the relevant range for $p_m$.

*Leader behavior*
For the regulator as leader, the leader price $p_r^{**}$ is given by

$$p_r^{**} = \arg\max_{p_r} W(p_r, f_m(p_r))$$

while the monopolist leader price is

$$p_m^{**} = \arg\max_{p_m} (p_m - 1)x_m(\phi(p_m), p_m)$$

Neither of these relationships leads to simple analytical comparisons with other solutions.

For the example given in the text, with $\sigma = 2$, $\beta = 2$, $\gamma = 1$ we have

$$f_m(p_r) = 1 + \sqrt{\frac{3p_r^2 + 1}{2p_r^2 + 1}}$$

$$\phi_r(p_m) = \frac{2p_m^2 + p_m}{2p_m^2 + 1}$$

from which numerical solutions for $p_r^{**}$ and $p_m^{**}$ are derived with little difficulty.

**Notes**
1. Originally delivered at a conference in honor or Richard Lipsey in August 1993.
2. Originally due to Kahn 1935, and valid only if distribution does not matter. See also Baumol and Bradford 1970, Guesnerie and Laffont 1975.
3. Regulation is often associated with sectors producing power, transportation, communication, or other intermediate products.
4. See also Lipsey and Lancaster 1956, Green 1961.

# 14    Productivity-geared wage policies[1]

It has become fashionable of late, in some quarters, to suppose that the problem of inflation can be solved by a national wages policy, in which wage increases are assessed, and granted, on the basis of increases in 'productivity', i.e., average labor productivity. To be sure, adherence to a belief in this kind of policy involves implicit acceptance of a 'cost–inflation' model of the economy, in which prices move in proportion to changes in costs, and the relevant costs are entirely, or largely, wage costs. One could easily quarrel with the whole basis of the cost–inflation model, but we shall accept it, for the purposes of argument, here.

Given simple wage–cost price determination, then it cannot be doubted that, if productivity increases by a uniform proportion throughout the economy, and wages are everywhere raised by that same proportion, then wage costs per unit of product are unchanged, all prices are unchanged, and any index of prices is unchanged. This argument is the seed from which has grown a whole complex of assertions which can loosely be classified as 'productivity-geared wage policies', not all of which have the validity of their progenitor.

What if productivity rises at different rates in different sectors of the economy? This, which must be accepted as very much the typical case, clearly presents problems, and it is these that we are going to examine in this paper. It is immediately obvious, however, that there are two extreme cases. On the one hand, it might be argued that all wages should rise by a common proportion equal to some assessment of the 'average' rise in productivity over the economy as a whole. On the other hand, it might equally be argued that wages in each industry should rise in proportion to the productivity increase in that industry.

The first argument, for a uniform wage rise throughout the economy, obviously heads straight into difficulties of an index number kind (i.e., in defining the appropriate 'average' productivity), but, abstracting from these, has a direct appeal in circumstances in which the general level of wages is subject to institutional determination. Such was the case with the Australian basic wage which, for more than 30 years, was geared to a cost of living index: during the post-war series of wage determinations it was the constant contention of employers' representatives that the basic wage (which virtually determined the level of all wages) should be geared to such an index of overall productivity, rather than to the cost of living index. It was on the grounds of the practical index number problems, rather than on grounds of principle, that the Commonwealth Arbitration Court rejected this contention.

The second argument, for a rise in wages industry by industry in proportion to each industry's increase in productivity, has not found great favor among advocates of a general wages policy, but is implicit in many industry bargaining situations.

Both these policies are clearly capable of giving wage increases which do not change the general level of prices: the first, by judicious choice of the definition of the 'average' increase in productivity, can maintain any chosen index of prices, while the second, by leaving individual prices unchanged, keeps all price index numbers constant.

Mere preservation of a constant index of prices cannot, however, be the sole aim of an economic policy which must profoundly affect many aspects of the economy. Indeed, those whose advocacy of a wages policy is based solely on this consideration are adopting the same attitude, in principle, as those advocates of banking policy prior to the 1930s whose sole consideration was preservation of the balance of payments at a constant exchange rate – a kinship that many supporters of naive wage policies are surely anxious to hide. Any wage policy is going to affect, *inter alia*, the relative demands for the products of the various industries and the relative supply of labor to the various industries: wages policy is every bit as capable of giving rise to unemployment as is monetary policy.

A uniform rise in wages will presumably leave the supply of labor to the various industries more or less unchanged. Since, however, there will be industries in which productivity has increased less than the 'average', wages, costs and prices will rise in those industries, the demand for the products will fall relative to other industries: it will only be by coincidence that the relatively greater use of labor in these industries (due to the lesser rise in productivity) exactly counterbalances the fall in relative demand. Similar effects will, of course, occur in industries in which productivity increases have been more than average, but in an opposite direction. Thus a policy of this kind will, except in special cases, lead to excess demand for labor in some industries, and excess supply in others, leading to regional unemployment or increases in earnings relative to nominal wages (so to breakdown of the carefully poised 'anti-inflationary' wages policy), or both.

If, on the other hand, wages rise in proportion to productivity increases in individual industries, the relative demands for the products will be more or less unchanged,[2] the relative demand for labor will fall in the industries with the greater productivity increases, while the relative supply of labor to these industries will rise. Again, there will be imbalance in the labor markets, leading to unemployment, breakdown of the wages policy, or both.

Intuitively, therefore, one would expect a successful wages policy (which maintained a constant price level *and* preserved balance in the markets for the various types of labor) to lie between the two extremes outlined above, and to be such that wages rose by something less than the increase in productivity in the more rapidly advancing industries, and by something more than the productivity increase in the less rapidly advancing industries. This general approach has been put forward both by the Cohen council[3] and by some of its critics: the Cohen council has even observed that it may be appropriate for wages to *fall* in industries in which productivity increases have been particularly large.

It is the purpose of the present paper to make some taxonomic observations on the nature of 'successful' possible wage policies under varying conditions of commodity demand and labor supply. The boxes which are offered may, or may not, be empty, but it is the writer's belief that some classificatory thinking is valuable at this point in the debate.

### The nature of the model

We shall concern ourselves with a simple two-sector economy with labor the only scarce factor. Prices are assumed to be proportional to (not necessarily equal to) wages multiplied by the reciprocal of the average labor productivity. This average productivity is assumed to be independent of the level of output (no diminishing marginal product) but subject to exogenous changes which are part of the data.

The variables in which we are interested are the outputs, demand for labor, supply of labor, prices, wages and productivities in the two sectors. We shall distinguish the two sectors A and B by the use of the subscripts $a$, $b$. Then we shall denote the outputs by $Z_a$, $Z_b$; the demands for labor by $L'_a$, $L'_b$; the supplies of labour by $L_a$, $L_b$; the prices by $P_a$, $P_b$; the wages by $W_a$, $W_b$; and the productivities by $X_a$, $X_b$.

Then wages and prices are related by the equation

$$P = k\frac{W}{X} \tag{1}$$

for both sectors, where $k$ is a constant of proportionality.

Output and the demand for labor are also related via productivity, as follows:

$$L' = \frac{Z}{X} \tag{2}$$

Now, in discussing wage and productivity problems and policies, it is usual to think in terms of proportional, rather than absolute, changes, and we shall couch our own analysis wholly in terms of proportional changes. We shall denote by lower case letters the proportional increase in the quantity which is represented by the corresponding capital letter, i.e., $z_a$ will stand for $dZ_a/Z_a$, the proportional increase in the output of sector A, and so on.

Since the changes with which we are likely to be concerned in real wage policy problems will be small proportional changes, we shall assume them to be small here. This enables us greatly to simplify our analysis since, for small proportional changes:

(i) the proportional change in a product is the sum of the proportional changes in the factors, and
(ii) the proportional change in a ratio is the proportional change in the numerator less the proportional change in the denominator.

These rules enable us to put (1) and (2) in the simplified forms

$$p = w - x \tag{3}$$
$$l' = z - x \tag{4}$$

where the constant $k$ of (1) has disappeared because we are dealing with changes.

**Preserving balance in the labor markets**
Whenever prices and wages change in one sector relative to the other, there will be direct effects both on the relative demands for the products of the two sectors and the relative supply of labor to the two sectors. Direct application of Marshallian partial elasticities is not, of course, possible in what is essentially a general equilibrium-type model. However, since we are concerned with small proportional changes, the most useful coefficients of behavior for our purposes are those of elasticity form. We shall, therefore, define two elasticities specifically suited to the present model – the elasticity of demand substitution, and the elasticity of labor mobility.

The *elasticity of demand substitution*, $s$, is defined as the ratio of the change in the ratio in which the products of the two sectors are consumed to the change in the ratio of their prices. That is (adopting the Marshallian convention of making the elasticity positive):

$$s = -\frac{\dfrac{d(Z_a / Z_b)}{Z_a / Z_b}}{\dfrac{d(P_a / P_b)}{P_a / P_b}} \tag{5}$$

Using our rules for proportional changes in ratios, and our convention of writing proportional changes in lower case letters, (5) can be put immediately in the form in which we shall use it, i.e.,

$$s = -\frac{(z_a - z_b)}{(p_a - p_b)} \tag{6}$$

If $p_b = 0$, and $z_b = 0$, then $s = -(z_a)/(p_a)$, and is equal to a Marshallian-type partial elasticity in which income is adjusted after the price change to bring the consumers to the point where they purchase the same amount of sector B's product as before. There is a symmetrical case obtained by putting $z_a = p_a = 0$.

To be able to use this elasticity, and treat it as a constant in our analysis, we must implicitly assume that the relationship between the relative consumption of the products and their relative prices is independent of the level of real income, that is, that the two products have identical income elasticities.

The *elasticity of labor mobility*, $m$, is defined, similarly, as the ratio of the change in the ratio in which labor offers itself to the two sectors to the change in the ratio of the wages in the two sectors. We shall write this immediately in the reduced form

$$m = \frac{(l_a - l_b)}{(w_a - w_b)} \tag{7}$$

Elasticities imply a response to a stimulus, and a response takes time. If there are considerable lags in the responses (compared to the frequency of perceptible productivity increases), and especially if the rates of response differ markedly in the product market and the labour market, then we should require to carry out a dynamic analysis of our problem. We shall, however, assume that the elasticities measure the extent of the response in a 'year', that productivity changes take place one a year, and that, when wages and prices change, all responses are geared to the new situation, the old being forgotten.

By assumption, changes in productivity are taken as the exogenous variables. Let us consider, therefore, the effects on the demand and supply of labour of some exogenous shift in the two productivities (expressed as proportional changes $x_a$, $x_b$) coupled with arbitrary proportional changes $w_a$, $w_b$ in the two wage rates.

Using (3), the proportional changes in the two prices will be given by

$$p_a = w_a - x_a$$
$$p_b = w_b - x_b$$

and

$$p_a - p_b = (w_a - w_b) - (x_a - x_b) \tag{8}$$

From (6), the proportional changes in the demand for the output of the two sectors, consequent upon the changes in relative prices, will be related by

$$z_a - z_b = - s(p_a - p_b)$$
$$= s[(x_a - x_b) - (w_a - w_b)] \tag{9}$$

The proportional change in the demand for labor in the two sectors will be related as follows, using (4):

$$l'_a - l'_b = (z_a - z_b) - (x_a - x_b)$$
$$= (s - 1)(x_a - x_b) - s(w_a - w_b), \text{ from (9)} \tag{10}$$

We now turn to the supply side of the labor market. The relationship between the proportional changes in the supply of labor to the two sectors is given directly from (7):

$$l_a - l_b = m(w_a - w_b) \tag{11}$$

Assuming that the initial position was one of equilibrium in the labor markets, this equilibrium will only be preserved under the combined change in productivities and wages if the proportional changes in demand are equal to the proportional changes in supply in both markets, so that $l_a = l'_a$ and $l_b = l'_b$, and thus $l_a - l_b = l'_a - l'_b$. From (10) and (11) this requires:

$$m(w_a - w_b) = (s - 1)(x_a - x_b) - s(w_a - w_b)$$
$$(m + s)(w_a - w_b) = (s - 1)(x_a - x_b)$$

or,

$$\frac{w_a - w_b}{x_a - x_b} = \frac{s - 1}{s + m} \tag{12}$$

Equation (12) is our fundamental relationship, for it expresses the relationship which must necessarily hold between relative wage changes and relative productivity changes in the two sectors if there is not to be relatively excess demand for labor in either sector. This relationship is so important that it is convenient to refer to it as the *structural elasticity* of the system, a term which is appropriate because it has the dimensions (or lack of them) of an elasticity, and is structural in the sense of involving all (i.e. both) the behavior coefficients of the system. We shall denote the structural elasticity by $E$, so that

$$E = \frac{s-1}{s+m} \qquad (13)$$

and the necessary condition for relative balance in the two labor markets is that the wage and productivity changes should be related by

$$w_a - w_b = E(x_a - x_b) \qquad (14)$$

$E$ is clearly positive if $s > 1$, negative if $s < 1$, and zero if $s = 1$, since both $s$ and $m$ have been defined so as to be essentially positive. The greatest positive value for $E$ is unity when $s$ is infinite, that is, when the outputs of the two sectors are perfect substitutes. In the negative range, $E$ has no limit, being negatively infinite when $s$ and $m$ are both zero, that is, there is no substitutability in demand and no labor mobility. $E$ approaches zero as $m$ approaches infinity; the smaller is $m$, other things being equal, the greater is the *numerical* value of $E$, either positive or negative.

## Maintaining a constant price level

Let the price index which it is required to keep constant have weights $g$, $1 - g$, attached to the outputs of sectors A and B respectively. Then any price changes which keep the value of this index constant must satisfy the condition:

$$g p_a + (1-g) p_b = 0 \qquad (15)$$

Using (3), we can put this in terms of two sets of variables, the wage changes and the productivity changes:

$$g(w_a - x_a) + (1 - g)(w_b - x_b) = 0 \qquad (16)$$

or the equivalent form,

$$w_b - x_b = -g[(w_a - w_b) - (x_a - x_b)] \qquad (17)$$
$$w_a - x_a = (1 - g)[(w_a - w_b) - (x_a - x_b)] \qquad (18)$$

These give the relationship which must hold between the wage and productivity increase in either sector, and the relative wage and productivity changes between the sectors. Equations (17) and (18) are not, of course, two separate conditions, but merely mirror images of each other.

## An effective wages policy

An effective productivity-geared wages policy, as we define it, is one which preserves balance in the labor market while maintaining constant the chosen price index. It must, therefore, satisfy the conditions (14) and (18) (or (17)) simultaneously. Using condition (14), we can substitute for $(w_a - w_b)$ in (17) and (18) and we obtain, immediately

$$w_b - x_b = -g(E - 1) - (x_a - x_b) \tag{19}$$
$$w_a - x_a = (1 - g)(E - 1)(x_a - x_b) \tag{20}$$

Taking the productivity changes as exogenous, (19) and (20) immediately give wage changes which will be appropriate to preserve the balance that we are after. Adopting the convention, to which we shall henceforth adhere, that the labeling of the sectors is so chosen as to make sector A that in which the productivity increase is the greater, so that $(x_a - x_b)$ is positive, and recalling that $E \leq 1$, we can rewrite (19) and (20) in a form in which all the factors are positive, so that the relative signs of the terms are immediately clear:

$$w_b = x_b + g(1 - E)(x_a - x_b)$$
$$w_a = x_a - (1 - g)(1 - E)(x_a - x_b) \tag{21}$$

The expression for the appropriate wage change consists of two terms. The first is simply the productivity change in that sector. The second contains an expression $(1 - E)(x_a - x_b)$ common to both sectors: this is the difference in the productivity changes multiplied by one minus the structural elasticity. This factor is, so to speak, split between the sectors in a manner *opposite* to the way in which they appear in the price index, being subtracted from the sector with the greater productivity increase and added to that with the lesser increase.

Unless the second, or adjustment, term is zero, therefore, we are justified in our intuitive view that the wage increase should lag behind the productivity increase in the sector with the greater productivity advance, and should move ahead of productivity in the other sector.

Before moving to examine a general classification of cases, we shall identify the circumstances in which the two limiting approaches to policy, to which reference was earlier made, are justified.

(i)  *Wages to rise in proportion to productivity in each sector.* This policy would be appropriate if (21) gave $w_a = x_a$ and $w_b = x_b$. This requires the adjustment term to be zero, which would be the case only if:

(a)  $x_a = x_b$ : i.e. both industries showed identical productivity changes. This is trivial.

(b)  $E = 1$: i.e., $s = \infty$ and the outputs of the two sectors are perfect substitutes.

Thus such a policy is not appropriate in any real, non-trivial circumstances.

(ii) *All wages to rise in the proportion of the 'average' productivity change.* Such a policy would be effective if the circumstances of our model led to $w_a = w_b$, i.e.

$$x_a - (1 - g)(1 - E)(x_a - x_b) = x_b + g(1 - E)(x_a - x_b)$$
$$x_a - x_b = (1 - E)(x_a - x_b)$$
$$E = 0 \qquad (22)$$

This is not a trivial case for, if the structural elasticity were zero (i.e., the elasticity of demand substitution between the outputs of the two sectors were unity), then a uniform rise in all wages could be appropriate for *all* productivity changes. The actual proportion in which wages should rise would be given from (21):

$$w = x_a - (1 - g)(1 - E)(x_a - x_b)$$
$$= x_a - (1 - g)(x_a - x_b) \quad (E = 0)$$
$$= gx_a + (1 - g)x_b \qquad (23)$$

and this shows that an appropriate index of 'average' productivity has the same weighting as the price index.

If there were reason for believing that the elasticity of demand substitution (as we have defined it) were approximately unity, so that the proportion of total expenditure between the outputs of the two sectors was nearly constant under a change in relative prices, *or* that the elasticity of labor mobility was very great,[4] then the policy of a uniform general rise in wages would be appropriate, and the extent of the rise would be given from a productivity index having the same weights as the price index.

**Some classificatory observations**
In general, as we have seen, an effective productivity-geared wage policy will involve wage rises less than the productivity increases in the sectors in which productivity is advancing most rapidly, and wage rises in excess of the productivity increases in those sectors in which the productivity advances are less rapid. Although this implies that the less rapidly advancing sector will always obtain a rise in wages at least equal to the productivity increase, no lower limit is implied to the extent of the wage rise in the more rapidly advancing sector – *a priori*, it might be less than in the other sector, and wages might even fall. Our aim here is to examine the conditions under which the wage rise is less in the more rapidly advancing sector, and the conditions under which the policy will call for a fall in wages in that sector. We shall then examine the effects of greater and lesser demand substitution, and greater and lesser labor mobility, on the nature of the wages policy.

*The relative wage increase in the two sectors*

From the analysis from which we obtained (22), it is obvious that $w_a \gtreqqless w_b$ according as $E \gtreqqless 0$. Thus it will be appropriate for wages to rise most in the more rapidly advancing sector so long as the structural elasticity is positive, that is, so long as the elasticity of demand substitution is greater than unity.

Thus, if the products of the two sectors are good substitutes ($s > 1$), the more rapidly advancing sector will receive the greater wage rise, but if the products of the sectors are poor substitutes, then the more rapidly advancing sector will receive the smaller wage rise. The relative wage increases, it will be noted, depend on demand conditions only and not on the extent of labour mobility.

*A fall in wages in the more rapidly advancing sector*

From (21) we have $w_a < 0$ if $x_a - (1-g)(1-E)(x_a - x_b) < 0$

$$\frac{x_a}{x_a - x_b} < (1-g)(1-E) \tag{24}$$

Examination of (24) makes it clear that the left-hand side is smaller, the greater is $x_a$ relative to $x_b$, being infinite when $x_a = x_b$ ($x_a \leq x_b$, of course) and unity when $x_a$ is infinite. The right-hand side is larger, the smaller is $g$ and the smaller is $E$ algebraically (i.e. the larger numerically, if it is negative). It is obvious that the absolutely necessary condition for a fall in wages in sector A is that $E$ be negative (see above). Given this, such a fall is the more likely:

(a)   the greater the productivity increase in the more rapidly advancing sector, relative to the productivity increase elsewhere;
(b)   the less important is that sector in the total economy, measured by the weight attached to its output in the price index (i.e. the smaller is $g$);
(c)   the more negative is the structural elasticity, that is, the lower are both the elasticity of demand substitution and the elasticity of labor mobility.

We can conclude that it would be appropriate for wages to fall, in general, in a sector only if productivity in that sector were advancing very rapidly, the sector was small ($g$ small), specialized ($s$ small) and using specialized labor ($m$ small). It is unlikely that a fall in wages would be appropriate in any substantial sector of the economy.

*The effects of the demand and labor mobility elasticities*

We have actually discussed these effects while examining effective wage policies from other points of view.

The critical value for the elasticity of demand substitution is unity. At this value the structural elasticity is zero, irrespective of the elasticity of labor mobility, and both wages will move together. The greater the extent to which the substitution elasticity differs from unity, the more divergent will be the wage changes in the two sectors, and the less successful will be a uniform-type wage policy. The greater the demand substitution, the more closely will the wages in each industry be geared to productivity in that industry; the lower the demand substitution, the more divergent will be the wage movement from the productivity change till, eventually, wages will rise rapidly in the least rapidly advancing industries, and fall in the most rapidly advancing sectors.

The effect of the elasticity of labor mobility is more straightforward. The larger this elasticity is, the more closely does the structural elasticity approach zero, and the more nearly do the wage changes coincide in the two sectors. The less the degree of labor mobility, the more divergent will be the wage movements in the two sectors.

## A numerical example

This example is given to illustrate, in a simple manner, the working of the model with which we are concerned. Let us suppose that there is a reasonable degree of both demand substitution and labor mobility in the economy, so that $s$ and $m$ are both, say, 2.0. Then the structural elasticity is given by $E = (s - 1)/(s + m)$ $= \frac{1}{4}$. Let the productivity increases be 3% in sector A and 1% in sector B. For simplicity, let the relative weights of the two sectors in the price index be $\frac{1}{3}$, $\frac{2}{3}$ $(g = \frac{1}{3})$.

Then the appropriate wage changes are given by (21):

$$w_a = 3\% - (\tfrac{2}{3})(\tfrac{3}{4}) \, (2\%)$$
$$= 2\%$$
$$w_b = 1\% + (\tfrac{1}{3})(\tfrac{3}{4}) \, (2\%)$$
$$= 1\tfrac{1}{2}\%$$

In this case, the wage increases more in the more rapidly advancing sector, since $E > 0$.

It is interesting to work out this example in full, as a check on the method. For sector A, we have, from (3),

$$p_a = 2\% - 3\% = -1\%$$

so that prices fall by 1%. For sector B we have

$$p_b = 1\tfrac{1}{2}\% - 1\% = \tfrac{1}{2}\%$$

Since the weights of the price index are in the ratio of 1:2, the condition for an unchanged price index is obviously satisfied.

From (6), the changes in demand for the two outputs are related thus:

$$z_a - z_b = -2(-1\% - \tfrac{1}{2}\%) = 3\%$$

the increase in the demand for sector A's output exceeding that for sector B's output by 3%. From (4) the relative change in the labor demands in the two sectors is given by:

$$1'_a - 1'_b = 3\% - 2\% = 1\%$$

while we have the supply side of the labor market given directly from (7)

$$1_a - 1_b = 2(2\% - 1\tfrac{1}{2}\%) = 1\%$$

so that the relative balance in the labor market is undisturbed.

**The problems of practical policy**
The greatest problem which would seem to confront the policy maker attempting to devise an effective wage policy of the kind we have outlined is that of assessing the value of the structural elasticity $E$. While, in a sense, this is true, there are aspects of a more political nature that probably present difficulties as great.

It is obvious that, if wage policy were determined on the basis of productivity estimates, then these estimates would be a matter of the highest interest and importance to all concerned, not least to the trade unions. Any discussion of the problems of wage policies of this kind must proceed, therefore, on the assumption of knowledge of the relative productivity changes on the part of the trade unions.

Now we have shown that the wage rise in the case of the more rapidly advancing sector will be less than the increase in productivity in that sector. The trade union concerned will be aware of this. No body of persons associated for mutual gain is likely to be unduly altruistic, and it seems more than probable that the trade union in the sector which is advancing more rapidly will tend to be of the opinion that, since its members are in the industry which is contributing most to the overall productivity increase, it is they who should receive the major wage increase. There will be a strong tendency for the union in this sector to attempt to obtain higher wages than the general wage policy considers appropriate. Furthermore, the employers in this sector will not feel any desperate need for resistance, since their unit costs will fall for any wage rise less than the increase in productivity.

This tendency towards upward pressure on wages in the more rapidly advancing sector would probably always be present; it would be greater the smaller (algebraically) is the structural elasticity and so the greater the gap between the wage increase and the productivity increase. It is difficult to conceive of a trade union in a free economy, finding that (as could be the case) its members were to have the smaller wage rise, although their industry showed the greater rise in productivity, not attempting to break out of the bounds of the wage policy apparatus and strike their own bargain with fairly unresisting employers. If the wage policy called for an actual decrease in the wages in this sector, surely only very considerable coercion could prevent a breakdown of the policy.

The trade union may have its doubts in the more rapidly advancing sector. In the less rapidly advancing sector, it will be the employers. In all cases, the wage policy will call for a wage rise in this sector greater than the increase in productivity. This will mean rising unit costs, which the employers will be reluctant to accept in a situation which is, by definition, not inflationary.

We can thus expect that, even if there is no excess supply or demand in either labor market, there will tend to exist, so long as trade unions and employer associations exist, an upward pressure on wages in the more rapidly advancing sector, and a downward pressure in the less rapidly advancing sector. To offset this, it would seem desirable not to strike quite the exact balance in the two labor markets which we have visualized so far, but to place a little pressure of excess supply into the labor market of the more rapidly advancing sector, and a little excess demand into the labor market of the other sector. That is to say, it might be wise to raise wages in the more rapidly advancing sector a little more, and in the less rapidly advancing sector a little less, than the amounts obtained by strict adherence to our formula. In terms of estimating the value of the structural elasticity, it would seem better to err on the side of being high (algebraically) rather than low.

Since it is, for institutional reasons, much simpler to put a floor on wages than a ceiling, and so easier to coerce employers into accepting a rise in wages greater than they would wish to grant than to prevent side bargains being struck to raise wages when employers are not unwilling, it is clear that it is the sector with the greater productivity advance which is crucial to the implementation of a productivity-geared wage policy. If wage rises in this sector can be kept down to the appropriate level, the other sector does not present great problems. In fact, if the 'government' can control wages in the sector with the greater rate of productivity change, little control may be needed in the less rapidly advancing sector.

It so happens, unfortunately, that the sector over which any central authority has control in the United Kingdom, the civil services in the widest sense, and the nationalized industries, are probably the sectors with the lower productivity increases, and attempts to combat inflation via wage control in these groups probably lead to distortion by granting lower increases than would be called for by an overall wages policy, while doing little to combat unduly great rises in wages (or earnings) in the sectors in which productivity is undergoing rapid change.

**Conclusion**

If we accept a simple wage cost inflation model as a macroeconomic framework, and this need only imply that we are concerned with a situation in which monetary policy is 'passive' or 'neutral', neither adding to, nor subtracting from, changes in prices which happen to be equal to changes in unit wage costs, then it is possible to determine a wage policy in which wages are geared to productivity changes in such a way as to preserve (*a*) a constant price level, and (*b*) balance in the labor markets of the sectors of the economy.

Such a policy will require wages to rise by less than the increase in productivity in the more rapidly advancing sector, and more than the increase in productivity in the less rapidly advancing sector, the exact relationships being determined from the 'structural elasticity' of the economy. For some value (or small range of values) of the structural elasticity, a wage rise uniform throughout the economy may be appropriate, but this will not be the general case.

Although the problems of estimating the relevant parameter – even were it believed stable in value – stand in the way of practical application of such a wages policy, the political problems are probably as great a barrier. It is the sector with the greatest productivity rise in which wages will be required to lag behind the productivity increase, so that wages may rise less in this sector than in the lagging sector, and could even be required to fall, so that it is control of wages in this sector which is most vital for successful implementation of the wages policy as a whole. If the central authority has no control over wages in the 'go-ahead' sector – and it rarely has in an uncontrolled economy – then it may well make things worse by attempting to exercise control over a lagging sector.

Even if there exist no control over wages, however, the notional framework of what an effective wage policy would be, in any circumstance, provides a useful measuring rod by which the possible effects of wage rises resulting from free bargaining may be judged.

**Notes**
1. Originally published in *Economica*, **25** (1958), 199–212.
2. Unless income effects differ markedly among different products.
3. Council on Prices, Productivity and Incomes, *First Report* (February 1958). London, H.M.S.O.
4. Since $E \to 0$ as $m \to \infty$.

# 15   The dynamic inefficiency of capitalism[1]

**Capitalism as a dynamic conflict**

It is said that Abba Lerner opened his lectures on Keynes at the New School with a remark something like the following: 'Marx, the socialist, devoted his life to the study of capitalism while Marshall, the capitalist economist, wrote about the economics of socialism. Keynes was the first capitalist economist to write about capitalism'.

The kernel of the epigram is, of course, that the Marshallian perfect competition was an 'ideal' configuration that might be achieved under market socialism but omitted the role of the capitalist as capitalist and concentrated on his role as entrepreneur. There is nothing in the Marshallian system inconsistent with a regime in which all capital is publicly owned and rented out to all comers at a market-clearing price. Capitalism (private ownership of capital) and private enterprise (private control over what to produce and how much) are related but not identical, and microeconomics is primarily concerned with the latter. The most extensive analyses of the market economy (Debreu 1959; Arrow and Hahn 1971) correctly refer to their model as that of a private enterprise economy or a competitive economy, not a capitalist one.

Malthus and Ricardo, and then Marx, perceived the essence of capitalism to be centered on the problems of capital accumulation and the distribution of income between workers and capitalists, a fruitful approach which has provided the basis for the 'paleoclassical' revival led by Joan Robinson (1956) and her Cambridge colleagues. Marx saw capitalism as essentially involved with capital accumulation, and therefore dynamic, and also as essentially involved with the division of output between workers and capitalists – but he concentrated only on the static aspects of the latter. The purpose of this paper is to present this conflict as a dynamic one, in which the struggle over distribution goes beyond that of a conflict over the proportion of current income to be devoted to current worker consumption and involves intertemporal decisions by both workers and capitalists.

This brings us to the role of Keynes, who did not concern himself with capital accumulation and had little to say on income distribution. He did, however, place his finger on one of the crucial properties of the modern capitalist system – the disjunction between the decision to forego present consumption in exchange for future consumption, and the decision actually to utilize that foregone consumption in order to increase the capital stock. We shall find this disjunction to be the key to the analysis of capitalism as a dynamic conflict.

## The workers' dilemma

Consider the simple but common classical model in which workers consume all their income while capitalists are merely investing machines who plough all their profits into accumulation. Suppose the workers receive a constant fraction, $c$, of total output. Do they 'lose' the fraction, $(1 - c)$, that goes to the capitalists? Only in the static, current-period sense, since the lost income becomes investment, increases the capital stock, increases future income, and thus increases the workers' future consumption. The investing-machine capitalist cannot be accused of exploiting the workers; he is merely enforcing current abstinence upon them for which they will later receive increased consumption.

The only effect of the investing-machine capitalist is to change the *time shape* of the workers' consumption pattern. Whether the time shape resulting from the capitalists' activities is better or worse, from the workers' point of view, depends on their intertemporal preferences. In principle, the intervention of the capitalist might given them a preferred time pattern. In any case, even if the time pattern is worse, the reasons for the workers becoming worse off as a result of the capitalists' activities are quite different from those which figure in the static theory of exploitation. Note that, so long as the capitalists *never* consume, the workers ultimately receive all output, whatever the relationship of wages to output at any particular time, and their only potential case for complaint is the time pattern in which it is received.

Now take the other extreme, in which the capitalists consume all the income they receive. If the ratio of wages to output is $c$, as before, the remaining fraction of output, $(1 - c)$, is truly and forever lost to the workers, since there is no increase in the capital stock and thus no increase in future consumption. From the workers' point of view, the income going to the capitalists is no longer enforced abstinence but simple expropriation because the workers need the capitalists only as agents for accumulation.

In the intermediate case, in which capitalists consume part of their income and invest part, that part which is consumed is lost to the workers forever while that part which is invested *may* not be – *if* the workers receive at least some of the increased income which results from the increased capital stock. Note that the extent of worker loss or 'exploitation' depends on the *whole time pattern* of capitalist consumption, not simply on the relationship of current capitalist consumption to current worker consumption. Even if the capitalists invest their whole income in early periods, there is no future gain to the workers if the whole increase in future income is converted into capitalist consumption.

If the workers have no control over any of the parameters of the system, they must simply grit their teeth and bear with whatever the capitalists choose to do. But we can assume that the workers do have some limited control over one of the key variables, the ratio of worker consumption to total output. There are at least three ways in which this control might be exercised:

1. Workers may have direct control over the share of wages in total output, exercised by bargaining or labor force variation, with the workers consuming the whole of their wages (the classical case).
2. Workers may save a variable fraction of their income. Since workers save but do not make investment decisions, this saving is equivalent to voluntarily handing over part of their income to the capitalists in the hope or belief (whether justified is a matter for later analysis) that the capitalists will use it for true capital investment and will not use the proceeds of new stock issues merely to support their mistresses or buy larger cars (the Keynesian case).[2]
3. Workers may play an important role in electoral politics, enabling them to influence the ratio of corporate and other profits taxes to personal income taxes. For a given level of government services, varying this ratio is equivalent to varying the ratio of disposable worker income to disposable private income, and thus of worker consumption to income available for private capital accumulation plus capitalist consumption (the modern case).[3]

Thus we have the workers' dilemma:

*Should they forego present consumption by handing over part of total income to the capitalists? If they do not, they will obtain no higher consumption in the future. If they do, they have no guarantee that the capitalists will actually invest sufficient of this income to bring about the desired level of increase.*

**The capitalists' dilemma**

The capitalists, of course, have full control over the investment decision, unlike the workers. At every point in time the capitalists can decide exactly what proportion of their current income they will consume and what proportion they will use for capital accumulation.

Malthus and Ricardo tended to regard the capitalist as a mere investing machine, for whom there was really no decision to be made. Marx recognized the importance of the capitalists' choice between consumption and investment, and wrote in one of his best-known passages:

> Although, therefore, the prodigality of the capitalist never possesses the bona-fide character of the open-handed feudal lord's prodigality ... yet his expenditure grows with his accumulation, without the one necessarily restricting the other. But along with this growth, there is at the same time developed in his breast, a Faustian conflict between the passion for accumulation, and the desire for enjoyment. (Marx 1906, 1:651)

In spite of castigating his predecessors for adopting the investment-machine approach to the capitalist, Marx did not embody the capitalist's consumption–investment choice in his analysis in an essential way. This is largely because he saw the choice as a static one, a balancing of a disembodied passion for accumulation against the pleasures of consumption, rather than as a dynamic choice involving intertemporal consumption patterns.

Capitalists can be presumed to invest only in order that their own future consumption will be greater as a result. The capitalist investment decision is therefore determined by the desired time shape of future consumption. Since the capitalists can determine exactly the rate at which they will accumulate, and thus the time shape of future output, it might seem that they (unlike the workers) are in full control of their own destiny. But they are not: although they have full control over the course of future total output, they do not have full control over the share of that output that will ultimately be available for their consumption. They may accumulate rapidly now in order to spend later, only to discover when the time comes that the workers are leaving them a much smaller share of output than they had anticipated, or that worker savings dry up just when capitalists plan to reduce investment in favor of consumption, or that profits taxes rise and reduce their disposable incomes.

Thus the capitalists, like the workers, face a dilemma:

*Should they spend now, or accumulate in order to spend more later? If they spend now, they know what they have available. If they accumulate, they may fail to obtain their expected share of the increased output when they come to spend.*

## A paradigm for capitalism

Putting together the workers' and capitalists' dilemmas, we perceive capitalism as dynamic conflict, a struggle over future as well as current levels of consumption for each of the two groups. Each group has control over one key variable – the workers over their consumption in each period, the capitalists over the rate of investment – but the outcome for both groups depends on the other group's decision variable as well as its own.

Thus capitalism can be viewed as a *differential game*[4] between workers and capitalists, with each group devising a strategy (a complete time pattern for its own decision variable, not just a single current move) so as to do best for itself while taking account of possible strategies of the other group and of the interactions between the strategies.

The remainder of this paper will be devoted to setting up and solving the simplest possible model embodying the above essential features, and to discussing the conclusions to be drawn from the solution. The purpose of the model is to illustrate the paradigm, not to set up a realistic model of a capitalist economy, which would require something much more complicated. In spite of the model's simplicity, we shall show the basic conclusions – especially the welfare loss from intergroup rivalry[5] – to be very robust with respect to added complexities.

## A simple differential game model

We assume a one-sector, single-technique economy, the output of which can be consumed directly or added to the existing capital stock. Labor is never limiting and capital lasts forever, so the ratio of output to capital is constant and all investment represents a net increase in the capital stock.

The behavioral features are as follows:

1. Workers can determine, between given upper and lower limits, the ratio of current worker consumption to current output, by varying the share of wages in output, the rate of worker saving, the ratio of profits taxes to total taxes, or a combination of these. The objective of the workers is to maximize total (undiscounted) consumption over a fixed time horizon.[6]
2. Capitalists can determine what proportion of that output not consumed by workers is to be invested and what proportion to be devoted to their own consumption. Like workers, capitalists aim to maximize total consumption over a fixed time horizon. The time horizons are assumed to be the same for workers and capitalists, and neither group has any interest in affairs beyond the horizon.[7]

Denote the proportion of total output devoted to worker consumption at any time by $u_1(t)$, and the proportion of the remainder which is invested by $u_2(t)$. We assume that $u_1(t)$, which is the workers' control variable, is bounded by lower and upper limits $c$ and $b$, respectively, with $0 < c < b < 1$. The capitalists' control variable, $u_2(t)$, is assumed to be free to vary over the whole closed interval $(0, 1)$.

Denoting the fixed output/capital ratio by $a$ and the capital stock at any time by $k(t)$, the basic technical relationships of the economy are, at time $t$:

| | |
|---|---|
| Total output | $= ak(t)$ |
| Worker consumption | $= ak(t)u_1(t)$ |
| Capitalist consumption | $= ak(t)[1 - u_1(t)][1 - u_2(t)]$ |
| Investment | $= ak(t)[1 - u_1(t)]u_2(t)$ |

Total worker consumption up to the horizon, $T$, is given by

$$J_1 = \int_0^T ak(t)u_1(t)dt \tag{1}$$

and total capitalist consumption, by

$$J_2 = \int_0^T ak(t)[1 - u_1(t)][1 - u_2(t)]dt \tag{2}$$

The dynamic path of the capital stock, the only state variable in the system, is given by

$$\dot{k}(t) = ak(t)[1 - u_1(t)]\, u_2(t)$$

(Henceforth we shall omit the time argument from $u_1$, $u_2$, and $k$.)

The structure of the situation is that workers try to maximize $J_1$ and capitalists to maximize $J_2$, both being constrained by the same dynamic relationship for the growth of the capital stock, equation (3). Workers can manipulate $u_1$ but not $u_2$, while capitalists can manipulate $u_2$ but not $u_1$.

This is a very simple differential game,[8] the solution of which will be given by the time paths $\bar{u}_1[0, T]$ and $\bar{u}_2[0, T]$ of the two control variables such that (1) $\bar{u}_1[0, T]$ is optimal for the workers' maximizing problem, given that the capitalists choose $\bar{u}_2[0, T]$ for the time path of their control variable; (2) $\bar{u}_2[0, T]$ is optimal for the capitalists' maximizing problem, given that the workers choose path $\bar{u}_1[0, T]$ for $u_1$.

We solve the total problem by finding the workers' optimal path of $u_1$ for each possible path of $u_2$, then the capitalists' optimal $u_2$ path for each possible path of $u_1$, finally searching for the matching pair that will be the paths of $\bar{u}_1$, $\bar{u}_2$.

**Solving the model**
The solution involves two separate maximizing problems, each involving the optimization of an integral subject to a differential equation constraint on the state variable $k$ and fixed constraints on the relevant control variable. Each problem is thus in the form to which the Pontryagin maximum principle may be directly applied.[9]

The workers' problem is to maximize

$$J_1 = \int_0^T aku_1 dt$$

subject to (3), to $c \le u_1 \le b$, and to an anticipated choice of $u_2$ by the capitalists.

The workers' Hamiltonian is

$$H_1 = aku_1 + y_1 ak(1 - u_1)u_2 \qquad (4)$$

where $y_1$ is the costate variable associated with $k$ in the workers' problem. This must satisfy the differential equation

$$\dot{y}_1 = -\partial H_1/\partial k = -[u_1 + y_1(1 - u_1)u_2]a \qquad (5)$$

In this problem, $y_1(t)$ represents the value to the workers (in terms of total consumption over the time horizon) of a marginal increase in the capital stock at time $t$.

Since workers do not look beyond the horizon, the marginal value of investment at the end of the program is zero; so we have the transversality condition $y_1(T) = 0$.

From the maximum principle, the optimal path for $u_1$ (given $u_2$) will maximize $H_1$ at each point in time, subject to the constraints on $u_1$ and the values of $k, y_1$ at that time. Thus the solution to the worker's problem will be given by

$$u_1 = c \quad \text{whenever } y_1 u_2 > 1$$
$$u_1 = b \quad \text{whenever } y_1 u_2 < 1$$

The simplicity and basic linearity of this model results in a 'bang-bang' solution, with the control variable always at one extreme of its permissible range or the other. Note that the optimal value of $u_1$ depends on both $y_1$ and $u_2$; $y_1$ in turn depends on $u_1$ as well as $u_2$.

Rather than waste our time investigating optimal paths for $u_1$ for arbitrary $u_2$ paths, we turn immediately to the capitalists' problem to find out what paths for $u_2$ are actually relevant.

The capitalists' problem is, for any time path for $u_1$, to choose a path for $u_2$ which maximizes

$$J_2 = \int_0^T ak(1 - u_1)(1 - u_2)dt$$

subject to (3), the constrains on $u_2$, and the anticipated choice of $u_1$ by the workers.

The capitalists' Hamiltonian is

$$H_2 = ak(1 - u_1)(1 - u_2) + y_2 ak(1 - u_1)u_2 \tag{6}$$

The costate variable $y_2$ is different from that in the workers' problem because, although it still represents the marginal value of investment, it represents the marginal value to the capitalists rather than to the workers.

The path of $y_2$ is determined by the differential equation

$$\dot{y}_2 = -\partial H_2/\partial k$$
$$= -[1 + (y_2 - 1)u_2](1 - u_1)a \tag{7}$$

and is subject to the boundary condition $y_2(T) = 0$ because the capitalists, like the workers, are presumed not to look beyond the horizon.

The capitalists' Hamiltonian, $H_2$ is linear in $u_2$ with coefficient $ak(1 - u_1)$ $(y_2 - 1)$, and since $(1 - u_1) > 0$, $H_2$ is maximized by values of $u_2$ which satisfy the conditions

$$u_2 = 0 \quad \text{whenever } y_2 < 1$$
$$u_2 = 1 \quad \text{whenever } y_2 > 1$$

Since optimal $u_1$ takes on only the values $c$ and $b$, and optimal $u_2$, only the values 0 and 1, there are only four possible combinations of the values of the two control variables that can be potential candidates for appearance in the solution. These combinations, together with the conditions that must be satisfied for each combination, are:

I     $u_1 = c$, $u_2 = 0$,     whenever $y_1 u_2 > 1$ and $y_2 < 1$
II    $u_1 = b$, $u_2 = 0$,     whenever $y_1 u_2 < 1$ and $y_2 < 1$
III   $u_1 = c$, $u_2 = 1$,     whenever $y_1 u_2 > 1$ and $y_2 > 1$
IV   $u_1 = b$, $u_2 = 1$,     whenever $y_1 u_2 < 1$ and $y_2 > 1$

It is obvious from inspection that combination I can never be optimal, since $u_2 = 0$ and $y_1 u_2 > 1$ are mutually incompatible.[10] This leaves only three combinations to be examined.

We start, as is usual in a problem of this kind, at the end rather than the beginning. We have a boundary condition $y_2(T) = 0$, and we know $y_2$ must be a continuous function of time; so we must have $y_2 < 1$ at the end and for some period prior to the end. Let us denote by $\hat{t}$ the beginning of the period for which $y_2 < 1$ (if $y_2 < 1$ everywhere, then $\hat{t} = 0$). In this final phase we must have combination II ($u_1 = b$, $u_2 = 0$) because $y_2 < 1$. Let us find out what is happening in this phase, by inserting the relevant values of the control variables in the differential equations (3), (5), and (7) that determine $k$, $y_1$, and $y_2$, respectively. We obtain.

$$\dot{k} = 0, \qquad\qquad k(t) = k(\hat{t}) \qquad\qquad \text{for } \hat{t} \le t \le T$$
$$\dot{y}_1 = -ab, \qquad\qquad y_1(t) = y_1(\hat{t}) - ab(t - \hat{t}) \qquad \text{for } \hat{t} \le t \le T$$
$$\dot{y}_2 = -a(1 - b), \qquad y_2(t) = y_2(\hat{t}) - a(1 - b)(t - \hat{t}) \qquad \text{for } \hat{t} \le t \le T$$

Since $y_1$ and $y_2$ are declining linearly during the final phase, and since $y_2(T) = 0$, we can compute $\hat{t}$ as the time at which $y_2(\hat{t}) = 1$ given that its behavior thereafter is determined as above. This gives

$$\hat{t} = T - \frac{1}{a(1 - b)} \tag{8}$$

Provided $T > 1/a(1 - b)$, the system enters its final phase at time $\hat{t}$ given by (8) above. Prior to time $\hat{t}$ we will have $y_2 > 1$, so that phase will be defined by combination II or combination III of control-variable values. Since we have $u_2 = 1$ in this phase, $y_1 u_2 = y_1$, and thus the value of $u_1$ depends on whether $y_1$ is greater or less than unity. Going back to the final phase, we note that $y_1(T) = 0$ and that $y_1$ declines linearly at time rate $ab$ during this phase. At $\hat{t}$, therefore, the value of $y_1$ is given by $y_1(\hat{t}) = ab(T - \hat{t}) = b/(1 - b)$ (from [8]).

Now $b$ is the maximum ratio of worker consumption to total output, and we shall take it to be $> \frac{1}{2}$, so that $b/(1 - b) > 1$ and $y_1(\hat{t}) > 1$. This means that the phase prior to the last will be characterized by combination III ($u_1 = c, u_2 = 1$). We insert these values of the control variables in the differential equations for $y_1, y_2$ and show that we have $y_1, y_2 > 1$ for all $t$ prior to $\hat{t}$. Thus there is no phase prior to that represented by combination III. Thus the solution consists of two phases,[11] commencing with III, then switching to II at time $\hat{t}$. In other words, workers consume minimally and capitalists accumulate up to time $\hat{t}$; then both groups switch to maximum consumption.

At this point the reader will probably be (and surely ought to be) asking the question, So what? There is certainly nothing very surprising in discovering that the optimal solution is one in which there is maximum accumulation in the first phase and maximum consumption in the second. The significance of the solution we have just derived does not lie in the general pattern but in the specifics – in particular, in the exact time at which the switch from the accumulation phase to the consumption phase takes place. We shall now go on to show that this switch takes place at the *wrong time* for social optimality, so that capitalist accumulation is suboptimal.

**The suboptimality of capitalism as a game**
Since both capitalists and workers are simply maximizing total consumption over a fixed time horizon, the appropriate social welfare index is simply the sum of capitalist and worker consumption. The social optimum is found by maximizing

$$J = J_1 + J_2 = \int_0^T ak\left[1 - (1 - u_1)u_2\right]dt$$

subject to the capital constraint (3) and assuming the same minimum ratio of worker consumption to total output ($c$) as before.

The problem can be shown to depend on a single control variable $(1 - u_1)u_2$ which we can denote by $v$, and which represents the ratio of investment to output. It must satisfy the constraint $0 \leq v \leq 1 - c$. It is easy to show that the optimal path consists of two phases, maximum accumulation ($v = 1 - c$) followed by maximum consumption ($v = 0$), the switch taking place at time $t^*$ given by

$$t^* = T - \frac{1}{a} \tag{9}$$

During the final phase, the costate variable $y$ (now the social value of investment) is declining linearly at rate $a$, and, as before, we assume that $y(T) = 0$, since neither workers nor capitalists look beyond the horizon.[12]

Note that the general pattern of the optimal program is exactly the same as for the capitalist program – both have consumption at the minimum level ($c$ times output) for the first phase, then a switch to the second phase in which accumulation drops to zero and all output is consumed. The only difference is in the time at which the switch is made, but it is this difference which is crucial.

Comparing the value of $t^*$ given by (9) with the value of $\hat{t}$ given by (8), we see that

$$t^* - \hat{t} = \frac{b}{a(1-b)} \tag{10}$$

Since $0 < b < 1$, this is positive, so that the optimal switch time is *later* than the capitalist switch time.[13]

The difference between the optimal and capitalist accumulation programs (illustrated in Figure 15.1) can most easily be seen by dividing the whole time span from start to horizon into three consecutive intervals:

*Interval 1 ($0 \leq t < \hat{t}$)*   In this interval, events are identical in both programs, with consumption equal to $cak(t)$ and $k$ growing exponentially at rate $a(1-c)$. At the end of the interval, capital has grown to $k(\hat{t}) = k_0 e^{a(1-c)\hat{t}}$, a level we shall denote by $\bar{k}$.

*Interval 2 ($\hat{t} \leq t \leq t^*$)*   The programs differ fundamentally during this period. In the capitalist program, accumulation has already ceased. Consumption jumped from $ca\bar{k}$ at the end of interval 1 to $a\bar{k}$ now (all output is consumed), and will remain steady at that level until the time horizon is reached. In the optimal program, on the other hand, accumulation is continuing with consumption still at $ca\bar{k}$ as we pass through $t = \hat{t}$, but increasing as the capital stock continues to grow at the same exponential rate as in interval 1. Whereas the capitalist program will give the same capital stock at the end of this interval as existed at the beginning, the optimal program will end with a higher stock.

*Interval 3 ($t^* \leq t \leq T$)*   Both programs will have all output devoted to consumption, but the optimal program will have a higher output and thus a higher level of consumption because of the larger capital stock resulting from the accumulation during interval 2.

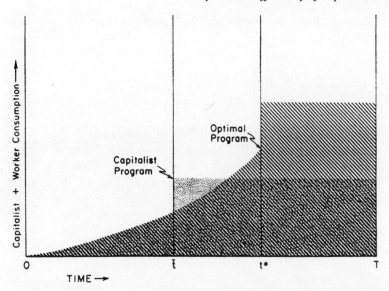

*Figure 15.1   Optimal and capitalist accumulation programs*

Total consumption over interval 1 will be identical in the two programs, and total consumption over interval 3 will obviously be higher for the optimal program than for the capitalist one, but the relationship in interval 2 is not clear. In order to show the suboptimality of capitalist accumulation, we must prove that total consumption over all three intervals is greater for the optimal program. We need only consider consumption over the last two intervals, since the two programs give identical results for interval 1.

Let us use the symbol $W^*$ for total consumption over the last two periods in the optimal program, and $\overline{W}$ for total consumption over those same intervals in the capitalist program. Since total consumption is equal to total output in the capitalist program, and output is constant at $a\overline{k}$, we have (using [8])

$$\overline{W} = a\overline{k}(T - i) = \frac{k}{1-b} \tag{11}$$

We must divide the optimal program into two parts. During interval 2, consumption is equal to $cak(t)$, and $k(t)$ is given by $k(t) = \overline{k}e^{a(1-c)(t-i)}$. During interval 3, consumption is constant at $ak(t^*)$.

Thus we have

$$W^* = \int_{i}^{t^*} ca\overline{k}e^{a(1-c)(t-i)}dt + a\overline{k}e^{a(1-c)(t^*-i)}(T - t^*)$$

Using the values for $i$ and $t^*$ from (8) and (9), the resulting integral can be reduced to give

$$W* = \bar{k}\left[\frac{1}{1-c}e^{(1-c)[b/(1-b)]} - \frac{c}{1-c}\right] \qquad (12)$$

The relationship between $W*$ and $\bar{W}$ is not obvious from a comparison of (11) and (12). However, we can make use of the inequality $e^x > 1 + x$ if $x > 0$. Since $(1-c)[b/(1-b)] > 0$, we have

$$e^{(1-c)[b/(1-b)]} > 1 + (1-c)\frac{b}{1-b}$$

$$\frac{1}{1-c}e^{(1-c)[b/(1-b)]} > \frac{1}{1-c} + \frac{b}{1-b}$$

Substituting in (12),

$$W* > \bar{k}\left(\frac{1}{1-c} + \frac{b}{1-b} - \frac{c}{1-c}\right)$$

$$> \frac{\bar{k}}{1-b}$$

$$> \bar{W}$$

thus finally proving that the capitalist accumulation program is suboptimal in the simple sense that the optimal program could provide more consumption for both workers and capitalists.

Note that the welfare loss from the capitalist game is dynamic, not a simple static loss, because it involves intertemporal rearrangement. Compared with the capitalist program, the optimal one cannot provide more consumption in every period – it provides more towards the end but less for some subinterval commencing at time $i$. At time $i + \varepsilon$, both capitalists and workers will be consuming more on the capitalist program than on the optimal one, so the intertemporal aspects of the social loss apply to both groups.

Because of the dynamic nature of the loss, neither group can induce the other to behave optimally by the use of bribe or compensation payments involving the current period only. Each would have to offer the other inducements in the form of irredeemable pledges about the division of output in the future.

## Analyzing the causes of loss

The welfare loss from the capitalist program arises, of course, from the failure of the system to accumulate during the interval ($\hat{t} < t < t^*$). During this interval, $y(t)$, which represents the social value of investment in terms of consumption, is greater than unity (since it falls to unity only at $t^*$), and thus the social value of a unit of output would be greater if it were invested rather than consumed. Yet output is consumed rather than invested during this period because the capitalists' valuation of investment, $y_2$, remains less than unity (it has already fallen to unity at time $\hat{t}$). The capitalists' valuation of investment is less than the social valuation because the capitalist will receive only a fraction $(1 - b)$ of the increased income generated, while society will receive the whole of it.

The workers' valuation of investment will be above unity for the early part of this period, but this does not count in the capitalist program because the workers cannot force the capitalists to accumulate against the latter's own best interests. Nor does the fact that the combined value of investment to workers and capitalists together is in excess of unity affect the program, because the groups make their decisions separately.

In the first interval ($t < \hat{t}$), the valuation of investment is greater than unity for the capitalists, the workers, and society as a whole. Since it is in the interest of the capitalists to invest in this period, and the workers gain from investment, workers will consume minimally because they are sure their unconsumed income will be used for accumulation. Thus there is maximum accumulation during this interval in both the capitalist and optimal programs.

In the last interval ($t > t^*$), the valuation of investment is less than unity for society as a whole, and for the workers and capitalists as individual groups. Thus there is no accumulation, and no desire for accumulation, in this period by society or either group, on either program.

All the problems which arise from the conflict between workers and capitalists are therefore centered in the middle interval, between $\hat{t}$ and $t^*$.

We can gain a considerable insight into the conflict inherent in this interval by considering the reactions of workers and capitalists to any program that involves switching between accumulation and capitalist consumption, or between minimum and maximum worker consumption, in this period.

Suppose, for example, that the workers, having read this paper, plan to adhere to the optimal program and consume minimally right through to time $t^*$. If the capitalists also adhere to the optimal program, then the workers are better off then under the capitalist program. But if we feed this worker consumption plan into the capitalists' optimizing problem, we find that the capitalists can then gain by switching from accumulating to consuming at some time $t'$ that is before $t^*$ (but after $\hat{t}$). Workers will then find themselves obtaining less than they expected from the optimal program. If the workers now take the capitalists' behavior (accumulate to time $t'$, then consume) as the basis for a new strategy, they will switch from minimum consumption to maximum consumption at a new time $t''$, which can be shown to be earlier than $t^*$. The capitalists' optimum reaction to this will be to cease accumulating even earlier than $t'$, and the workers' counter-reaction will be to switch to maximum consumption earlier than $t''$. The process will continue, and can be shown to converge to $\hat{t}$.[14] It can also be shown that an attempt by the capitalists to get onto the optimal timetable and accumulate through to $t^*$ will lead to workers switching to maximum consumption prior to $t^*$, and to another reaction and counterreaction process converging to $\hat{t}$.

Any switch time from accumulation to consumption by capitalists or from minimum to maximum consumption by workers which lies in this middle interval is game-unstable and will set up a process that will bring both switch times into coincidence back at $\hat{t}$.

Thus the welfare loss from capitalism is due to the game-type situation which arises from the separation of the consumption decision from the investment decision. In this sense, the weakness of capitalism is of a Keynesian, rather than a Marxian, kind.

**Robustness of the conclusions**
The model on which we have based our conclusions to this point is characterized by the extreme simplicity of its properties – non-diminishing returns to capital, no discounting of the future, no vision beyond the horizon, among other things. Do the conclusions we have drawn from this model depend on the simplicity of its properties, or do they survive into more complex models? That is the question to which we now address ourselves.

For the simple linear model we were able to compute and compare the levels of total consumption on the optimal and capitalist programs, to prove the social loss under capitalism quite directly and explicitly. In more complex models, such computations are difficult at best and impossible (except for specific numerical examples) in some cases.

We can always demonstrate the existence of a loss, however, by comparing the costate variables in the two programs. Let us preserve the notation $t^*$ for the time at which the socially optimal program switches from accumulation to consumption, and $\hat{t}$ for the time at which the capitalist program switches. If we can then show that all the costate variables decrease monotonically with time, and that $\hat{t} < t^*$, then we will have shown that the social value of investment (costate variable $y$ in the optimal program) indicates accumulation is socially optimal over the interval $(\hat{t} \le t \le t^*)$, even though the capitalist program has ceased investing at $\hat{t}$. Thus we need only ensure that the additional complexities we add to our model do not upset the monotonicity of decline of $y$, $y_1$, $y_2$ and preserve the relationship $\hat{t} < t^*$.

## Discounting the future

Assume initially that workers and capitalists both discount the future at rate $r$, so that the social rate of discount must also be $r$. The introduction of discounting gives more complex differential equations for the costate variables, but they all decline monotonically with time. Switches now occur when the relevant costate variables pass through the value $e^{-rt}$, rather than unity, because the relevant comparison is between the value of investment and the discounted value of consumption at that time. Over the final phase $(t > t^*)$ we can easily show that $\dot{y}_2(t)$ (rate of change of the capitalists' valuation of investment) is equal to $(1 - b)$ $\dot{y}(t)$ (where $\dot{y}$ is the rate of change of the social value of investment) for all $t$, so that $y_2(t^*) < y(t^*) = e^{-rt^*}$ because we must have $y_2(T) = y(T) = 0$. Thus $\hat{t} < t^*$, and the capitalist program ceases investing before it is socially optimal to do so.[15]

We can show that the conclusion holds even if the three rates of discount are all different, provided the social rate of discount is no greater than the lesser of the workers' or capitalists' rates.

## Diminishing returns to capital

Instead of assuming a single technique and sufficient labor to assure that the output/capital ratio is constant, we can assume a neoclassical production function of the traditional kind, $f(k)$, with $f'(k) > 0$ and $f''(k) < 0$, so that the output/capital ratio diminishes as capital accumulates relative to labor. In the final phase of both the optimal and capitalist programs there is no accumulation, so (assuming constant labor) the output/capital ratios are constants given by $a^* = f(k^*)/k^*$ in the optimal program, and $\bar{a} = f(\bar{k})/\bar{k}$ in the capitalist program, with $a^* \gtreqless \bar{a}$ according as $k^* \lesseqgtr \bar{k}$. The solutions in the terminal phases are exactly the same as in the basic model except that we replace $a$ (formerly common to both programs) by $a^*$ in the optimal program and $\bar{a}$ in the capitalist one. The costate variables decline linearly at rates given by $a^*$ (for $y$ in the optimal program) and $\bar{a}(1 - b)$ (for $y_2$ in the capitalist program). Since $a^*$ and $\bar{a}$ are not the same, we must investigate the possibility that $\bar{a}(1 - b) \geq a^*$, which would have $y_2$ declining at least as rapidly as $y$ and thus $\hat{t}$ no earlier than $t^*$. But we could have $\bar{a}(1 - b) \geq a^*$ only if we had $\bar{a} > a^*$, and this would require $\bar{k} < k^*$ but imply $\hat{t} \geq t^*$ – that is, that the capitalist program should be accumulating at the same rate as the optimal program, for at least as long, but end up with less capital. This is contradictory, so we must have $\bar{a}(1 - b) < a^*$ and thus $\hat{t} < t^*$, leading once more to a social loss from failure to accumulate in the interval $(\hat{t} \leq t \leq t^*)$.

## Looking beyond the horizon

Suppose that the capitalists have interests that extend beyond the horizon. This means that their valuation of investment in the final period is no longer zero, but has some positive value $y_2(T) = m < 1$.[16] The effect of this will be to make the switch time $\hat{t}$ later than it would be with $y_2(T) = 0$, because $y_2$ now needs to fall only from the switch value to $m$, instead of from the switch value to zero, in the final phase from $\hat{t}$ to $T$. The change is only in the boundary condition and affects none of the dynamic relations within the system, so the rates of change of the costate variables are unaffected. But if the capitalists' valuation of investment at time $T$ is $m$, society's valuation of terminal investment must be at least this, since any post-horizon benefits that can accrue to the capitalists alone can also accrue to society as a whole.[17] Thus $y(T) \geq m$, and $y$ now has a lesser distance to fall from $t^*$ to $T$. Thus $t^*$ is necessarily moved back along with $\hat{t}$. It is perhaps easier to work backward, noting that $y$ is always increasing more rapidly than $y_2$ as we move back from the horizon; and since $y$ starts from a terminal value at least as great as $y_2$, we have $y_2(t^*) < y(t^*)$, and thus the capitalist program is already in the consuming phase when the optimal program switches over. Once again we have $\hat{t} < t^*$ and a social loss on the capitalist program.

The three modifications discussed above are not, of course, mutually exclusive. We can indeed have discounting, looking beyond the horizon, and diminishing returns to capital all in the same model, without our essential conclusion – that capitalism is dynamically inefficient – being changed. The conclusion is very robust.[18]

### A concluding remark

Although the analysis has been described as being that of capitalism, with the two groups being workers and capitalists, the essential feature is that there be two groups, one of which controls its own consumption but does not control capital accumulation, while the other controls the allocation of the remainder of output between investment and its own consumption. We might choose labels for these two groups other than 'workers' and 'capitalists'.

As a matter of fact, the analysis might apply very well to some socialist societies, with the two groups characterized as 'ordinary citizens' and 'privileged bureaucrats'.

### Notes

1. Originally published in the *Journal of Political Economy*, **81** (1973), 1092–109.
2. Keynes was concerned with the short-run problem of effective demand, for which capitalist consumption was as useful as capitalist accumulation. He missed the opportunity to discuss the long-run consequences of capitalists consuming rather than investing.
3. I am indebted to E.W. Phelps for suggesting this mechanism.
4. Intriligator 1971 gave a brief discussion of differential games, using examples from the engineering and missile problems on which the early work in the field was based.
5. In other words, capitalism is a non-zero sum game in which rivalry may lead to social loss, and not merely a scramble to distribute the product.
6. The no discounting assumption will later be relaxed, but not the assumption of a fixed horizon.

7. The cases in which horizons differ, and in which there is interest in events beyond the horizon, are discussed later.
8. The extreme simplicity of the model gives us the rarest of prizes in differential game models – a full explicit solution in algebraic parameters.
9. See Pontryagin et al. 1962, Intriligator 1971, Hadley and Kemp 1971.
10. That is, workers will never accept minimum consumption if capitalists are not accumulating, whatever the value $(y_1)$ they place on investment – because that investment will not take place.
11. If $b < \frac{1}{2}$, instead of $> \frac{1}{2}$ as assumed here, the solution has two switches and three phases. It commences with combination III as here, but the workers switch to maximum consumption before capitalists stop accumulating, and we have combination IV as an intermediate phase. The final phase commences at $\hat{t}$, computed as here, and is combination II, as here. None of the major conclusions of the analysis are affected if we have $b < \frac{1}{2}$, but it seems more unrealistic than the case given.
12. The case in which society looks over the horizon, even though workers and capitalists do not, is considered later.
13. That the capitalist switch time differs from the optimal switch time is itself an indication of suboptimality. In this model, the existence of the loss can be shown explicitly.
14. If the workers plan to switch from minimum to maximum consumption at time $\hat{t} + \tau$ $(\tau > 0)$ and capitalists optimize with respect to the worker plan, they will switch from accumulation to consumption at time $\hat{t} + \tau'$, where $\tau' = (b - c)/(1 - c)\,\tau$. Since workers always lose by consuming minimally when capitalists are not accumulating, their reaction to the capitalist move would be to move their switch time forward to $\hat{t} + \tau'$ at the latest. This will give a new switch time for capitalists, and so on. Since $0 < \tau < \tau'$, $\tau' \to 0$ as $\tau \to 0$ and the strategies converge to a common switch time at $\hat{t}$.
15. Provided the rate of discount is not so great, compared with the length of the horizon, as to move $t^*$ forward to 0, as the very impatient society does not accumulate on either program, but consumes from the beginning.
16. It is assumed that the value of post-horizon events is not so large as to lead to accumulation right up to the horizon.
17. If the workers, rather than the capitalists, look over the horizon, then the terminal social value of investment would be at least as great as that of the workers. In this case $t^*$ will move back while $\hat{t}$ is unchanged, leading to even greater inefficiency of the capitalist program. No matter what the relative valuations of terminal investment by the workers and the capitalists, the capitalist program will always be suboptimal so long as the social valuation of terminal investment is at least as great as the capitalists' valuation.
18. The time horizon can never be made infinite in a 'bang-bang' model of this kind, even with discounting. But the conclusions hold for all finite time horizons, even 10,000 years. A smooth trajectory infinite time model requires a complete reformulation.

# References

Archibald, G.C., Eaton, B.C. and Lipsey, R.G. 1986. 'Address models of value theory'. In J.E. Stiglitz and G.F. Mathewson (eds), *New Developments in the Analysis of Market Structure*, Cambridge, Mass., MIT Press.

Archibald, G.C. and Rosenbluth, G. 1975. 'The "new" theory of consumer demand and monopolistic competition', *Quarterly Journal of Economics*, **89**, 569–90.

Arrow, Kenneth J. and Hahn, F.H. 1971. *General Competitive Analysis*, San Francisco, Holden-Day.

Auld, D.A.L. 1972. 'Imperfect knowledge and the new theory of demand', *Journal of Political Economy*, **80**, 1287–94.

Bailey, E.E. and Friedlaender, A.F. 1982. 'Market structure and multiproduct industries', *Journal of Economic Literature*, **20**, 1024–48.

Balassa, Bela 1966. 'Tariff reductions and trade in manufactures among the industrialized countries', *American Economic Review*, **56**, 466–78.

Balassa, Bela 1975. *European Economic Integration*, Amsterdam, North-Holland.

Baumol, W.J. and Bradford, D.F. 1970. 'Optimal departures from marginal cost pricing', *American Economic Review*, **60**, 265–83.

Baumol, W.J., Panzar, J.C. and Willig, R.D. 1982. *Contestable Markets and the Theory of Industry Structure*, San Diego, Harcourt Brace Jovanovich.

Beckmann, M. 1968. *Location Theory*, New York, Random House.

Benoit, J.P. and Krishna, V. 1987. 'Dynamic duopoly: prices and quantities', *Review of Economic Studies*, **54**, 23–36.

Bernardo, J.J. and Blin, J.M. 1977. 'A programming model of choice among multi-attributed brands', *Journal of Consumer Research*, **4**, 111–18.

Bhagwati, J. 1971. 'The Generalized theory of distortions and welfare'. In J. Bhagwati et al. (eds), *Essays in Honor of Gottfried Haberler*, Chicago and Amsterdam, Rand McNally and North-Holland.

Bonanno, Giacomo 1987. 'Location choice, product proliferation and entry deterrence', *Review of Economic Studies*, **54**, 37–45.

Brander, J.A. and Eaton, J. 1984. 'Product line rivalry', *American Economic Review*, **74**, 323–34.

Brander, J., and Spencer, B. 1984. 'Tariff protection and imperfect competition'. In Kierzkowski 1984.

Brumat, C.M. and Tomasini, L.M. 1979. 'A probabilistic extension of Lancaster's approach to consumer theory', *Zeitschrift für Nationalökonomie*, **39**, 381–3.

Capozza, D. and van Order, R. 1978. 'A generalized model of spatial competition', *American Economic Review*, **68**, 896–908.

Capozza, D. and van Order, R. 1980. 'Unique equilibria, pure profits and efficiency in location models', *American Economic Review*, **70**, 1046–53.

Capozza, D. and van Order, R. 1982. 'Product differentiation and the consistency of monopolistic competition: a spatial perspective', *Journal of Industrial Economics*, **31**, 27–40.

Chamberlin, E.H. 1933. *The Theory of Monopolistic Competition*, Cambridge, Mass., Harvard University Press.

Cheng, L. 1988. 'Assisting domestic industries under international oligopoly: the relevance of the nature of competition to optimal policies', *American Economic Review*, **78**, 746–58.

Corden, W.M. 1974. *Trade Policy and Economic Welfare*, London, Oxford University Press.

Corlett, W.J. and Hague, D.C. 1953. 'Complementarity and the excess burden of taxation', *Review of Economic Studies*, **21**, 21–30.

D'Aspremont, C., Gabszewicz J. and Thisse, J.-F. 1979. 'On Hotelling's "Stability in competition"', *Econometrica*, **47**, 1145–50.

Davies, R. 1975. 'Product differentiation and the structure of United Kingdom trade', *Bulletin of Economic Research*, **27**, 27–41.

Davies, R. 1977. 'Two-way international trade: a comment', *Weltwirtschaftliches Archiv*, **113**, 179–81.

Debreu, Gerard 1959. *Theory of Value*, New York, Wiley.

de Palma, A., Ginsburgh, V., Papageorgiu, Y. and Thisse, J.-F. 1985. 'The principle of minimum differentiation holds under sufficient heterogeneity', *Econometrica*, **53**, 767–81.

Dixit, A. 1984. 'International trade policies for oligopolistic industries', *Economic Journal*, **94**, 1–16.

Dixit, A.K. and Norman, V. 1980. *Theory of International Trade,* Cambridge, Cambridge University Press.

Dixit, A.K. and Stiglitz, J.E. 1977. 'Monopolistic competition and optimum product diversity', *American Economic Review*, **67**, 297–308.

Dorward, N. 1982. 'Recent developments in the analysis of spatial competition and their implications for industrial economics', *Journal of Industrial Economics*, **31**, 133–52.

Downs, A. 1957. *An Economic Theory of Democracy*, New York, Harper and Row.

Dreze, J. 1961. 'Les exportations intra-C.E.E. en 1955 et la position belge', *Recherches Economiques de Louvain*, **27**, 717–38.

Eaton, J. and Grossman, G. 1986. 'Optimal trade and industrial policy under oligopoly', *Quarterly Journal of Economics*, **101**, 383–406.

Eaton, B.C. and Lipsey, R.G. 1975. 'The Principle of minimum differentiation reconsidered: some new developments in the theory of spatial competition', *Review of Economic Studies*, **42**, 27–49.

Eaton, B.C. and Lipsey, R.G. 1976. 'The non-Uniqueness of equilibrium in the Löschian location model', *American Economic Review*, **66**, 132–57.

Eaton, B.C. and Lipsey, R.G. 1979. 'The theory of market preemption: barriers to entry in a growing spatial market', *Economica*, **46**, 149–58.

Eaton, B.C. and Lipsey, R.G. 1980. 'The block metric and the law of markets', *Journal of Urban Economics*, **7**, 337–47.

Eaton, J. and Kierzkowski, H. 1984. 'Oligopolistic competition, product variety, and international trade'. In Kierzkowski 1984.

Economides, N. 1984. 'The principle of minimum differentiation revisited', *European Economic Review*, **24**, 345–68.

Finger, J.M. 1975. 'Trade overlaps and intra-industry trade', *Economic Inquiry*, **13**, 581–9.

Flam, H. and Helpman, E. 1987. 'Industrial policy under monopolistic competition', *Journal of International Economics*, **22**, 79–102.

Gabszewicz, J.J. and Thisse, J.-F. 1979. 'Price competition, quality and income disparities', *Journal of Economic Theory*, **22**, 340–59.

Geistfeld, L.V. 1977. 'Consumer decision making: the technical efficiency approach', *Journal of Consumer Research*, **4**, 48–56.

Graitson, D. 1982. 'Spatial competition à la Hotelling: a selective survey', *Journal of Industrial Economics*, **31**, 13–26.

Gray, H.P. 1973. 'Two-way international trade in manufacturing: a theoretical underpinning', *Weltwirtschaftliches Archiv*, **109**, 19–39.

Gray, H.P. 1977. 'Two-way trade: a reply', *Weltwirtschaftliches Archiv*, **113**, 182–4.

Green, H.A.J. 1961. 'The social optimum in the presence of monopoly and taxation', *Review of Economic Studies*, **29**, 66–78.

Greenhut, M.L. and Ohta, H. 1975. *Theory of Spatial Pricing and Market Areas*, Durham NC, Duke University Press.

Greeno, D.W., Sommers, M.S. and Wolff, R.N. 1977. 'An empirical evaluation of investigating mode attributes for commodities', *Operational Research Quarterly*, **28**, 829–38.

Grubel, H.G. 1967. 'Intra-industry specialization and the pattern of trade', *Canadian Journal of Economics and Political Science*, **33**, 374–88.

Grubel, H.G. 1970. 'The theory of intra-industry trade'. In I. McDougall and R. Snape (eds), *Studies in International Economics*, Amsterdam, North-Holland.

Grubel, H.G. and Lloyd, P.J. 1971. 'The empirical measurement of intra-industry trade', *Economic Record*, **47**, 494–517.

Guesnerie, R. and Laffont, J.J. 1975, 'Taxing price makers', *Journal of Economic Theory*, **9**, 423–55.

Hadley, G. and Kemp, M. 1971. *Variational Methods in Economics*, New York, American Elsevier.

Hart, O.D. 1985a. 'Monopolistic competition in the spirit of Chamberlin: a general model', *Review of Economic Studies*, **52**, 529–46.

Hart, O.D. 1985b. 'Monopolistic competition in the spirit of Chamberlin: special results', *Economic Journal*, **95**, 885–908.

Hay, D.A. 1976. 'Sequential entry and entry-deterring strategies in spatial competition', *Oxford Economic Papers*, **28**, 240–57.

Hauser, John R. and Shugan, Steven M. 1983. 'Defensive marketing strategies', *Marketing Science*, **2**, 319–60.

Heckscher, Eli 1919. 'The effect of foreign trade on the distribution of income', *Ekonomisk Tidskrift*, **21**, 497–512.

Helpman, E. 1981. 'International trade in the presence of product differentiation, economies of scale and monopolistic competitors: a Chamberlin–Heckscher–Ohlin approach', *Journal of International Economics*, **11**, 305–40.

Horn, H. 1984. 'Product diversity, trade, and welfare'. In Kierzkowski 1984.

Horstmann, I. and Slivinski, A. 1985. 'Location models as models of product choice', *Journal of Economic Theory*, **36**, 367–86.

Hotelling, H. 1929. 'Stability in competition', *Economic Journal*, **39**, 41–57.

Intriligator, M.D. 1971. *Mathematical Optimization and Economic Theory*, Englewood Cliffs NJ, Prentice-Hall.

Ireland, N.J. 1985. 'Product diversity and monopolistic competition under uncertainty', *Journal of Industrial Economics*, **33**, 501–13.

Itoh, M. 1983. 'Monopoly, product differentiation and economic welfare', *Journal of Economic Theory*, **31**, 88–104.

James, S.F. and Pearce, I.F. 1951. 'The factor price equalisation myth', *Review of Economic Studies*, **19**, 111–20.

Kahn, R.F. 1935. 'Some notes on ideal output', *Economic Journal*, **45**, 1–35.

Kaldor, N. 1955. 'Alternative theories of distribution', *Review of Economic Studies*, **23**, 83–100.

Kierzkowski, H. (ed.) 1984. *Monopolistic Competition and International Trade*, Oxford, Clarendon Press.

Kreps, D. and Scheinkman, J. 1983. 'Quantity precommitment and Bertrand competition yield Cournot outcomes', *Bell Journal of Economics*, **14**, 326–37.

Krugman, P.R. 1979. 'Increasing returns, monopolistic competition and international trade', *Journal of International Economics*, **9**, 858–64.

Krugman, P.R. 1980. 'Scale economies, product differentiation, and the pattern of trade', *American Economic Review*, **70**, 151–75.

Ladd, G.W. and Zober, M. 1977. 'Model of consumer reaction to product characteristics', *Journal of Consumer Research*, **4**, 89–101.

Lancaster, K. 1966. 'A new approach to consumer theory', *Journal of Political Economy*, **74**, 132–57. Reprinted as Chapter 2 in Lancaster 1991.

Lancaster, K. 1971. *Consumer Demand: A New Approach*, New York, Columbia University Press.

Lancaster, K. 1975. 'Socially optimal product differentiation', *American Economic Review*, **65**, 567–85. Reprinted as Chapter 10 in Lancaster 1991.

Lancaster, K. 1976. 'The measurement of changes in quality', *Review of Income and Wealth*, **23**, 157–72. Reprinted as Chapter 6 in Lancaster 1991.

Lancaster, K. 1979. *Variety, Equity and Efficiency*, New York, Columbia University Press.

Lancaster, K. 1979a. 'Product uniqueness under perfect monopolistic competition', Columbia University Economics Workshops.

Lancaster, K. 1979b. 'Monopolistic competition with a nonuniform distribution of consumers', Columbia University Economics Workshops.

Lancaster, K. 1980. 'Intra-industry trade under perfect monopolistic competition', *Journal of International Economics*, **10**, 151–75. Reprinted as Chapter 2 in this volume.

Lancaster, K. 1980a. 'Perfect monopolistic competition in a multi-characteristic setting', Paper presented at Fourth World Congress of the Econometric Society, Aix-en-Provence.

Lancaster, K. 1981. 'Trade in differentiated products: comment'. In J. Bhagwati (ed), *Import Competition and Response*, Chicago, University of Chicago Press, 208–16.

Lancaster, K. 1982. 'Innovative entry: profit hidden beneath the zero', *Journal of Industrial Economics*, **31**, 41–56. Reprinted as Chapter 8 in this volume.

Lancaster, K. 1984. 'Protection and product differentiation'. In Kierzkowski 1984. Reprinted as Chapter 3 in this volume.

Lancaster, K. 1988. 'Product differentiation and industrial policy for two-tiered industries'. Conference paper, published in J. Alec Gee and George Norman (eds) 1992. *Market Structure and Strategy*, London, Wheatsheaf. Reprinted as Chapter 9 in this volume.

Lancaster, K. 1990. 'The economics of product variety: a survey', *Marketing Science*, **9**, 189–206. Reprinted as Chapter 11 in this volume.

Lancaster, K. 1991. *Modern Consumer Theory*, Aldershot UK, Edward Elgar.

Leland, H.E. 1977. 'Quality choice and competition', *American Economic Review*, **67**, 127–37.

Leontief, Wassily 1953. 'Domestic production and foreign trade: the American capital position re-examined', *Proceedings of the American Philosophical Society*, **97**, 332–49.

Lerner, A.P. 1944. *The Economics of Control*, New York, Macmillan.

Lerner, A.P. 1952. 'Factor prices and international trade', *Economica*, **19**, 1–15.

Lerner, A.P. and Singer, H. 1937. 'Some notes on duopoly and spatial competition', *Journal of Political Economy*, **45**, 145–86.

Linder, S.B. 1961. *An Essay on Trade and Transformation*, New York, Wiley.

Lipsey, R.G. 1957. 'The theory of customs unions: trade diversity and welfare', *Economica*, **24**, 40–46.

Lipsey, R.G. and Lancaster, K.J. 1956. 'The general theory of second best', *Review of Economic Studies*, **24**, 11–32.

Little, I.M.D. 1950. *A Critique of Welfare Economics*, Oxford, Clarendon Press.

Little, I.M.D. 1951. 'Direct versus indirect taxes', *Economic Journal*, **61**, 577–84.

Lösch, A. 1954. *The Economics of Location*, New Haven, Yale University Press.

McKenzie, Lionel 1951. 'Ideal output and the independence of firms', *Economic Journal*, **61**, 785–803.

Manning, H.P. 1914. *Geometry of Four Dimensions*, London, Macmillan.

Marx, Karl 1936. *Capital*, New York, Random House.

Meade, J.E. 1955a. *The Theory of Customs Unions*, Amsterdam, North-Holland.

Meade, J.E. 1955b. *Trade and Welfare*, London, Oxford University Press.

Meade, J.E. 1974. 'The Optimal balance between economies of scale and variety of products', *Economica*, **41**, 359–67.

Metzler, Lloyd 1945. 'Stability of multiple markets: the Hicks condition', *Econometrica*, **13**, 277–92.

Mills, E.S. and Lav, M. 1964. 'A model of market areas with free entry', *Journal of Political Economy*, **72**, 278–88.

Mirrlees, J.A. 1971. 'An exploration in the theory of optimum income taxation', *Review of Economic Studies*, **38**, 175–208.

Moorthy, K. Sridhar 1984. 'Market segmentation, self-selection, and product line design', *Marketing Science*, **3**, 288–307.

Moorthy, K. Sridhar 1986. 'Product and price competition in a duopoly', *Marketing Science*, **5**, 141–68.

Mussa, M. and Rosen, S. 1978. 'Monopoly and product quality', *Journal of Economic Theory*, **18**, 301–17.

Negishi, T. 1960. 'The perceived demand curve in the theory of second best', *Review of Economic Studies*, **28**, 196–201.

Nelson, P. 1970. 'Information and consumer behavior', *Journal of Political Economy*, **78**, 311–29.

Nelson, P. 1982. 'Advertising as information', *Journal of Political Economy*, **82**, 729–54.

Neven, D. 1985. 'Two stage (perfect) equilibrium in Hotelling's model', *Journal of Industrial Economics*, **33**, 317–25.

Novshek, W. 1980. 'Equilibrium in simple spatial (or differentiated product) models', *Journal of Economic Theory*, **22**, 313–26.

Ohlin, Bertil 1933. *Interregional and International Trade*, Cambridge, Mass., Harvard University Press.

Ozga, S.A. 1955. 'An essay in the theory of tariffs', *Journal of Political Economy*, **63**, 489–99.

Panzar, J.C. and Willig, R.D. 1981. 'Economies of scope', *American Economic Review*, **72**, 268–72.

Perloff, J. and Salop, S.C. 1985. 'Equilibrium with product differentiation', *Review of Economic Studies*, **52**, 107–20.

Pontryagin, L.S. et al. 1962. *The Mathematical Theory of Optimal Processes*, New York, Wiley-Interscience.

Prescott, E.C. and Visscher, M. 1977. 'Sequential location among firms with foresight', *Bell Journal of Economics*, **8**, 378–93.

Ramsey, F.P. 1927. 'A contribution to the theory of taxation', *Economic Journal*, **37**, 47–61.

Ratchford, B.T. 1975. 'The new economic theory of consumer behavior: an interpretive essay', *Journal of Consumer Research*, **2**, 65–75.

Ratchford, B.T. 1979. 'Operationalizing economic models of demand for product characteristics', *Journal of Consumer Research*, **6**, 76–85.

Riley, J.G. 1975. 'Competitive signaling', *Journal of Economic Theory*, **10**, 174–86.

Robinson, Joan 1956. *The Accumulation of Capital*, London, Macmillan.

Rothschild, M. 1973. 'Models of market organization with imperfect information', *Journal of Political Economy*, **81**, 1283–308.

Rothschild, M. 1974. 'Searching for the lowest price when the distribution of prices is unknown', *Journal of Political Economy*, **82**, 689–711.

Rybczynski, T.M. 1955. 'Factor endowments and relative commodity prices', *Economica*, **22**, 336–41.

Salop, S. 1973. 'Systematic job search and unemployment', *Review of Economic Studies*, **40**, 191–202.

Salop, S. 1979. 'Monopolistic competition with outside goods', *Bell Journal of Economics*, **10**, 141–56.

Salop, S. and Stiglitz, J. 1976. 'Bargains and Ripoffs', *Review of Economic Studies*, **44**, 493–510.

Samuelson, P.A. 1947. *Foundations of Economic Analysis*, Cambridge, Mass., Harvard University Press.

Samuelson, P.A. 1953. 'Prices of factors and goods in general equilibrium', *Review of Economic Studies*, **21**, 1–20.

Scherer, F.M. 1979. 'The welfare economics of product variety: an application to the ready-to-eat cereals industry', *Journal of Industrial Economics*, **28**, 113–34.

Scherer, F.M. 1984. 'Measuring surplus attributable to differentiated products: reply', *Journal of Industrial Economics*, **33**, 133.

Schmalensee, R. 1978. 'Entry deterrence in the ready-to-eat breakfast cereal industry', *Bell Journal of Economics*, **9**, 305–27.

Shaked, A. 1975. 'Non-existence of equilibrium for the two-dimensional three firms location problem', *Review of Economic Studies*, **42**, 51–6.

Shaked, A. and Sutton, J. 1982. 'Anti-Hotelling: relaxing price competition through product differentiation', *Review of Economic Studies*, **49**, 3–14.

Shaw, R.W. 1982. 'Product proliferation in characteristics space: the UK fertilizer industry', *Journal of Industrial Economics*, **31**, 69–92.

Smithies, A. 1936. *Explorations in Economics*, London, McGraw-Hill.

Spence, A.M. 1973. 'Job market signaling', *Quarterly Journal of Economics*, **87**, 355–79.

Spence, A.M. 1974. 'Competitive and optimal responses to signals: analysis of efficiency and distribution', *Journal of Economic Theory*, **9**, 296–332.

Spence, A.M. 1976a. 'Product differentiation and welfare', *American Economic Review*, **66** (Papers and Proceedings), 407–14.

Spence, A.M. 1976b. 'Product Selection, Fixed Costs and Monopolistic Competition', *Review of Economic Studies*, **43**, 217–35.

Stahl, K. 1982. 'Differentiated products, consumer search and locational oligopoly', *Journal of Industrial Economics*, **31**, 97–114.

Stigler, G.J. 1961. 'The economics of information', *Journal of Political Economy*, **69**, 296–332.

Stiglitz, J.E. 1975. 'Information and economic analysis'. In Parkin, M. and Nobay, A.R. (eds), *Current Economic Problems*, Cambridge University Press.

Stokey, Nancy L. 1988. 'Learning by doing and the introduction of new goods', *Journal of Political Economy*, **96**, 701–17.

Stolper, W.F. and Samuelson, P.A. 1941. 'Protection and real wages', *Review of Economic Studies*, **9**, 58–73.

Swan, P.L. 1970. 'Market structure and technological progress: the influence of monopoly on product innovation', *Quarterly Journal of Economics*, **84**, 627–38.

Swann, G.M.P. 1985. 'Product competition in microprocessors', *Journal of Industrial Economics*, **34**, 33–54.

Truman, E.M. 1972. 'The production and trade of manufactured products in the E.E.C. and E.F.T.A.: a comparison', *European Economic Review*, **3**, 271–90.

Valavanis-Vail, Stefan 1954. 'Leontief's scarce-factor paradox', *Journal of Political Economy*, **62**, 523–28.

Viner, Jacob 1950. *The Customs Union Issue*, New York, Carnegie Endowment.

White, L.J. 1977. 'Market structure and product varieties', *American Economic Review*, **67**, 179–82.

Wildman, S. 1984. 'Measuring surplus attributable to differentiated products', *Journal of Industrial Economics*, **33**, 123–32.

Williamson, Oliver E. 1975. *Markets and Hierarchies*, New York, Free Press.

Wilson, Charles A. 1988. 'On the Optimal Pricing Policy of a Monopolist', *Journal of Political Economy*, **96**, 164–76.

Wolinsky, A. 1984. 'Product differentiation with imperfect information', *Review of Economic Studies*, **51**, 53–61.

# Index